AN INTRODUCTION

TO THE

STUDY OF THE CIVIL LAW.

BY

DAVID IRVING, LL. D.

The Fourth Edition.

THE LAWBOOK EXCHANGE, LTD.
Clark, New Jersey

ISBN-13: 978-1-58477-993-3
ISBN-10: 1-58477-993-4

Lawbook Exchange edition 2010

The quality of this reprint is equivalent to the quality of the original work.

THE LAWBOOK EXCHANGE, LTD.

33 Terminal Avenue
Clark, New Jersey 07066-1321

*Please see our website for a selection of our other publications
and fine facsimile reprints of classic works of legal history:*
www.lawbookexchange.com

Library of Congress Cataloging-in-Publication Data

Irving, David, 1778-1860.
 An introduction to the study of the civil law / by David Irving.
-- 4th ed.
    p. cm.
 Originally published: London : A. Maxwell [etc.], 1837.
 Includes bibliographical references and index.
 ISBN-13: 978-1-58477-993-3 (hardcover : alk. paper)
 ISBN-10: 1-58477-993-4 (hardcover : alk. paper)
 1. Civil law--Study and teaching. 2. Roman law--Study and
teaching. I. Title.
 K623.I7454 2009
 340.071'1--dc22

                              2009034422

Printed in the United States of America on acid-free paper

AN INTRODUCTION

TO THE

STUDY OF THE CIVIL LAW.

BY

DAVID IRVING, LL. D.

The Fourth Edition.

LONDON:

A. MAXWELL, 32, BELL YARD, LINCOLN'S INN,
Law Bookseller to His Majesty:

T. CLARK, EDINBURGH; AND MILLIKEN & SON, DUBLIN.

1837.

LONDON :

W. M'DOWALL, PRINTER, PEMBERTON-ROW,
GOUGH-SQUARE.

TO

GUSTAF HUGO, LL. D.

KNIGHT OF THE GUELPHIC ORDER, PRIVY COUNSELLOR OF

JUSTICE, AND PROFESSOR OF THE CIVIL LAW

IN THE

UNIVERSITY OF GÖTTINGEN,

THESE OBSERVATIONS ARE INSCRIBED

IN TESTIMONY OF THE AUTHOR'S HIGH RESPECT

FOR

HIS TALENTS AND LEARNING.

AN INTRODUCTION

TO THE

STUDY OF THE CIVIL LAW.

—◆—

THE system of Roman jurisprudence has for many cen-
tūries been regarded as one of the most conspicuous
monuments of human wisdom and genius; and its powerful influence on modern legislation has been felt and
acknowledged by every civilized nation of Europe.
Although it has long ceased to retain the full authority
of written law, it can never cease to attract the notice,
and to excite the admiration of lawyers who are capable
of ascending to this clear and copious fountain of juridical
knowledge.

A learned professor in a foreign university thought it
expedient to pronounce and publish an academical oration
on the excessive study of the civil law.[1]   This is a species
of excess which no person, interested in the prosperity of
the British universities, need at present anticipate with

[1] Henr. Gulielmi Tydeman Oratio de eo quod nimium est in Studio
Juris Romani. Daventriæ, 1802, 4to.

B

any painful degree of anxiety ; and if too much learning should seem to have made some lawyers mad, it must at least be admitted that a very small portion of their learning is drawn from the recondite sources of the Roman jurisprudence.   Nothing indeed is more common than to hear them declare their decided opinion as to the utter inutility of such a study : it is equally common to hear certain worthy denizens of the republic of letters profess the utmost contempt for classical learning, and both opinions rest on the same unstable foundation ; they are in every instance the opinions of individuals who endeavour to derive some consolation to themselves, by pretending to despise what they do not understand. That the study of the civil law is however of real importance, that a competent knowledge of it may be extremely useful to the classical scholar, as well as to the practical lawyer, may be asserted with at least some degree of confidence.

In those countries most remarkable for the extent and solidity of their erudition, namely, in Germany and Holland, this study has long constituted an essential branch of a liberal education ; and they persuade themselves that many advantages result from such a plan of academical discipline.   Many of their professed scholars are excellent civilians, and many of their professed civilians are excellent scholars.   It is sufficiently obvious that those who are acquainted with the phraseology and with the spirit of the Roman law, will readily understand many passages of the Latin classics which to others must remain obscure and unintelligible.[2]   Even the poets admit

---

[2] " Neque enim ignorabat," says Ernesti, " quam multa essent in libris Latinis, quæ sine juris illius scientia satis intelligi et explicari non possent." (Narratio de J. M. Gesnero: Opuscula Oratoria, p. 327).—Capperonnier,

of such illustration: Plautus, Horace, and Ovid may frequently be explained from the writings of the civilians.

These general assertions will best be confirmed by a particular example; and the examples are so abundant that the chief difficulty lies in the necessity of making a selection. The subsequent passage in one of the epistles of Pliny, may however be regarded as sufficient for our purpose: " Tu quidem pro cætera tua diligentia admones me, codicillos Aciliani, qui me ex parte instituit heredem, pro non scriptis habendos, quia non sint confirmati testamento : quod jus ne mihi quidem ignotum est, quum sit iis etiam notum qui nihil aliud sciunt. Sed ego propriam quandam legem mihi dixi, ut defunctorum voluntates, etiamsi jure deficerent, quasi perfectas tuerer. Constat autem, codicillos istos Aciliani manu scriptos. Licet ergo non sint confirmati testamento, a me tamen, ut confirmati, observabuntur." [3] This point of law, says Pliny, is even known to those who are ignorant of every other ; but it seems nevertheless to have been completely misapprehended by a late respectable writer, who has thus stated the doctrine of codicils : " When additions were made to a will, they were called *codicilli*. They were expressed in the form of a letter

who published a splendid edition of Quinctilian (Paris. 1725, fol.) has betrayed great ignorance of the Roman law, for which he is sufficiently chastised by his able and unrelenting adversary Burman. (Epistola ad C. Capperonnerium de nova ejus Quinctiliani Editione, p. 85-92. Leidæ, 1726, 4to.) " Senties, spero," says Burman, p. 90, " ubi hanc epistolam legeris, opus esse aliqua juris peritia, qui Fabium tractare et intelligere velit."

[3] Plinii Epistolæ, lib. ii. ep. xvi. edit. Gesner.—Dr. Schneither has published a " Dissertatio juridica inauguralis, qua Loca e Plinii Junioris Scriptis, quæ ad Jus Civile pertinent, recensentur et illustrantur." Groningæ, 1827, 8vo.

addressed to the heirs, sometimes also to trustees (ad fideicommissarios). It behoved them however to be confirmed by the testament. Plin. Ep. ii. 16." [4] The first of these sentences contains a definition of a modern codicil; but, according to the civil law, a codicil was a less solemn form of a will. It might be made by a person who was either testate or intestate; in other words, it could either accompany or subsist without a testament. A person might leave several codicils; whereas no *pagan*, that is, no person who was not a soldier, could leave more testaments than one. It was essential to the character of a testament that it should institute an heir; but a codicil was in all cases incompetent for that purpose, and could only bequeath legacies and trusts: it therefore could not disinherit one heir, or substitute another. As the law stood in the age of Caius, a legacy bequeathed by a codicil, and not ratified by a testament, was null and void; [5] and according to the doctrine which, in more general terms, was afterwards stated by Papinian, where the codicil was of a date prior to the will, it was held to be ineffectual unless confirmed by that will, or by another codicil. [6] The notion of this writer, that a codicil must succeed a testament, and that

---

[4] Adam's Roman Antiquities, p. 58. Major's edit. Lond. 1835, 8vo. —Dr. Adam has stated that testaments were always written in Latin, and that a legacy expressed in Greek was not valid. The assertion was true in the age of Ulpian, to whose authority he refers, and, in a work on classical antiquities, this statement might perhaps be sufficient; but in the year 439 it was expressly enacted that any person might write his testament in Greek; " ut etiam Græce omnibus liceat testari." (Cod. lib. vi. tit. xxiii. fr. 21. § 4). I will only add that a very elaborate dissertation on the public use of foreign languages among the Romans, has lately been published by an eminent civilian. (Dirksen's Civilistische Abhandlungen, Bd. i. S. i. Berlin, 1820, 2 Bde. 8vo.)

[5] Caii Institutiones, lib. ii. § 270.   [6] Digest. lib. xxix. tit. vii. fr. 5.

it must nevertheless be confirmed by a testament, cannot very easily be comprehended; but the statement of Pliny, when properly understood, is conformable to the established doctrine of the civilians. The individual whom he mentions had first made a codicil and afterwards a testament, and had neglected to confirm in the one a legacy which had been bequeathed in the other: a direct bequest could not be effectually made in this manner, but Pliny expresses his determination to take no advantage of the legal informality.

From their ignorance of the peculiar language of the civilians, men of real erudition have sometimes felt themselves much at a loss, or have been betrayed into great mistakes. Gisbert Cuper, for example, having occasion to quote a passage from a letter of Brenkman, is obliged to confess himself unable to comprehend the meaning of a particular expression. " Perinde autem est, an per folia, an per aversionem *(je ne sai ce que ce mot veut dire)* pretium constituatur."[7] To sell any thing *aversione* or *per aversionem*, corresponds to our vulgar phrase of selling by the lump.[8] Cujacius supposes the term to have been thus applied, "quod scilicet quasi *aversi* quodammodo negotium ita contrahamus, re omni neque perspecta nec explorata bene."[9]

It is related of the celebrated Poliziano, by whom the study of the Roman law had by no means been neglected,[1]

[7] Gebaveri Narratio de H. Brenkmanno, p. 33. Gotting. 1764, 4to.

[8] Dukeri Opuscula de Latinitate Jurisconsultorum Veterum, p. 437. Vicat, Vocabularium Juris utriusque, tom. i. p. 150.

[9] Cujacius ad Institut. lib. iii. tit. xxiii. § 3.

[1] Hauboldi Institutiones Juris Romani Litterariæ, p. 48. Hugo's Lehrbuch der juristischen und meist civilistischen gelehrten Geschichte, S. 201. Savigny's Geschichte des Römischen Rechts im Mittelalter, Bd. vi. S. 375.

that when consulted respecting the signification of *suus
heres*,[2] he was unable to offer any explanation; and yet
this technical phrase is not entirely excluded from those
classical writings with which he was so familiar. It occurs in the following passage of Ovid:

> Vivit enim in vobis facundi lingua parentis,
> Et res heredem reperit illa suum.[3]

Heredes sui were natural and domestic heirs, the children
or other descendants of the deceased, such as were under
his power, and were not to fall under the power of another after his death.[4] To express their peculiar rights,
the modern civilians frequently employ the barbarous
substantive *suitas*. It is related of Schurzfleisch, a German philologer, that when some person presented him
with a tract " De Jure *Suitatis*," he laughed at the
civilians for discussing the rights of hogs.[5]

---

[2] " De cujus vocis significatione," says Alciatus, " interrogatus a Socyno
Angelus Politianus obmutuit, cum tamen gloriatus esset in glossematis
juris civilis se vel Accursium superare posse." (De Verborum Significatione, lib. iv. p. 102. edit. Lugduni, 1537, fol.)   See likewise his Dis-
punctiones, lib. iii. cap. xviii.

[3] Ovidii Epist. ex Ponto, lib. ii. ep. ii. v. 53.—See Grotius, Florum
Sparsio ad Jus Justinianeum, p. 56. The juridical science of Ovid has
been illustrated in a work published under this title: " Dissertatio philolo-
gico-juridica de insigni in poeta Ovidio Romani Juris Peritia, quam Thesi-
bus suis inauguralibus adjectam voluit auctor J. van Iddekinge, J. U. D."
Amst. 1811, 8vo.

[4] " Sui quidem heredes ideo appellantur quia domestici heredes sunt,
et vivo quoque parente quodammodo domini existimantur." (Caii Institutiones, lib. ii. § 157.)

[5] Otto ad Institutiones, p. 301. " Risisse fertur jurisconsultos, qui de
jure porcorum disputarent." He jocularly derived the word from *sus*,
instead of *suus*.

The history of the Roman law, and the general history of the Roman state, if studied to much advantage, must be studied in conjunction with each other.[6] Without a familiar knowledge of the institutions, manners, and character of a people, it is always difficult, if not impossible, to comprehend the spirit of their laws: many legal forms and enactments must appear unmeaning or absurd, if we are unable to trace the origin of those forms and enactments in the peculiar habits and circumstances of the age and nation.[7] An intimate acquaintance with the history and antiquities of Rome is therefore indispensable to a civilian;[8] and a comprehensive knowledge of the

[6] "Ut in jurisprudentiæ Romanæ studiis," says Balduinus, "jus ab historia tanquam facto discernendum est, sic est etiam utrunque conjungendum, ut et in jure Romano historiam, et in historia jus ipsum observemus." (Ad Edicta Veterum Principum Rom. de Christianis, p. 6. Basil. s. a. 8vo.)

[7] See Schultingii Oratio de Jurisprudentia Historica, subjoined to his Jurisprudentia Ante-Justinianea, p. 908.—"Ideoque," says Burman, "maxime semper mihi arridebat ea ratio tractandi juris, quæ subsidium ex historia et antiquitate peteret." (De Vectigalibus Populi Romani, præf. edit. Leidæ, 1734, 4to.)

[8] The *glossatores*, or early commentators on the civil law, were not unfrequently betrayed into the grossest misconceptions. Being generally very ignorant of classical antiquity, they were necessarily left to grope their way. The merits of this class of commentators have however been highly extolled by an able though somewhat paradoxical writer. "Ad me quod attinet," says Wieling in his Oratio pro Glossatoribus, "fremant omnes licet, dicam quod sentio: unus mehercle Irnerius, unus item Accursius, in vulgato glossarum corpore, omnes omnium recentiorum commentarios, si quis legum causas, et fori usum viderit, et auctoritatis pondere, et utilitatis ubertate, longissime exsuperat." (Lectiones Juris Civilis, &c. p. 309. edit. Traj. ad Rhen. 1740, 8vo.) Of their mode of illustrating the text of the civil law, I shall produce one specimen, which will probably be deemed sufficient: it is from the gloss of Accursius on the second title of the Institutions, *de jure naturali, gentium, et civili*. "Casus. Quidam scholaris accessit ad principem, et talem proposuit

Roman jurisprudence is not less requisite to him who is
anxious to understand the genuine history of Rome. Of
the light which ancient history may derive from the civil
law, I shall here introduce a single illustration.

It is commonly regarded as a very curious and remarkable fact, that although the Romans were disposed
to tolerate every other religious sect,[9] yet they fre-

quæstionem: Domine Imperator, dicite mihi quæ differentia est inter jus
gentium et jus civile: et ideo quæro, quia volo unum jus ab alio scire
discernere. Imperator respondit: amice, dico tibi quod omnes populi,
qui utuntur jure scripto et jure non scripto, pro parte utuntur suo proprio
jure, seu civili, et pro parte utuntur jure communi omnium hominum.
Secundo dicit scholaris: Domine Imperator, vos loquimini sic obscure,
quod non intelligo vos. Quid est hoc dicere, quod omnes populi, quo
utuntur jure scripto et jure non scripto, pro parte utuntur suo proprii
jure, et pro parte utuntur jure communi omnium hominum? Dicit
imperator: quod dixi tibi, quod utuntur pro parte suo proprio jure, sic
intellige," &c. (Institutiones, Fr. Accursii Glossis illustratæ, p. 14. edit.
1555, 8vo.) Ælius Antonius Nebrissensis, or Antonio de Lebrixa, the
great restorer of polite learning in Spain, published a work entitled
"Sanctissimi Juris Civ. Lexicon, adversus insignes Accursii leguleii
Errores editum." Antverpiæ, 1527, 8vo. See Savigny's Geschichte des
Römischen Rechts im Mittelalter, Bd. vi. S. 391. This lexicon was
afterwards printed with an anonymous "Vocabularium utriusque Juris."
Venetiis, 1575, 8vo.

[9] Bynkershoek de Cultu Religionis Peregrinæ apud Veteres Romanos:
Opera, tom. iii. p. 237.—See however what is stated in Bishop Watson's
Apology for Christianity, p. 104, and in Sir George Colebrooke's *Six
Letters on Intolerance*, p. 295. Lond. 1791, 8vo. The last of these
writers places great reliance on what he conceives to have been one of
the laws of the twelve Tables: " Apart let no one have new gods. Those
of strangers let no one worship privately, unless they be publicly allowed."
He proceeds to state that "no words can be more precise to prohibit the
private exercise of a religion not warranted by the state. As this law was
never repealed, I do not see on what authority authors have asserted that
at Rome every family was left to worship in its own way." It is however
very material to remark, that this is not one of the laws of the twelve
Tables, but one of those devised by Cicero for the government of an ima-

quently persecuted the Christians with unrelenting cruelty. This exception, so fatal to a peaceable and harmless sect, must have originated in circumstances which materially distinguished them from the votaries of every other religion.. The causes and the pretexts of persecution may have varied at various periods; but there seems to have been one general cause, which will readily be apprehended by those who are intimately acquainted with the Roman jurisprudence. From the most remote period of their history, the Romans had conceived extreme horror against all nocturnal meetings of a secret and mysterious nature. A law prohibiting nightly vigils in a temple has even been ascribed, though with little probability, to the founder of their state.[1]

ginary republic. (De Legibus, lib. ii. cap. viii.) " Nam quas," says Gravina, " e Ciceronis libris de Legibus in XII. Tabul. retulerunt, non veras arbitramur, sed a Cicerone confictas, exemplo legum Platonicarum; quamvis multas legum decemviralium sententias propter æquitatem, quam continebant, ex intima philosophia ductam Cicero suis legibus comprehenderit." (Origines Juris Civilis, p. 172.) There is much truth in the remark of Dr. Prideaux, that to the heathen nations one sort of idolatry was as acceptable as another. (Connection, vol. ii. p. 176). " Romani sigillatim," says Mosheim, " publicam licet religionem amplificari et peregrinis Diis ac institutis augeri haud facile paterentur, civibus tamen amplissimam facultatem concedebant, exteras religiones sequendi, et alienos Deos sacellis, templis, aris, sacris et lucis colendi." (De Rebus Christianorum ante Constantinum Magnum Commentarii, p. 6. Helmstadii, 1753, 4to.)

[1] Balduinus ad Leges Romuli, p. 7. edit. Paris. 1554, fol.—" Sed eruditis," says Funccius, " illæ non pari modo probantur omnibus: cum et maximus Cujacius illas fuisse confictas asserere nullus dubitaverit. Revera positiones ipsæ, earum formæ, numerus, et ordo, cum insigni figmentorum acervo, nemini non prima fronte apparent." (Leges XII. Tabularum, p. 5. Rintelli, 1744, 4to.) The laws of Romulus are more particularly discussed by Dirksen, Versuche zur Kritik und Auslegung der Quellen des Römischen Rechts, S. 261. See likewise Idsinga, Varia Juris Civilis, p. 1. Harlingæ, 1738, 8vo.

The laws of the twelve Tables declared it a capital offence to attend nocturnal assemblies in the city.[2] And,
to omit other authorities, the " Senatusconsultum Mar-
cianum de Bacchanalibus "[3] is of a similar tendency;
though it is indeed directed against a particular institution, which was believed to have been productive of the
greatest enormities.[4] This then being the spirit of the
law, it is obvious that the nocturnal meetings of the primitive Christians must have rendered them objects of
peculiar suspicion, and exposed them to the animadversion of the magistrate. It was during the night that
they usually held their most solemn and religious assemblies;[5] for a practice which may be supposed to have
arisen from their fears, seems to have been continued from
the operation of other causes. Misunderstanding the
purport of certain passages of Scripture, they were led to
imagine that the second advent, of which they lived in
constant expectation,[6] would take place during the
night; and they were accustomed to celebrate nightly
vigils at the tombs of the saints and martyrs. In this
case therefore they incurred no penalties peculiar to the
votaries of a new religion, but only such as equally at-

[2] Gothofredus ad XII. Tab. p. 143.   Gravina, p. 226.

[3] Maffei, Istoria Diplomatica, p. 125.   Mantova, 1727, 4to.   Bynkershoek de Religione Peregrina, p. 259. Livius ex edit. Drakenborch, tom.
vii. p. 197.   Taylor's Elements of the Civil Law, p. 546.   Bynkershoek
has added notes, and Taylor a very copious and learned commentary.
This curious relique may be found in various other works.

[4] Livii Hist. lib. xxxix. cap. viii.

[5] Böhmeri Dissertationes Juris Ecclesiastici Antiqui ad Plinium Secundum et Tertullianum, p. 35.   Lipsiæ, 1711, 8vo.

[6] See Bishop Kaye's Ecclesiastical History of the second and third
Centuries, illustrated from the writings of Tertullian, p. 364.   Cambridge,
1826, 8vo.

tached to those who, professing the public religion of the state, were yet guilty of this undoubted violation of its laws.[7]

The legislation of Rome under the regal dynasty must have been extremely simple. Of this era however

[7] " Adfirmabant autem," says the younger Pliny, " hanc fuisse summam vel culpæ suæ, vel erroris, quod essent soliti stato die ante lucem convenire." (Epistolæ, lib. x. ep. xcvii.) This application of the existing laws to the case of the Christians has been noticed by various writers. " Sed tempore Tertulliani, plane injuria, cœtus omnes Christianorum hoc nomine suspecti, et infames vulgo erant, dum profani homines sanctissimos piorum congressus tantum non pro Bacchanalibus habent." (Balduinus ad Leges Romuli, p. 15). " Sed hoc ipso Christiani rei Romanis legibus; cautum enim 12 Tab. ne nocturni cœtus in urbe agitarentur." (Wowerus ad Minucium Felicem, p. 73. edit. Ouzelii. Lugd. Bat. 1672, 8vo.) " Hæc cum ita sint, facile apparet quare nocturnæ coitiones Christianorum in crimen traherentur publicum, causamque tot persecutionum præberent." (Böhmeri Dissertationes, p. 38.)

Dr. Taylor did not therefore, as an angry antagonist avers, make any *discovery* when he illustrated this application of the Roman law, but it may perhaps be admitted that he expressed himself with too great latitude. " It is not true," he remarks, " that the primitive Christians held their assemblies in the night time, to avoid the interruptions of the civil power; but the converse of that proposition is true in the utmost latitude, viz. that they met with molestations from that quarter, because their assemblies were nocturnal." (Elements of the Civil Law, p. 579.) This position was attacked by Bishop Warburton, with his usual ability, and in his usual style. (Divine Legation of Moses, vol. iii. p. xxxv.) " Perhaps," says the late Dr. Parr in a letter to the writer of these pages, " it may not be amiss for me to tell you that Taylor had one day dropped in conversation that Warburton did not understand Greek. The story reached Warburton's ears, and he most unmercifully wreaked his vengeance upon the offender." See Nichols's amended account of Dr. Taylor, in a publication entitled " Two Music Speeches at Cambridge, by Roger Long and John Taylor," p. xix. Lond. 1819, 8vo. In Warburton's letters to Hurd, a singular monument of the strength and weakness of the human understanding, Taylor is treated as a learned dunce. (Letters from a late eminent Prelate to one of his Friends, p. 225. edit. Lond. 1809, 8vo.)

very few reliques have been preserved, nor are the genuine sufficiently distinguished from the spurious. The *Leges Regiæ* have been collected by Lipsius,[8] and other men of learning; and of the supposed laws of Romulus a separate collection was published by Balduinus.[9]

After the expulsion of the last king, the want of a regular code of laws appears to have been felt by the Romans, who were yet an inconsiderable and a rude people. According to the uniform testimony of their own writers, they had recourse to the expedient of sending a deputation to Greece, in order to procure information respecting the laws of a kindred nation. The commonly received account of this embassy was called in question by Giambattista Vico,[1] a professor of rhetoric, who ought to have been a professor of law, at Naples: he has been followed by Bonamy,[2] Gibbon, and many other writers, both civilians and historians. The current of opinion

[8] Lipsii Opera, tom. iv. p. 277. Antverpiæ, 1637, 4 tom. fol. On the laws of the Roman kings there is an elaborate dissertation by Dirksen, Versuche zur Kritik und Auslegung der Quellen des Römischen Rechts, S. 234. Leipzig, 1823, 8vo.

[9] Balduini libri duo in Leges Romuli, et Leges XII. Tab. quibus Fontes Juris Civilis explicantur. Paris. 1554, fol. This edition, which is not the earliest, is subjoined to the author's copious commentary on the Institutions.

[1] J. B. Vicus de Constantia Jurisprudentis, p. 224. Neapoli, 1721, 4to. See likewise the same author's *Principj di Scienza nuova d'intorno alla comune Natura delle Nazioni*, tom. i. p. 120. ed. Milano, 1801, 3 tom. 8vo. —"Hoc opus," says Fabroni, in allusion to the latter work, " ei in amore et deliciis fuit, et glorians affirmabat se posteris monumentum reliquisse, ex quo judicium facere possent, quantum in hoc studiorum genere valeret, quantumque elaborasset." (Vitæ Italorum Doctrina excellentium, tom. xii. p. 295).

[2] Dissertation sur l'Origine des Loix des XII. Tables, par M. Bonamy: Mémoires de l'Académie des Inscriptions et Belles Lettres, tom. xii. p. 27.

in Germany is decidedly in favour of his conclusion, which however we are not yet fully prepared to admit.[3]

It is stated by Livy, and by Dionysius of Halicarnassus, that ambassadors were sent to Greece, in order to collect information respecting the laws of that country; and the same account, or nearly the same, is repeated by many other ancient writers. Angelo Mai, adopting the opinion of Vico, has urged as an objection against this account, that it is nowhere mentioned in the writings of Cicero:[4] but if we were to admit the fact, it would not be necessary to admit the inference; for Cicero might or might not find occasion to refer to an event which, so far as we can discover, no person regarded as doubtful. The following expressions however seem to contain a manifest allusion to the influence of the Athenian upon the Roman laws: "Adsunt Athenienses, unde humanitas, doctrina, religio, fruges, jura, leges ortæ, atque in omnes terras distributæ putantur."[5] This passage occurs in one of his orations; and, in another work, Cicero notices the coincidence or identity of certain decemviral laws with those of Solon.[6] In the subsequent

[3] On the subject of this controversy, two articles, written by Berriat St. Prix, may be found in that valuable repository the *Thémis, ou Bibliothèque du Jurisconsulte*, tom. iv. p. 304, tom. vi. p. 269.

[4] "Nullam tamen facit Cicero mentionem Romanorum in Græciam legatorum ad Solonis leges petendas: cujus rei altum silentium est in aliis quoque Tullii scriptis. Immo is de Or. i. 44. leges Romanas aperte anteponit inconditis et ridiculis, ut ait, Lycurgi, Draconis, Solonisque legibus, quod facere vix debuit, si jus Romanum e Græco haustum putavisset." (Maius ad Ciceronem de Republica, lib. ii. cap. xxxvi. p. 201. Romae, 1822, 8vo.)

[5] Ciceronis Orat. pro Flacco, § 26.

[6] Cicero de Legibus, lib. ii. cap. xxiii. xxv.

passage, Tacitus evidently alludes to a fact which must have been considered as incontrovertible : " Creatique decemviri, et accitis quæ usquam egregia, compositæ duodecim Tabulæ, finis æqui juris." [7]   The younger Pliny thus addresses one of his friends : " Habe ante oculos, hanc esse terram quæ nobis miserit jura, quæ leges non victa acceperit, sed petentibus dederit; Athenas esse, quas adeas; Lacedæmonem esse, quam regas." [8] Pomponius has likewise adopted the same account : " Postea, ne diutius hoc fieret, placuit publica auctoritate decem constitui viros, per quos peterentur leges a Græcis civitatibus, et civitas fundaretur legibus." [9]   Many other passages of ancient writers might be accumulated, not to strengthen the original authority on which we find the fact stated, but to evince that this fact was generally, if not universally, admitted.

Dr. Macieiowski, professor of the civil law in the university of Warsaw, has directed the edge of his criticism against the character of Livy and Dionysius as historians ; [1] and we are not unwilling to admit that on this subject his opinion is entitled to attention.   The value and importance of Dionysius's work for the early history

[7] Taciti Annal. lib. iii. cap. xxvii.

[8] Plinii Epistolæ, lib. viii. ep. xxiv.—" Allatas a Græcia leges," says Florus, " decem principes lecti, jubente populo, conscripserant; ordinataque erat in duodecim Tabulis tota justitia." (Epitome Rer. Rom. lib. i. cap. xxiv.)

[9] Digest. lib. i. tit. ii. fr. 2. § 4. These words of Pomponius, as they now stand, are at variance with the account given by Livy; and Bynkershoek very ingeniously conjectures that they ought to be transposed in the following manner: " Placuit publica auctoritate peterentur leges a Græcis civitatibus, et decem constitui viros, per quos civitas fundaretur legibus."

[1] Macieiowski Opusculorum Sylloge prima, p. 102. Varsaviæ, 1823, 8vo. Having, in the first edition of his history, expressed his disbelief in

of the Roman law, has been discussed by Dr. Schulin;[2] and with respect to the character of Livy, we only think it necessary to remark that we regard him as no incompetent authority for such a fact as he has recorded. Had the fact of such a mission been very absurd or very incredible in itself, the state of the question would have been essentially different. It is further urged by the same learned professor, that all the ancient monuments of Roman history must have perished when the city was burnt by the Gauls. But it is not to be doubted that the laws of the twelve Tables, or at least ample portions of them, survived the destruction of the city: those laws are repeatedly mentioned by Cicero, as we should now mention the Great Charter, not as what has existed, but as what still exists;[3] at a later period they were the subject of various commentaries, nor do we meet with any hint or suggestion that such commentaries related to fragments, instead of the entire collection. It is indeed stated by Livy that, after this calamity, an attempt was made by public authority to recover the regal and decemviral laws;[4] and we learn from Cyprian that, during the third

the story of the embassy to Greece, his opinion was publicly controverted by Professor Ciampi, in a work entitled Novum Examen Loci Liviani, de Legatis, &c. Vilnæ, 1821, 8vo. To this antagonist he replies, but without mentioning his name, in an Excursus ad Livii Historiarum lib. iii. cap. 31. sqq. See likewise the second edition of his Historia Juris Romani, p. 54. Varsaviæ, 1825, 8vo.

[2] De Dionysio Halicarnasseo Historico, præcipuo Historiæ Juris Romani Fonte, Dissertatio inauguralis, in Academia Heidelbergensi præmio ornata. Scripsit Phil. Frid. Schulin, Moeno-Francofurtanus, Juris utriusque Doctor. Heidelbergæ, 1820, 4to.

[3] "Discebamus enim pueri XII. ut carmen necessarium; quas jam nemo discit." (Cicero de Legibus, lib. ii. cap. xxiii.)

[4] "In primis fœdera et leges (erant autem eæ duodecim Tabulæ, et quædam regiæ leges) conquiri quæ comparerent, jusserunt." (Livii Hist. lib. vi. cap. i.)

century, the laws of the twelve Tables were still to be
found engraved on tablets of brass.[5] If then the laws
themselves were rescued from the ruins of the city, is
there any difficulty in imagining, or any absurdity in believing, that their genuine history was likewise preserved? Let us even suppose that every written monument perished in the common wreck, yet the nation
itself was not exterminated; and the oral tradition of
one generation became the lettered record of the
next.

Some writers have involved the subject in unnecessary
doubt and difficulty, by misapprehending the real state
of the question; for it has been seriously asked whether
the decemvirs transferred the entire laws of Solon to the
twelve Tables. If any person imagines that they transferred the entire laws of Solon, or any other legislator,
he manifestly entertains a very crude opinion; and he
who opposes such an opinion, can only be thought to
combat a phantom. Let us examine the passage of Livy
as our original text: " Quum de legibus conveniret, de
latore tantum discreparet, missi legati Athenas Sp. Pos-
tumius Albus, A. Manlius, Ser. Sulpicius Camerinus;
jussique inclytas leges Solonis describere, et aliarum
Græciæ civitatum instituta, mores, juraque noscere." [6]

---

[5] " Incisæ sint licet leges duodecim tabulis, et publice ære præfixo jura
præscripta sint, inter leges ipsas delinquitur, inter jura peccatur." (Cypriani Opera, p. 4. edit. Baluz. Paris. 1726, fol.) Whether this is not
rather to be considered as a rhetorical flourish, than as the statement of
an historical fact, may perhaps admit of some doubt.

[6] Livii Hist. lib. iii. cap. xxxi.—According to Dionysius of Halicarnas·
sus, they were partly indebted to the Greek colonies in Italy. Ἐν δὲ τῷ
αὐτῷ καιρῷ παρεγίνοντο ἀπό τε Ἀθηνῶν καὶ τῶν ἐν Ἰταλοῖς Ἑλληνίδων
πόλεων οἱ πρέσβεις, φέροντες τοὺς νόμους. (Antiquitates Romanæ, lib.
x. cap. liv. p. 646. edit. Hudson.) See the learned work of Dempster, De

He soon afterwards states that those ambassadors were nominated among the decemvirs for two reasons : " His proximi legati tres habiti, qui Athenas ierant; simul ut pro legatione tam longinqua præmio esset honos ; simul peritos legum peregrinarum ad condenda nova jura usui fore credebant." Nothing can be more plain and intelligible than this account. Three ambassadors, or as we might with equal propriety describe them, three messengers, were sent to Greece, with instructions to procure a copy of the laws of Solon, and to acquaint themselves with the laws and institutions of other states of Greece besides Athens.[7] In the commission for preparing a body of laws, these three individuals were included, in order that this honour might compensate them for their former labours, and that the knowledge which they had acquired of foreign jurisprudence might be rendered useful in the compilation of a new body of laws. The ex-

---

Etruria Regali, tom. i. p. 445. Florent. 1723-4, 2 tom. fol. Niebuhr is decidedly of opinion, that, with regard to personal rights, and the forms of legal procedure, the Romans were indebted to no Greek cities except those of Italy. He however considers it as an historical fact, that ambassadors were sent beyond the sea; but he supposes they may have found nothing that appeared applicable to the existing circumstances of their own republic. "Und konnten denn nicht die Gesandten ausgehen eine in weiter Ferne verehrte Weisheit zu vernehmen, diese aber hernach nicht anwendbar befunden werden?" (Römische Geschichte, Th. ii. S. 344.) See Wachsmuth's ältere Geschichte des Römischen Staates, S. 369. Halle, 1819, 8vo.

[7] " Sunt igitur duodecim Tabulæ fons omnis publici privatique juris: duodecim Tabularum fons Græcorum leges, Atheniensium maxime." (Ruhnkenii Oratio de Græcia Artium ac Doctrinarum Inventrice: Opuscula, tom. i. p. 99). " It is perhaps worth while to remark," says Dr. Smith, " that though the laws of the twelve Tables were, many of them, copied from those of some ancient Greek republics, yet law never seems to have grown up to be a science in any republic of ancient Greece." (Wealth of Nations, vol. iii. p. 176).

pression *ad condenda nova jura* certainly does not suggest
the idea of transferring laws already made.   If therefore
any enquirer should succeed in proving, what it will however be very difficult to prove, that there is not a single
coincidence between any existing fragment of the twelve
Tables, and any existing fragment of the laws of Athens
or any other state of Greece, no argument could thence
be deduced against Livy's account of the mission.   The
Romans, at that period a rude and simple nation, were
anxious to obtain some knowledge of the laws, customs,
and institutions of a kindred people, before they attempted to reduce their own laws to something approaching to a systematic form; and in order to procure this
knowledge, they adopted an expedient which must strike
every person, who reflects on the state of society at that
remote era, as the most obvious and practicable that
could have been devised.   But of the new laws with
which they thus became acquainted, it is evident that
many were utterly to be rejected, some to be abhorred;
and they might learn what to avoid, as well as what to
imitate.   We might as rationally expect one nation to
adopt the entire language as the entire laws of another
nation.   When the decemvirs were employed in their
important task, the city of Rome had seen three centuries of years, and during that period had partly been
governed by written, and partly by unwritten laws.   It is
therefore to be supposed that the twelve Tables chiefly
consisted of a digest of what was regarded as the best
portion of their municipal enactments and customs:
customary law, which acquires its vigour and consistency
in the early stages of society, was doubtless a very essential part; and some modifications, perhaps various
regulations entirely new, might be derived from a fo-

reign source.　This I conceive to be the authentic
history, and these the genuine effects, of the famous
mission into Greece; and in the general texture of this
story I find nothing that exceeds the limits of rational
belief.

Dr. Dunbar has well remarked that "the Romans,
while yet a rude people, disdained not to appoint an embassy to enquire into the jurisprudence of the Greeks,
and to supply, from that fountain, the deficiencies in their
civil code.　This embassy seems to have been suggested
by Hermodorus, an exiled citizen of Ephesus, who afterwards eminently assisted in interpreting the collection of
laws brought from Greece.　His public services met with
a public reward.　A statue was erected to him in the
Comitia at the public expense; an honour which the
jealousy of Rome would have denied to a stranger in a
less generous age.　But, at this period, she acted from
a nobler impulse; and the statue erected to Hermodorus was erected, in reality, to her own honour.　Yet the
name of this Ephesian, which casts a lustre upon Rome,
seemed to cast a shade upon his native city; and that
people, according to Heraclitus, deserved to have been
extirpated to a man, who had condemned such a citizen
to exile."[8]　This agency of Hermodorus is not mentioned
by Livy: but the erection of his statue is recorded by

[8] Dunbar's Essays on the History of Mankind in rude and cultivated
Ages, p. 161.　Lond. 1780, 8vo.—See likewise Dr. Wallace's Dissertation on the Numbers of Mankind in antient and modern Times, p. 238.
Edinb. 1753, 8vo.　"Les Grecs," says Voltaire, "fournirent aux Romains la loi des douze Tables.　Un peuple qui va chercher des loix et des
dieux chez un autre, devait être un peuple petit et barbare; aussi les pre-
miers Romains l'étaient-ils."　(Philosophie de l'Histoire, p. 282.　Amst
1765, 8vo).

the elder Pliny;[9] and his connexion with the decemvirs is likewise stated by Pomponius: " Et ita ex accidentia appellatæ sunt Leges duodecim Tabularum: quarum ferendarum auctorem fuisse decemviris Hermodorum quendam Ephesium, exulantem in Italia, quidam retulerunt."[1] By the word *auctor*, as used in this passage, we are evidently to understand a person who advised or influenced the decemvirs; and, according to Pliny, his services were those of a translator or expounder. It is therefore highly probable that he was chiefly employed in expounding to them the Greek laws, of which they had obtained a transcript. As he appears to have been a person of superior talents,[2] his own comments might be useful and important; but I am by no means inclined to estimate his services so highly as Vico and Gratama, who represent him as the real author of the laws of the twelve Tables.[3]

Before I dismiss the history of the twelve Tables, I am tempted to notice an opinion which another modern author has delivered respecting one of their enactments. " Ancient histories," says Lord Kames, " are full of incredible facts that passed current during the infancy of reason, which at present would be rejected with contempt. Every one who is conversant in the history of ancient nations, can recal instances without end. Does any person believe at present, though gravely reported by

[9] " Fuit et Hermodori Ephesii in Comitio, legum quas decemviri scribebant interpretis, [statua] publice dicata." (Plinii Natur. Hist. lib. xxxiv. cap. xi.)

[1] Digest. lib. i. tit. ii. fr. 2. § 4.

[2] See Menagii Observationes in Diogenem Laertium, p. 393.

[3] J. B. Vici Opera Latina, tom. ii. p. 385. Serpii Gratama Oratio de Hermodoro Ephesio vero XII. Tabularum Auctore. Groningæ, 1817, 4to.

historians, that in old Rome there was a law for cutting into pieces the body of a bankrupt, and distributing the parts among his creditors?"[4]   This is the speculation of an ingenious man, who is sometimes too precipitate in his conclusions.   Annæus Robertus[5] and Heraldus[6] have each proposed a mitigating interpretation of this law of the twelve Tables: Bynkershoek was solicitous to prove that the creditors were entitled to divide, not the body, but the price of the insolvent debtor;[7] and his opinion has been adopted by the learned Dr. Taylor,[8] and by some other civilians.   But this opinion can neither be reconciled with the obvious meaning of the words, nor with the ancient mode of understanding them.[9]   Those

[4] Kames's Sketches of the History of Man, vol. iii. p. 253.

[5] Roberti Rerum Judicataram libri iv. f. 137, b. edit. Paris. 1597, 4to.

[6] Heraldi de Rerum Judicatarum Auctoritate libri ii. p. 518.   Paris. 1640, 8vo.—The common opinion is maintained by Salmasius in several of his works, and with his usual erudition.   De Usuris liber, p. 546. Lugd. Bat. 1638, 8vo. De Modo Usurarum liber, p. 809.   Lugd. Bat. 1639, 8vo.   Miscellæ Defensiones de variis Observationibus et Emenda-tionibus ad Jus Atticum et Romanum pertinentibus, p. 317.   Lugd. Bat. 1645, 8vo.   This latter work is directed against Heraldus, who prepared, but did not himself live to publish, a very ample and a very learned reply, under the title of " Desiderii Heraldi Observationes ad Jus Atticum et Romanum, in quibus Claudii Salmasii Miscellæ Defensiones, ejusque Specimen expenduntur."   Paris. 1650, fol.   See more particularly p. 288. One of the works which he here undertakes to confute is a " Specimen Confutationis Animadversionum Desiderii Heraldi; sive Tractatus de Subscribendis et Signandis Testamentis, item de antiquorum et hodier-norum Sigillorum Differentia."   Lugd. Bat. 1648, 8vo.   This is the most learned controversy that occurs in the annals of jurisprudence.

[7] Bynkershoek Observationes Juris Romani, lib. i. cap. i.

[8] Taylori Commentarius in L. Decemviralem de inope Debitore in par-tis dissecando.   Cantabrigiæ, 1742, 4to.

[9] Dr. Valpy, a learned divine, has confuted the opinion of Bynkershoek and Taylor, in a long note subjoined to his *Sermons preached on public Occasions*, vol. ii. p. 1.   Lond. 1811, 2 vols. 8vo.

who consider such an enactment as altogether incredible, ought at the same time to consider the real character of the Roman people at that period of their history.[1] They certainly were not distinguished by the gentler virtues; and if their laws were altogether silent as to the treatment of debtors, we ascertain from other sources of information that it was extremely harsh and cruel. In more rude communities, where commerce is almost entirely unknown, and where the poor are completely subjected to the rich, the insolvent debtor is very apt to be treated as a criminal. In ancient Rome, we know from historical records, not merely from the letter of the law, that he might be reduced to the condition of a slave; and it is obvious to every person acquainted with ancient history, that the unrelenting treatment of debtors was a ground of open dissension between the different orders of the people. The same laws which conferred on the father of a family the power of life and death over his wife and children, and which awarded capital punishment against the author of a satirical poem, may without much difficulty be conceived to have disposed of a poor debtor's person in the most summary manner.

It was in the 302d year from the building of the city that the decemvirs were appointed, and were invested with extraordinary powers, for the purpose of compiling a body of laws. They accordingly completed ten tables, which in the following year were confirmed by the comitia centuriata; but as some deficiencies were still to be supplied, decemvirs were again created, and the labour was thus brought to a conclusion. The laws of the twelve

[1] " Hæc tam horribilis atrocitas," says Salmasius, "non in alium finem instituta, quam, ut fraudatores essent pauciores, et fœnebris pecuniæ commercium in tuto ac solido locaretur." (De Usuris liber, p. 546).

Tables were illustrated by the commentaries of several ancient lawyers, and among the rest of Antistius Labeo and Caius: the fragments of those laws have been collected and explained by many of the moderns, by Balduinus, Rævardus, Marcilius, Augustinus, Gravina, Funccius, Bouchaud, and others;[2] but the most able and conspicuous labourer in this province is the younger Gothofredus, whose edition of the Theodosian Code has rendered his name illustrious in the history of jurisprudence.[3]

Law assumed the form of a science during the latter ages of the republic; and jurisprudence, like philosophy, was at length subdivided into sects.[1] The chief splendour of the Roman lawyers is to be traced from the reign of Augustus to that of Alexander Severus;[5] and the last name of great celebrity is that of Herennius Modestinus.[6] With this pupil of Ulpian, the oracles of the civilians be-

[2] See Dirksen's Uebersicht der bisherigen Versuche zur Kritik und Herstellung des Textes der Zwölf-Tafel-Fragmente. Leipzig, 1824, 8vo.

[3] Gothofredus's Fragmenta XII. Tabularum are to be found in his Fontes quatuor Juris Civilis. Genevæ, 1653, 4to. They are reprinted among his Opera Juridica minora. Lugd. Bat. 1733, fol.

[1] Mascovii de Sectis Sabinianorum et Proculianorum in Jure Civili Diatriba. Lipsiæ, 1728, 8vo. Dirksen's Beiträge zur Kunde des Römischen Rechts, S. 1. Leipzig, 1825, 8vo. On the schools of the Roman lawyers, the more recent of these authors has written a dissertation of 158 pages.

[5] See the collection edited by Dr. Franck under the title of "Vitæ tripartitæ Jurisconsultorum veterum, a Bernardo Rutilio, Joanne Bertrando, et Guilielmo Grotio conscriptæ." Halæ Magd. 1718, 4to.

[6] The fragments of Modestinus have been illustrated by many different civilians, and, among others, by Brenkman, in a work entitled " De Eurematicis Diatriba : sive, in Herennii Modestini librum singularem Περὶ Εὐρηματικῶν Commentarius." Lugd. Bat. 1706, 8vo. See Bachii Historia Jurisprudentiæ Romanæ, p. 506. edit. Stockmann. Lipsiæ, 1807, 8vo.

came mute:[7] the succeeding lawyers are only known as compilers or expounders; and although the law was long afterwards taught at Rome, Constantinople, and Berytus, we cannot in those declining annals discover any vestiges of ancient genius. The reign of Constantine was not conspicuous for legal science; and by fixing the seat of empire at Byzantium, he diminished all the chances or probabilities of improvement. To the great body of those who inhabited the new metropolis, the language of the law was a foreign language; nor was this the only circumstance unfavourable to the cultivation and progress of jurisprudence.[8]

It is well known that the decisions of certain lawyers obtained the force of law.[9] In a rescript of Constantine, dated in the year 327, we find the highest authority ascribed to the opinions of Julius Paulus,[1] who flourished at the close of the second and the commencement of the third century. After an interval of nearly one hundred

[7] "Atque hic jurisconsultorum finis est, hic oracula jurisconsultorum obmutuere; sic ut ultimum jurisconsultorum Modestinum dicere liceat, cessim et retro collapsa jam jurisprudentia." (Gothofredi Hist. Juris Civilis, p. 14).

[8] "Sæpe nostra clementia dubitavit, quæ causa faceret, ut tantis propositis præmiis, quibus artes et studia nutriuntur, tam pauci raroque extiterint qui plena juris civilis scientia ditarentur, et in tanto lucubrationum tristi pallore, vix unus aut alter receperit soliditatem perfectæ doctrinæ." (Novell. Theod. tit. i.)

[9] "Responsa prudentium sunt sententiæ et opiniones eorum, quibus permissum est jura condere: quorum omnium si in unum sententiæ concurrant, id quod ita sentiunt, legis vicem obtinet; si vero dissentiunt, judici licet, quam velit sententiam sequi; idque rescripto divi Hadriani significatur." (Caii Institutiones, lib. i. § 7). This is one of the numerous instances in which the Institutions of Caius reflect a strong light on the history of the Roman law. Before their discovery, this rescript of Hadrian was totally unknown to modern civilians.

[1] Theodosiani Codicis genuini Fragmenta, p. 34.

years, appeared another imperial constitution, intended
to regulate the number and weight of legal opinions. In
the judges themselves very little confidence seems to be
reposed, nor is it difficult to imagine that their general
merits are not undervalued: they are bound to decide
points of law, according to the number of accredited
opinions; when the numbers are equal, and the decision
of Papinian can be produced on one side of a question,
his authority must be allowed to preponderate, " qui, ut
singulos vincit, ita cedit duobus;" and it is only in the
case of a perfect equilibrium of legal opinions, that they
are left to the full exercise of their own discrimination.[2]
This arrangement is so entirely mechanical, that it is
manifestly adapted to the lowest standard of attainment
in those entrusted with the administration of the law.

Of the writings of the ancient lawyers, innumerable
fragments are incorporated in the Pandects, and various
others have been collected by Schulting. The recent
discovery of several reliques of the Roman law has given a
fresh impulse to the continental civilians. New portions
of the Theodosian Code have been brought to light by
Clossius and Peyron. To the Vatican Fragments, published by Angelo Mai,[3] we can only make a transient
allusion; but the recovery of the long-lost Institutions of

[2] Cod. Theodos. lib. i. tit. iv. p. 24. edit. Wenck.

[3] The edition of Mai has been followed by several others. The most
elaborate that I have seen bears the subsequent title : " Juris Civilis An-
tejustinianei Vaticana Fragmenta, e codice rescripto ab Angelo Maio edita,
recognovit, commentario tum critico tum exegetico, nec non quadruplici
appendice instruxit Alex. Aug. de Buchholtz, Doctor Juris utriusque."
Regimonti Borussorum, 1828, 8vo. These fragments, revised by Beth-
mann-Hollweg, are inserted in the first fasciculus of the *Corpus Juris
Romani Antejustiniani*, a valuable collection now in the course of publication.

the law.[5]   After much laborious preparation, the Institutions of Caius or Gaius were published in a very able and satisfactory manner by Professor Göschen,[6] who, since that period, has been removed to the university of Göttingen. Although the manuscript has been exposed to frequent and material mutilations, much remains to instruct and to interest the learned enquirer; and the book has accordingly been received by the foreign civilians with a degree

[5] Zeitschrift für geschichtliche Rechtswissenschaft, herausgegeben von Savigny, Eichhorn und Göschen, Bd. iv. S. 480.

[6] Gaii Institutionum commentarii IV. e codice rescripto Bibliothecæ Capitularis Veronensis, auspiciis Regiæ Scientiarum Academiæ Borussicæ, nunc primum editi.   Accedit Fragmentum veteris Jurisconsulti de Jure Fisci, ex aliis ejusdem Bibliothecæ membranis transcriptum. Berolini, 1820, 8vo. A second edition followed in 1824. The text was reprinted in a collection edited by Jourdan, in concert with Blondeau and Du Caurroy, two professors of the civil law in the university of Paris. The collection is entitled Juris Civilis Ecloga. Paris. 1822, 12mo. Several other editions have since appeared; and among these, the following is entitled to particular notice: "Gaii et Justiniani Institutiones Juris Romani.   Recognoverunt, annotationem adjecerunt, conjunctasque ediderunt Clem. Aug. Car. Klenze, Juris utriusque Doctor, et in Universitate Frid. Guil. Berol. Professor Publ. Ordinarius, et Eduardus Böcking, Juris utriusque Doctor." Berolini, 1829, 4to. The Institutions of Caius, revised by Heffter, form the first part of the Corp. Jur. Roman. Antejust. The editor had previously evinced his competency for such a task by the publication of " Gaii Jurisconsulti Institutionum commentarius quartus, sive de Actionibus. Recensuit, restituere conatus est, adnotationem perpetuam, librumque observationum adjecit Augustus Guilelmus Heffter, Antecessor Bonnensis." Berolini, 1827, 4to. An edition of Caius, with notes and emendations, was long ago promised by Pietro Ruga, professor of the civil law in the university of Rome. (Giornale Arcadico di Scienze, Lettere, ed Arte, tom. xiii. p. 14. Roma, 1822, 8vo.) Göschen and other editors have apparently erred in the orthography of the author's name. From the testimony of Quinctilian and Terentianus Maurus it is evident, that, although the ancients pronounced Gaius, they wrote Caius. (Dausquii Orthographia Latini Sermonis vetus et nova, vol. ii. p. 70. edit. Paris. 1677, fol.)

of ardour and exultation, not easily conceived by those who are unacquainted with the progress of such studies among some of the continental nations. Its value in elucidating the history of the Roman law has been discussed by Schrader.[7] Caius has already been illustrated in many other publications, and, in some of the German universities, has been illustrated in separate courses of lectures. It may safely be affirmed, that the discovery of the Institutions of Caius forms a new era in the history of jurisprudence.

Before we proceed to examine the legislative labours of Theodosius, it will be proper to state that, in the compilation of a code of laws, he had been preceded by two private lawyers, Gregorius or Gregorianus, and Hermogenes or Hermogenianus, for their respective names are not completely ascertained.[8] From the order in which their codes are mentioned by ancient writers, it is to be inferred that the labours of Gregorius preceded those of Hermogenianus.[9] Some fragments of both codes have been

---

[7] Was gewinnt die Römische Rechtsgeschichte durch Caius Institutionen? untersucht von Eduard Schrader, Professor in Tübingen. Heidelberg, 1823, 8vo.—The learned author has prosecuted similar enquiries in an article entitled " Neuentdeckte Quellen Römischer Rechtskunde," which occurs in the Kritische Zeitschrift für Rechtswissenschaft, Bd. i. S. 137. Elvers has published a very useful work under the title of *Promptuarium Gaianum.* Gœtingæ, 1824, 8vo.

[8] Gothofredi Prolegomena ad Codicem Theodosianum, cap. i. Schultingii Jurisprudentia Ante-Justinianea, p. 683. Menagii Juris Civilis Amœnitates, cap. xi. Reinoldi Opuscula Juridica, p. 404. C. F. Pohlii Dissertatio de Codicibus Gregoriano atque Hermogeniano. Lipsiæ, 1777, 4to.

[9] Blume supposes Gregorius to have lived in the reign of the emperors Diocletian and Maximian. One of the rescripts inserted in his code bears a very mutilated inscription, from the fragments of which this learned civilian raises the words " Diocletianus et (Maximianus) Domini

preserved by Anianus.[1] Gregorius appears to have collected the imperial constitutions belonging to the intermediate reigns, from Adrian to Constantine the Great. Hermogenianus is supposed to have formed a supplementary collection; and the remaining fragments consist entirely of the constitutions of Diocletian and Maximian. Of the former of these compilers, the personal history is involved in complete obscurity. According to the conjectures of modern civilians, the latter must have flourished in the reign of Constantine; and he is supposed to be the same Hermogenianus whose works are quoted in the Pandects. Both compilations are apparently to be considered as the undertakings of private individuals: the ancient commentator on the Theodosian Code has indeed averred that their authority is confirmed by a law, "sub titulo de Constitutionibus Principium et Edictis,"[2] and Gothofredus has naturally enough relied on this averment;

---

nostri." (Lex Dei, sive Mosaicarum et Romanarum Legum Collatio, p. 10. 156. Bonnæ, 1833, 8vo.) This expression, if we admit it as genuine, must obviously have been applied to the princes then reigning; but the notice rests on the credit of a conjectural emendation, which, however ingenious, cannot be received as infallibly certain.

[1] Schultingii Jurisprudentia Ante-Justinianea, p. 681. Lugd. Bat. 1717, 4to. Jus Civile Ante-Justinianeum, tom. i. p. 263. Berolini, 1815, 2 tom. 8vo. The most critical and most valuable edition was recently published by Hänel: "Codicis Gregoriani et Codicis Hermogeniani Fragmenta. Ad xxxv. librorum manuscriptorum et priorum editionum fidem recognovit et annotatione critica instruxit Gustavus Haenel Lipsiensis." Bonnæ, 1835, 4to. Copies are to be found in a separate form; but this edition constitutes part of a great collection, of which the first fasciculus has appeared with the following title: " Corpus Juris Romani Antejustiniani. Consilio Professorum Bonnensium E. Böckingii, A. Bethmann-Hollwegii, E. Puggæi, curaverunt iidem assumptis sociis L. Arndtsio, A. F. Barkovio, F. Blumio, G. Haenelio, G. Hefftero, aliisque. Præfatus est Eduardus Böckingius." Bonnæ, 1835, 4to.

[2] Cod. Theodos. lib. i. tit. iv. fr. 1.

but the commentator probably alluded to a constitution
which has recently been discovered, and which certainly
affords no adequate support to such an opinion.   The
emperor merely declares his resolution of forming a collection of imperial constitutions, "ad similitudinem Gregoriani atque Hermogeniani Codicis :" he thus acknow-
ledges the propriety of such a model, but is silent with
respect to any public sanction of those antecedent codes.[3]
It is however probable that they obtained some degree of
authority in the forum.[4]   This circumstance may naturally be imputed to the intrinsic value of such a collection
of laws; and we may conceive the two codes to have
obtained the same degree of authority as might belong
to the publication of an English author, who had prepared a digest or an abridgment of the Statutes.   In
either case the credit of the compiler must depend,
not upon any formal sanction, but upon the fidelity with
which he is generally believed to have executed his
undertaking.

The Theodosian Code occupies a very prominent place
in the annals of jurisprudence; and, in this country at
least, its history is so imperfectly known that I am induced
to exhibit a particular account of the code itself, and of
the most material circumstances attending its transmission to our times.   Sir Edward Sugden, if I rightly guess
at his meaning, supposes it to be partly a code of the
public laws of the empire, partly a digest of the opinions
of private lawyers.   " Rome began," as he avers, "with
the laws of the twelve Tables, and in the time of Justinian, many camels would have been required to carry the
codes and laws of the empire, and the comments upon

---

[3] Theodosiani Codicis genuini Fragmenta, p. 6.
[4] Heineccii Hist. Juris Civilis, p. 478. edit. Ritter.

them.[5]   Amongst the Roman lawyers, many individuals
left behind them hundreds of books of their own composition on the laws.   These overwhelming masses rendered
a methodical collection and digest of the laws necessary.
This was all that was attempted by the Theodosian
Code." [6]   Of the origin and nature of the Theodosian
Code, this is certainly a very learned and satisfactory
exposition.   But, says Mr. Humphreys, "for the digest,
as well as for any selection from individual commentators,
I have searched the *four* folios of my Codex Theodosianus in vain [which copy appears to want two entire
volumes]; while, on the other hand, the numerous

---

[5] The writer who speaks of the ἄχθος καμήλων πολλῶν is Eunapius,
who lived, not in the time of Justinian, but in the time of Arcadius and
Honorius. (Fabricii Bibliotheca Græca, tom. vii. p. 536. edit. Harles.)
The passage may be found in Eunapii Vitæ Sophistarum, recensuit
notisque illustravit Jo. Fr. Boissonade, accedit annotatio Dan. Wyttenbachii, tom. i. p. 42. Amst. 1822, 2 tom. 8vo. This passage appears to
have been misunderstood by Heineccius and other writers, who have
misled Sir Edward Sugden. "Atque nexus ipse verborum," says Wyttenbach, "ostendit hæc dici de pragmaticorum scriptiunculis, quæ in
testamentis, emtionibus, venditionibus, stipulationibus, similibus argu-
mentis versantur: hæ Latinis dicuntur *libelli*, Græcis βιβλίδια, de quibus
docuit Brissonius de Verborum Significatione, p. 546, 547: et est versus
Juvenalis, allatus ab Arnaldo, Satir. vii. 107:
       Dic igitur, quid caussidicis civilia præstent
       Officia, et magno comites in fasce libelli.
Si veterum jurisconsultorum libros significare voluisset, honestiori eos
nomine συγγράμματα, συντάγματα, συντάξεις, et simili modo, vocasset."
(Tom. ii. p. 140). See likewise G. d'Arnaud Variarum Conjecturarum libri
duo, p. 204. Franequeræ, 1738, 4to. This explanation of a passage which is
so frequently quoted, and so frequently misunderstood, has not escaped
the notice of a very learned English lawyer. (Cooper, Lettres sur la
Cour de la Chancellerie, et sur quelques Points de la Jurisprudence
Anglaise, p. 17, edit. Paris, 1830, 8vo.)
[6] Sugden's Letter to James Humphreys, Esq. p. 53, 3d edit. Lond.
1827, 8vo.

novels of Theodosius II., which both authenticate and form a supplement to his code, exhibit an attempt (using your own expression) to effect something beyond a mere compilation of anterior laws." [7] As this same code is not written in Arabic, or even in Greek, it was reasonably enough to be expected that such individuals as these might have found means of acquainting themselves, if not with its tenor and contents, at least with its history and external form; and I will venture to affirm that there is scarcely a notary public in all Germany, who, if he had thought it incumbent upon him to write, would thus have written about the Theodosian Code.

This code of laws, which is sometimes erroneously ascribed to Theodosius the Great, derived its origin from his grandson Theodosius the younger. [8] On the decease of the first Theodosius, the Roman empire was divided between his two sons, the provinces of the east being allotted to Arcadius, those of the west to Honorius. From the sovereign of the east descended Theodosius the Second : after the death of his father and of his uncle, he again united the dominions which had thus been par-

[7] Humphreys's Letter to Edward B. Sugden, Esq. p. 7. Lond. 1827, 8vo.

[8] The late Bishop Müller, who was a man of solid learning and of sound judgment, published a work which greatly contributes to illustrate the history of an interesting period embraced by the Theodosian Code. It is in the form of a disquisition on the genius, manners, and luxury of the age of Theodosius the Great. The author's materials are to a great extent derived from the writings of Chrysostom, from the Code itself, and from the admirable commentary of Gothofredus; but he likewise appears to have consulted almost all the ancient writers, whether Christian or pagan, who could furnish him with any gleanings of information. (Commentatio Historica de Genio, Moribus, et Luxu Ævi Theodosiani, auctore Petro Erasmo Müller Havniensi, Philos. Doct. Particula I. Havniæ, 1797. Particula II. Goettingæ, 1798, 8vo.)

titioned; but conferring the titles of Cæsar and Augustus upon Valentinian the Third, who married his daughter Licinia Eudoxia, he assigned to him the western provinces of the empire. This son-in-law, who became his successor at Constantinople, was likewise his cousin, being the son of Constantius Cæsar, and of Galla Placidia, the daughter of Theodosius the Great.[9]

It appears to have been the original intention of Theodosius to compile two codes, arranged according to different plans; but his second code was never completed, nor is it easy to conjecture, from this description, what specific plan he contemplated. The emperor had thus divulged his intention in the year 429, and the Theodosian Code received his sanction on the fifteenth day before the calends of March, 438. The compilers of the Code were eight in number; and, as Gothofredus has remarked, they all occupied stations which required an acquaintance with the laws. Antiochus, who was placed at the head of this important commission, has been confounded by him, as well as by Heineccius, with Antiochus the eunuch, and likewise with a third individual of the same name.[1]

[9] In illustrating the history of Galla Placidia, the celebrated Ruhnkenius exhibited the first public specimen of his erudition. (Opuscula, tom. i. p. 1. Lugd. Bat. 1823, 2 tom. 8vo.) He was then a *Magister Legens* in the university of Wittemberg, and, although a very young writer, he afforded an ample promise of that profound and various learning by which he was afterwards so much distinguished. The first of his two disputations was held *præside J. D. Rittero.* Ritter was professor of history, but he likewise read lectures on law. (Wyttenbachii Vita Ruhnkenii, p. 14.) To his connexion with this learned and able man, we may ascribe his relish for the study of jurisprudence. Twelve of his letters to Ritter have been published, and many portions of them relate to juridical subjects. (Opuscula, tom. ii. p. 767, 862.)

[1] See Ritter ad Novell. Theod. p. 6.

D

By a constitution, which has recently been discovered, and which bears the date of 435, the emperor had invested the compilers of his code with power to retrench what was superfluous, to add what was necessary, to change what was ambiguous, and to correct what was incongruous.[2] " Quod, ut, brevitate constrictum, claritate luceat, aggressuris hoc opus et demendi supervacanea, et adjiciendi necessaria, et mutandi ambigua, et emendandi incongrua tribuimus potestatem." Justinian afterwards invested his commissioners with more ample powers: they were even authorized to consolidate several constitutions into one; and we may presume that neither of the two codes exhibited the imperial laws, or at least a large proportion of them, in their original state. In the novel which sanctions the Theodosian Code, the emperor evidently admits that the compilers whom he had employed were not mere copyists: " Manet igitur, manebitque perpetuo, elimata gloria conditorum, nec in nostrum titulum demigravit nisi lux sola brevitatis."

This code contains the edicts and rescripts of sixteen emperors; and its chronology extends from 312 to 438, thus embracing a period of 126 years.[3] It commences with the reign of the first Christian emperor, and there is a systematic exclusion of the constitutions issued by the military adventurers who, during that interval, were

---

[2] Codicis Theodosiani Fragmenta inedita, p. 29.

[3] " Si species constitutionum quæras, hic occurrunt non edicta tantum, sed et rescripta varia ad consultationes magistratuum emissa; epistolæ item, seu litteræ ad magistratus, orationes ad senatum, pragmaticæ, acta habita in consistoriis principum, itemque in principiis, mandata denique data rectoribus provinciarum, censitoribus, peræquatoribus missis, cognitoribus futuris in collatione de religione. Huc inquam congesta omnia illa, quæ aliquam juris scientiam et definitionem continerent." (Gothofredi Prolegomena ad Codicem Theodosianum, cap. ii.)

Caius is too remarkable an event to be noticed in the same manner. An unsatisfactory abridgment of these Institutions had long been known ; but the genuine text of Caius was not discovered till the year 1816. In the library of the chapter of Verona, the celebrated Niebuhr, author of the Roman history, found a juridical manuscript of great antiquity; and when a short extract was communicated to Savigny, he easily ascertained that it formed a portion of the original work of this ancient lawyer, who flourished about the age of Antoninus. In the course of the following year, the Royal Academy of Berlin despatched to Verona two distinguished members of the university, Professor Göschen, a civilian, and Professor Bekker, a philologer, entrusted with the important commission of executing a transcript of the manuscript; and in the performance of this very formidable task, they were greatly aided by the spontaneous and indefatigable services of Dr. Bethmann Hollweg, who is now a professor of law at Bonn. The manuscript is a *codex rescriptus,* and to a considerable extent *bis rescriptus ;* nor is it easy to conceive the difficulty of deciphering an ancient relique in this condition. Without the aid of a chemical process, it would have been impossible to succeed in the attempt to read what had thus been written and erased.[4] According to the opinion of Kopp, the learned author of the Palæographia Critica, who is allowed to possess great knowledge of ancient monuments, the manuscript must have been written before Justinian's reformation of

---

[4] Abhandlungen der historish-philologischen Klasse der Königlich-Preussischen Akademie der Wissenschaften aus den Jahren 1816-1817, S. 307. Berlin, 1819, 4to. Thémis, tom. i. p. 287. Goescheni præf. in Gaium.

finally unsuccessful in their attempts to usurp the government; but the selection is not limited to the constitutions of the Christian princes, for here we find the apostate Julian among other imperial lawgivers. The code is divided into sixteen books, and the laws which compose each title are arranged in chronological order.

The body of laws thus prepared by the emperor of the east, was immediately adopted by the emperor of the west. A very curious document, containing the " Gesta in Senatu Urbis Romæ de recipiendo Theodosiano Codice," has been discovered by Clossius.[4] At this period the Roman senate only exhibited a shadow of its former greatness: the stern and dignified republicans had long been supplanted by the minions of an imperial court; and a senate, possessing a very slender remnant of authority, was embodied in each of the two great divisions of the empire.[5] The senate of Rome having assembled on this occasion, one of the consuls, Anicius Acilius Glabrio Faustus, proceeded to acquaint the fathers with the legislative enterprise of the one emperor, and the zealous concurrence of the other. " Quam rem æternus princeps, dominus noster Valentinianus, devotione socii, affectu filii comprobavit." He afterwards read the constitution, which has already been mentioned, relative to the project of forming two different codes ; and this recitation was succeeded by many exclamations in the highest strain of

---

[4] Clossius, p. 3. Wenck, p. 3.

[5] M. C. Curtii Commentarii de Senatu Romano post Tempora Reipublicæ liberæ, p. 206. Halæ, 1768, 8vo. Del Senato Romano opera postuma del Conte Antonio Vendettini. Roma, 1782, 4to. The first chapter of the count's work treats "dello stato del senato Romano sotto gl' imperatori, ed i rè Goti;" the second, " del senato dall' anno 553 fin al secolo X.;" and the last, "delle mutazioni occorse ne' pontificati di Martino V. e di Eugenio IV."

panegyric. In the midst of various exclamations of kindness and regard for the consul, they afterwards hazard a
few suggestions respecting the custody and transcription
of this new code of laws; but we perceive no traces of
free discussion, or of real deliberation, which always im-
plies the power of adopting either the one or the other
of two conflicting opinions. They might presume to regulate certain matters of detail, but were without any
real influence in the administration of public affairs. In
the instance now before us, their chief functions were
manifestly confined to the ready approval of what the
consul informed them was the will of the emperor.

The Theodosian Code was thus promulgated in the
western, as well as in the eastern empire. The Gothic
conquerors of the west permitted their Roman subjects
to enjoy the benefit and the protection of their own laws;
and a compendium of those laws was even prepared
under the auspices of Alaric, king of the Visigoths,
whose dominions comprehended certain provinces of Spain
and Gaul.[6] This collection contains an abridgment of the
three codes of Gregorius, Hermogenianus, and Theodosius, together with some novels, or new constitutions, an
epitome of the Institutions of Caius, and extracts from
the Sententiæ of Paulus. It was completed in the year
506, " regnante domino Alarico rege, ordinante viro illustri Goiarico comite ;" and we must apparently conclude
that the superintendence of the work had been committed
to Goiaric, who was doubtless an officer of the king's
court. But it has for several centuries been known
under the title of ANIANI BREVIARIUM, or the Abridg-

      [6] C. G. Bieneri Commentarii de Origine et Progressu Legum Jurium-
que Germanicorum, part. i. p. 280. Lipsiæ, 1787-95, 2 part. 8vo.

ment of Anianus. The different copies appear to have been attested by his signature; and, according to the opinion of Gothofredus, he presents himself, not as the compiler of the book, but merely as the king's referendary.[7] " Anianus, vir spectabilis, ex præceptione D. N. gloriosiss. Alarici regis, hunc Codicem de Theodosiani legibus, atque sententiis juris, vel diversis libris electum, Aduris anno xxii. eo regnante, edidi atque subscripsi." This attestation is followed by a date, which states the day of the month, and repeats the year of the king's reign; and such a date we may suppose to apply to the act of verifying the copy, not to that of compiling the work itself. We might indeed have expected to find the words "edidi atque subscripsi" arranged in a different order, "subscripsi atque edidi;" but this remark is alike applicable, whether we conceive Anianus to have been the compiler, or merely the collater. To the formation of this collection it is highly probable that several individuals contributed their assistance, under the general direction of Goiaric.[8] To all the books contained in the

---

[7] Gothofredi Prolegomena, cap. v. Brunquelli Dissertatio de Codice Theodosiano ejusque in Codice Justinianeo Usu: Opuscula ad Historiam et Jurisprudentiam spectantia, p. 68. Halæ Magd. 1774, 8vo. Savigny's Geschichte des Römischen Rechts im Mittelalter, Bd. ii. S. 42. The more common opinion is however maintained by Schulting, Jurisprudentia Ante-Justinianea, præf. and by Hugo, Geschichte des Römischen Rechts, S. 732. " Codicem Theodosianum exscribi jussit," says Cironius, "ut illo uterentur quod Anianus cancellarius suus Aduris promulgavit, cum interpretationibus suis, sub titulo Legis Romanæ." (Observationes Juris Canonici, p. 72. Tolosæ, 1645, fol.)

[8] I therefore adopt the opinion of Gothofredus, that in the following passage Sigebertus Gemblacensis has misunderstood the proper sense of the word edere: " Anianus vir spectabilis, jubente Athalarico R. volumen unum de legibus Theodosii Imperatoris edidit; et monente Oruntio episcopo librum Joannis Chrysostomi in Matthæum de Græco in Latinum transtulit." (De Scriptoribus Ecclesiasticis, p. 101. edit. Fabricii.)

collection, with the exception of the epitome of Caius,
is added an *interpretatio,* or explanation. The manuscripts of the Theodosian Code do not all contain the
same explanation, and two different explanations are
sometimes subjoined to the same law.   It appears from
the *auctoritas* that explanations were inserted by order of
King Alaric, and we must suppose others to have been
derived from a different source.   The ancient commentary is to be found in Gothofredus's edition of the Theodosian Code; and a very cursory inspection of it seems
to have betrayed Sir Edward Sugden into the error of
supposing that code partly to consist of a digest of the
public laws, and partly of the discussions of private lawyers.   This commentary obtained so much credit, that
it appears in some measure to have superseded the text.
When the writers of the middle ages quote the Theodosian laws, they very commonly refer, not to the text, but
to the commentary.   Such ancient explanations as these
are not without some degree of interest or utility;[9]
though they cannot but be supposed to bear sufficient
marks of the age to which they belong.

   It is only in this ancient abridgment that a considerable proportion of the Theodosian Code has apparently
been transmitted to our times.[1]   For the first edition of

---

   [9] This collection of laws, says the archbishop of Tarragona, is accompanied " cum interpretationibus non ineptis." (Augustinus de Nominibus Propriis τοῦ Πανδέκτου Florentini, not. col. 27.   Tarracone, 1579,
fol.) The merits and defects of these interpretations are minutely discussed by Gothofredus, Prolegomena, cap. vi.   See likewise Savigny's
Geschichte, Bd. ii. S. 54.
   [1] Respecting the newly discovered manuscripts of this Breviarium, the
reader will find much information in Haubold's Opuscula Academica,
vol. ii. p. 897.   Lipsiæ, 1825-9, 2 tom. 8vo. See likewise the preface to
the same volume.

the Code, which was printed at Basel in the year 1528, we are indebted to the commendable zeal of Joannes Sichardus.[2] He had access to several manuscripts; but all of them appear to have been so defective, that very many titles are not to be found in his publication, and indeed several books present themselves in the most mutilated form. He has subjoined the ancient *interpretatio*, together with a collection of the *Novellæ Constitutiones* of Theodosius, Valentinian, and some other emperors. His edition is without annotations, but he has inserted various readings in the margin. After an interval of twenty-two years, a more complete edition of the Theodosian Code was published by Jean du Tillet, or Tillius, who has however omitted the ancient commentary.[3] In 1566, his edition was followed by that of Cujacius, who, among other appendages, has subjoined the ancient commentary, and a collection of the Novels. According to the title page, the sixth, seventh, eighth, and sixteenth books, " nunc primum prodeunt, cæteri aucti sunt innumeris constitutionibus."[4] Another edition by the same illustrious civilian, but without his name, was published at Paris in 1586; and, in the course of the same year, his name appeared in the title of an edition printed at Geneva.[5] These were followed by other editions of the

[2] Codicis Theodosiani libri xvi. quibus sunt ipsorum Principum autoritate adjectæ Novellæ, Theodosii, Valentiniani, Martiani, Majoriani, Severi. Caii Institutionum lib. ii. Julii Pauli Receptarum Sententiarum lib. v. Gregoriani Codicis lib. v. Hermogeniani lib. i. Papiniani tit. i. Hiis nos adjecimus ex vetustissimis bibliothecis, eo quod ad jus civile pertinerent, et alterius etiam Responsa passim in Pandectis legerentur, L. Volusiani Metiani lib. de Asse, Julii Frontini lib. de Controversiis Limitum, cum Aggeni Urbici Commentariis. Excudebat Basileæ Henricus Petrus, mense Martio, anno M.D.XXVIII. Fol.

[3] Parisiis, 1550, 8vo.   [4] Lugduni, 1566, fol.

[5] Parisiis, 1586, fol. Aureliæ Allobrogum, 1586, 4to.

Theodosian Code; and all the editions include other reliques of ancient jurisprudence.

But the great editor and expounder of the Theodosian Code was Jacobus Gothofredus, or Godefroy, who stands in the first rank of modern civilians. This very learned and able man was born at Geneva on the 13th of September 1587. His father, Dionysius Gothofredus, belonged to a noble family in France, but, as he professed the protestant religion, he was constrained to abandon his native country after the atrocious massacre of St. Bartholomew : he was successively appointed a professor of law in several universities, and has left various monuments of his learning and industry, particularly his exegetical edition of the *Corpus Juris Civilis.*[6] His second son, who now claims our attention, betook himself with great ardour to the study of jurisprudence, and in the year 1619 was appointed a professor in his native city. He afterwards filled the highest offices of this little republic : in the year 1629 he became a member of the council; he was appointed secretary of state, was employed in several embassies, and was five times chosen syndic. In the year 1637, after the death of Petrus Cunæus, professor of the civil law in the university of Leyden, he was invited to fill the vacant chair; but although the emoluments of the office were not inconsiderable, he could not be induced to abandon a country to which he felt much attachment.[7] He had now acquired

---

[6] Terrasson, Hist. de la Jurisprudence Romaine, p. 472.

[7] Gothofredus dedicated to the States General of Holland " Philostorgii Cappadocis Ecclesiasticæ Historiæ libri xii." Genevæ, 1643, 4to. To this elaborate edition he has appended two juridical dissertations, " De Nuptiis Consobrinorum," and " De Testamento tempore Pestis, vel a Testatore Peste contacto, condito."

a very high reputation as a lawyer of deep and extensive erudition, and in this respect he is only equalled by Cujacius. To his ample stores of philological learning he added a masterly knowledge of history, both civil and ecclesiastical : his industry appears to have been indefatigable, and his reading unbounded. Uniting with his other qualifications a complete knowledge of ancient jurisprudence in all its branches, and applying to his multifarious investigations an acute understanding and a sober judgment, he has produced various works, which cannot but be supposed to rise very far above the ordinary standard of merit.[8] Although he has not undertaken any extensive work on a plan strictly historical, no other writer has more effectually contributed to illustrate the history of the Roman law. The value of his *Manuale Juris*[9] and of his *Fontes quatuor Juris Civilis* is well known to all those who are not entirely unacquainted with the progress of this science : he is the author or editor of many other productions; but the great and lasting monument of his talents and learning is his edition of the Theodosian Code, on which he bestowed the assiduous labour of thirty years. This edition he did not himself live to complete, having died at Geneva on the 24th of June 1652.[1] His library, including all his manuscripts as well as printed books, was purchased by

[8] The merits of Gothofredus are very elaborately discussed by Otto, Thesaurus Juris Romani, tom. iii. p. xxxi.

[9] Of this very useful work there is a recent edition, published by the late Professor Berthelot. Parisiis, 1806, 8vo.

[1] C. H. Trotz præf. in Jacobi Gothofredi Opera Juridica minora. Lugd. Bat. 1733, fol. Senebier, Histoire Littéraire de Geneve, tom. ii. p. 144. Geneve, 1786, 3 tom. 8vo.—This splendid edition of Trotz includes all the juridical works of Gothofredus, except his illustrations of the Theodosian Code.

Antoine Marville, professor of law in the university of Valence; nor was it a little fortunate that his literary treasures fell into such hands.[2]   Of the intrinsic value of

[2] The personal history of Antoine Marville is somewhat curious.   His father, Claude de Vignemonte, "greffier en chef du presidial" at Amiens, having destined him for the church, he reluctantly prosecuted his theological studies, and passed through the inferior orders till he became a subdeacon or deacon; but he had fully resolved to devote himself to the profession of law, and as his father would not consent to this change of plan, he secretly withdrew to Paris, where he assumed a new name along with the habit of a layman.   The place of his nativity was a village named Marteville; and from the name of this village, shortened of its middle syllable, he adopted the appellation of Marville, which was likewise retained by his descendants.   His remuneration as a private tutor enabled him to maintain himself at Paris, and to prosecute his favourite study: after a course of four years, he took the degree of doctor of laws, and next found employment as a "repetiteur en droit."   But as this abandonment of the clerical profession exposed him to legal animadversion, he was afraid of being recognized in the capital; and having resided there for seven or eight years, he removed in 1640 to Grenoble, where he was admitted as an advocate, but was apparently more employed in giving private lessons in jurisprudence.   A vacancy in the law-faculty having occurred at Valence, Marville was appointed a professor in that university in the year 1648.   The *primicerius antecessor*, or first professor of law, having died in the course of the following year, the office was first destined for the learned Fabrot, well known as the editor of Theophilus and the Basilica; but as he was then occupied with the edition of the Byzantine historians, his residence in Paris was indispensable; and for a certain sum of money, paid with the knowledge of the keeper of the seal, he acquiesced in the appointment of Marville.   A short while before obtaining this preferment, he had married a lady of Valence, and here he spent the remainder of a long life, having died in 1693, in the eighty-fifth year of his age.   He is represented as a person amiable in his character, and gentle in his manners.   His original works are neither considerable for their number nor for their value; but his name is inseparably connected with that of Gothofredus, and is therefore familiarly known to all those who are conversant with the history of the Roman law.   At the close of his preface, he states that this great civilian had recommended to him the care of his edition of the Theodosian Code, in the event of its not being

such a possession, Marville was sufficiently aware, and he was both able and willing to bestow the labour necessary for arranging the vast collections which Gothofredus had accumulated. Nor was this labour inconsiderable; for the commentary abounded with erasures and corrections, many of the notes were written on separate slips of paper, and many others on the margin of a printed copy of the original work. Having with no small assiduity and perseverance digested the papers into a proper form, he at length committed the edition to the press; and the Theodosian Code, with the notes and commentary of Gothofredus, was published at Lyon in the year 1665.[3]

If the illustrious civilian of Geneva had himself prepared this edition for the press, it would doubtless have appeared to greater advantage; but even in its present form it is a work of the highest value to the lawyer and to the historian; it is indeed an immense storehouse of juridical and historical knowledge. The commentator has collected a stupendous mass of learning, and his information is derived from every accessible source. To the text of the Code he subjoins the ancient explanation: this is followed by his notes, in which he adverts to the various readings, to the emendation of the text,

completed in his own lifetime: "Ne fatear me adductum fuisse prævia authoris dum viveret admonitione in civitate Parisiensi, ut id officium præstarem, si ante excusum opus, e vivis decederet."

[3] Codex Theodosianus, cum perpetuis Commentariis Jacobi Gothofredi, viri senatorii et Jureconsulti hujus sæculi eximii. Præmittuntur Chronologia accuratior, cum Chronico Historico, et Prolegomena: subjiciuntur Notitia Dignitatum, Prosopographia, Topographia, Index Rerum, et Glossarium Nomicum. Opus posthumum, diu in foro et schola desideratum, recognitum et ordinatum ad usum Codicis Justinianei, opera et studio Antonii Marvillii, Antecessoris Primicerii in Universitate Valentina. Lugduni, 1665, 6 tom. fol.

and to the parallel or conflicting passages in the Theodosian and Justinian laws; and the illustration of each title
is completed by his ample commentary, in which he dis-
cusses the scope and tendency of the various enactments,
and pours around every subject of importance an immense stream of erudition, drawn from the deepest recesses of jurisprudence and history.   But in addition to
his perpetual commentary, he has composed different
tracts which greatly contribute to the elucidation of this
collection of laws.   To the first volume is prefixed a
Chronologia Codicis Theodosiani,[4] which is of great importance both in a juridical and historical point of view;
and this elaborate chronology is succeeded by his *Prolegomena in Codicem Theodosianum,* in which the history
of the Code is fully detailed.   The last volume contains
a " Notitia Dignitatum seu Administrationum tam civi-
lium quam militarium, in Partibus Orientis et Occi-
dentis, confecta e Codice Theodosiano;" a " Prosopographia, seu Index Personarum omnium quarum fit
mentio in Codice Theodosiano;" a " Topographia Theo-
dosiana; sive Orbis Romanus, ex Codice Theodosiano
depromptus;" and, besides an Index of subjects and of
words, a " Glossarium Nomicum Codicis Theodosiani."
The value of such a work as this can only be adequately
understood by those who have bestowed much attention
on the study of the Roman law and history.   " Im-
mortale opus est," says Hugo, " quod Gothofredus perfecit, in quo neque præivit ei quisquam neque ejus vestigia premere ausus est.   Nemo Codicem Theodosianum

---

[4] Hommel is evidently mistaken in supposing this chronology to be the
work of Marville. (Litteratura Juris, p. 58). That it was written by
Gothofredus, is sufficiently ascertained from the general preface of the
editor.

illustrare studuerat; qui primus id consilium cepit, ita quoque perfecit ut præter spicilegium nil prorsus superesse videretur." [5] This is the ample testimony of a great civilian, who is not commonly disposed to bestow commendation with too lavish a hand; and to his testimony it may not be superfluous to add that of a great historian, who must likewise be regarded as a very competent judge of a work so much connected with history as well as jurisprudence. "Among the books which I purchased," says Gibbon, "the Theodosian Code, with the commentary of James Godefroy, must be gratefully remembered. I used it (and much I used it) as a work of history, rather than of jurisprudence; but in every light it may be considered as a full and capacious repository of the political state of the empire in the fourth and fifth centuries." [6]

About seventy years after the appearance of this edition, the Theodosian Code, with the commentary of Gothofredus, was republished by Jo. Daniel Ritter, who commenced his undertaking when he was professor of philosophy at Leipzig, and completed it after he had been appointed professor of history at Wittemberg.[7] For a task of this kind he possessed eminent qualifications: being familiarly acquainted with the Roman law and history, he was equally conversant with ancient literature, and he displayed the talents of a skilful critic. To his

[5] Hugonis Index Editionum Fontium Corporis Juris Civilis, p. 187.

[6] Gibbon's Memoirs of his own Life and Writings, p. 213, 8vo.

[7] Codex Theodosianus, &c. editio nova, collata cum antiquissimo Codice MS. Wurceburgensi et Libris editis, iterum recognita, emendata, variorumque observationibus aucta, quibus adjecit suas Joan. Dan. Ritter, P.P. Lipsiæ, 1736-45, 6 tom. fol. Ritter's edition was soon afterwards reprinted in Italy. Mantuæ, 1740-50.

edition he has added various prefaces, and many shorter notes, and has corrected the text by the collation of manuscripts, and of the former editions. He has reprinted the spurious *Appendix Codicis Theodosiani*,[8] which had been published in 1631 by Sirmond, a French Jesuit of uncommon erudition ; and to the Novels, which had received no illustration from Gothofredus, he has subjoined many annotations.[9] This publication of Ritter procured him a high reputation. As a testimony of his conspicuous merit, the university of Göttingen conferred upon him the honorary degree of doctor of laws ;[1] and as such gratuitous honours are by no means common in Germany, this fact may here deserve a passing notice.

Of the novels which accompany this code, it is not necessary to enumerate the different editions; but it may not be improper to mention that not many years after the conclusion of Ritter's labours, the printed collection received an accession of five constitutions of Theodosius and Valentinian, which were published by two different editors from the Ottobonian manuscript that now belongs to the Vatican Library. These editors were Zirardini and Amaduzzi, who had both engaged in this undertaking without being aware of each other's intentions : they have each extended their illustrations so as to complete a considerable volume; the latter has indeed produced a

---

[8] Appendix Codicis Theodosiani novis Constitutionibus cumulatior; cum Epistolis aliquot veterum Conciliorum et Pontificum Romanorum, nunc primum editis; opera et studio Jacobi Sirmondi, Presbyteri Societatis Iesu. Parisiis, 1631, 8vo.

[9] Ruhnkenius to Ritter: "In quo opere cum alii alia mirantur, ego nihil tantopere miror, quam εὐστοχίαν illam criticam, qua locis depositis ac prope desperatis Novellarum Theodosii, Valentiniani etc. et lucem et medelam attulisti." (Ruhnkenii Opuscula, tom. ii. p. 770).

[1] Hommelii Litteratura Juris, p. 57. Lipsiæ, 1761, 8vo.

splendid folio of more than four hundred pages. The one edition appeared in 1766,[2] the other in 1767;[3] and a long period elapsed before the legislation of Theodosius received any new elucidation.

The discovery of the Institutions of Caius gave a renovating and powerful impulse to the civilians of the continent; and the recesses of many libraries were explored in the eager expectation of detecting other reliques of ancient jurisprudence. In the library of the university of Turin, Professor Peyron discovered a mutilated and undescribed volume in large octavo, and on a more particular examination he found that it was a palimpsest. This volume, as he is led to conjecture, had formed a part of the literary reliques collected in the monastery of Bobbio, which was founded by St. Columbanus, a native of Ireland, about the beginning of the seventh century.[4] It once contained a curious library, but the monks were not very competent judges of its value, or very faithful guardians of its treasures; and from the close of the fifteenth century, the

---

[2] Imperatorum Theodosii Junioris et Valentiniani III. Novellæ Leges, cæteris Antejustinianeis, quæ in Lipsiensi anni 1745, vel in anterioribus editionibus vulgatæ sunt, addendæ. Ex Ottoboniano MS. Codice edit, Commentario illustrat, ex eodemque Codice alia profert Antonius Zirardinus Ravennas, Jureconsultus. Faventiæ, 1766, 8vo.

[3] Leges Novellæ V. anecdotæ Imperatorum Theodosii Junioris et Valentiniani III. cum cæterarum etiam Novellarum editarum Titulis et variis Lectionibus, &c. opera et studio Johannis Christophori Amadutii, qui præfationem et annotationes adjecit. Romæ, 1767, fol.

[4] Some of the compositions of Columbanus, in verse as well as prose, may be found in Archbishop Usher's *Veterum Epistolarum Hibernicarum Sylloge*, p. 7-18. Dublinii, 1632, 4to. Dempster, according to his usual custom, has claimed this saint as a native of Scotland. (Historia Ecclesiastica Gentis Scotorum, p. 142. Bononiæ, 1627, 4to.)

manuscripts of Bobbio were gradually suffered to enrich
the libraries of Italy.   Of this monastic repository Peyron has given an elaborate account in another publication, and has there inserted a catalogue of the manuscripts, which had been compiled in the year 1461.[5]   In
the manuscript thus detected at Turin, the second writing
consisted of Julius Valerius's Latin version of a narrative
of the exploits of Alexander the Great, written by a
Greek of the name of Æsop.   From another copy, preserved in the Ambrosian Library at Milan, this version
was published for the first time by Dr. Angelo Mai, and
it contains nothing that can reconcile us to the mutilation
or erasure of the Theodosian Code.[6]   On the application
of a proper acid, the version of Valerius, written with

[5] M. Tulli Ciceronis Orationum pro Scauro, pro Tullio, et in Clodium
Fragmenta inedita, pro' Cluentio, pro Cælio, pro Cæcina, etc. Variantes
Lectiones, Orationem pro T. A. Milone a lacunis restitutam, ex Membranis palimpsestis Bibliothecæ R. Taurinensis Athenæi edidit, et eum
Ambrosianis parium Orationum Fragmentis composuit Amedeus Peyron,
&c. Idem præfatus est de Bibliotheca Bobiensi, cujus Inventarium anno
MCCCCLXI. confectum edidit atque illustravit. Stuttgardiæ et Tubingæ, 1824, 4to. Peyron has made one statement which to British
readers is curious and interesting. "Ad primam hanc ætatem pertinet
primus bibliothecæ fundus, veneranda illa scilicet codicum supellex a D.
Columbano ejusque discipulis Bobium comportata. Vidi in Ambrosiana,
atque Taurinensis habet libros Latinos Saxonicis litteris descriptos, glos-
sisque Saxonicis illustratos; hos pro varia eorum antiquitate vel a D. Columbano ex Hibernia, vel a Cumiano ex Scotia, aliisque Anglicis mo-
nachis allatos autumo." (De Bibliotheca Bobiensi Commentatio, p. vi.)

[6] Julii Valerii Res gestæ Alexandri Macedonis, translatæ ex Æsopo
Græco, prodeunt nunc primum, edente notisque illustrante Angelo Maio,
Ambrosiani Collegii Doctore. Mediolani, 1817, 8vo.— In the same vo-
lume, this work is preceded by the " Itinerarium Alexandri ad Constan-
tium Augustum, Constantini M. filium, edente nunc primum Angelo
Maio," &c.

evanescent ink, was very easily effaced, and the more ancient writing became disentangled. Peyron supposes
that this manuscript of the Code was transcribed during
the earlier part of the sixth century; but, according to
Mai, the peculiarities of writing rather belong to the
century following. In this manner are preserved thirteen
leaves, comprehending portions of the first five books,
and two pages, which contain a fragment of the sixth
book of the Theodosian Code. Nor are these leaves
without mutilation: the vellum, in the course of its preparation for a new purpose, has been cut at one side, so
that in one page the beginning, and in another the end
of the lines, are regularly shorn away; and, in some instances, the tops or bottoms of the leaves are likewise
curtailed. The words or fragments of words which the
editor has conjecturally supplied, are sufficiently distinguished by being printed in Italics. The text is first
exhibited, not in fac-simile, but according to the original
arrangement of the lines, and without any separation of
words. To the skill and industry of Peyron we are indebted for eighty-three constitutions, or fragments of
constitutions, exclusive of the fragment belonging to the
sixth book. He has subjoined various readings from
those portions of the manuscript which include constitutions formerly published.[7]

When the professor of oriental languages made this
important discovery, he began to regret that something

Codicis Theodosiani Fragmenta inedita. Ex codice palimpsesto
Bibliothecæ R. Taurinensis Athenæi in lucem protulit atque illustravit
Amedeus Peyron, Linguarum Orientalium Professor. Augustæ Tau-
rinorum, 1824, 4to.—This publication of Peyron was inserted in the Me-
morie della Reale Academia di Torino, tom. xxviii , and only a few copies have appeared in a separate form.

more congenial to his previous studies had not rather
presented itself; for, having already attained to his seventh lustre, he had never been initiated in the mysteries
of jurisprudence. He however possessed sufficient elas-
ticity of mind to betake himself to a new course of study;
and instead of consigning this ancient relique to some
juridical critic, he resolved to become acquainted with
the Roman law, and to write a commentary himself. He
has added notes and a commentary after the model of
Gothofredus; and he appears to have executed this part
of his task much better than could have been expected
from a person who had only prepared himself in such a
manner.

About the same period when Peyron made this discovery at Turin, a similar discovery was made at Milan
by Dr. Clossius, who is now a professor of law in the
university of Dorpat. In the Ambrosian Library he found
a quarto volume, containing the treatise *De Officiis*, and
several of the orations of Cicero, the Institutions of Justinian,[8] a portion of *Aniani Breviarium*, and *Rhythmus de
Assumptione Virginis Mariæ*. The manuscript, which
he supposes to belong to the middle of the twelfth century, is written in small, regular, and not inelegant characters, but with pale ink; and the different works contained in the volume appear to have been transcribed by
the same hand. All the peculiarities of the manuscript
are minutely described in the editor's preface, which extends to thirty-eight pages. The " Gesta in Senatu
Urbis Romæ de recipiendo Theodosiano Codice," cannot but be regarded as a very curious document; and,
besides this historical relique, he has rescued from ob-

---

[8] Prodromus Corporis Juris Civilis, a Schradero, Clossio, Tafelio, Professoribus Tubingensibus, edendi, p. 53. Berolini, 1823, 8vo.

livion a considerable number of constitutions, chiefly belonging to the first book of the Theodosian Code.[9]
The new materials, thus prepared by Peyron and Clossius, have been incorporated with the older stock, and
have received much additional illustration from Dr.
Wenck, professor of the civil law in the university of
Leipzig.[1] The first five books of the Theodosian Code,
which long appeared so defective and mutilated, are now
exhibited in a form materially improved; and the annotations of Wenck will not be despised, even by such
readers as are most familiarly acquainted with those of
Gothofredus and Ritter. His notes are sufficiently copious, and afford abundant proofs of the extent of his
erudition, and the soundness of his judgment. This
edition I consider as essential to the library of every
scholar who feels a particular interest in the study, and
more especially in the historical study, of the Roman
law.

After an interval of a century, the example of Theodosius was followed by Justinian.[2] To ten individuals

[9] Theodosiani Codicis genuini Fragmenta. Ex membranis Bibliothecæ
Ambrosianæ Mediolanensis nunc primum edidit Waltherus Fridericus
Clossius, Phil. et J. U. Doctor, et Juris Professor Publicus Ordinarius in
Regia Universitate Tubingeni. Tubingæ, 1824, 8vo.

[1] Codicis Theodosiani libri v. priores. Recognovit, additamentis insignibus a Walthero Friderico Clossio et Amedeo Peyron repertis aliisque
auxit, notis subitaneis, tum criticis tum exegeticis, nec non quadruplici
appendice instruxit Car. Frid. Christianus Wenck, Antecessor Lipsiensis.
Lipsiæ, 1825, 8vo.

[2] Spangenberg's Einleitung in das Römisch-Justinianeische Rechts-
buch, oder Corpus Juris Civilis Romani. Hannover, 1817, 8vo. This
learned and laborious author, who fills a judicial situation at Zelle, has
more recently published a curious work entitled "Juris Romani Tabulæ
Negotiorum sollemnium, modo in ære, modo in marmore, modo in charta
superstites." Lipsiæ, 1822, 8vo. Dr. Spangenberg has performed an-

learned in the laws he in the year 528 entrusted the important task of compiling a new Code; and at the head of this commission he placed Tribonian, who makes so conspicuous a figure in the history of his reign.[3] The materials for their undertaking were contained in the three Codes which have already been mentioned, and in the constitutions of the intervening emperors. Their collection includes the edicts and rescripts of a long series of princes, from Hadrian to Justinian; and they were authorized to select what was most important, to retrench what was superfluous, to rectify what was erroneous, and even to consolidate several constitutions into one. This task they performed with sufficient dispatch: the new Code, which was to supersede all the former, received the imperial sanction on the 7th of April 529. But soon after its completion, Justinian found it necessary to issue fifty new decisions, for the purpose of reconciling conflicting principles; and having in the course of a very few years promulgated various other constitutions, he granted a commission to Tribonian and other four persons to revise the Code, and insert the additional laws in their proper places. The first edition was suppressed, and the new edition, *Codex repetitæ prælectionis*, was sanctioned on the 16th of November 534. It is divided into twelve books, and each book into a variety of titles.

During this interval, however, Tribonian had been engaged in a work of greater difficulty. On the 15th of

other important service by editing a posthumous work of Haubold: " Antiquitatis Romanæ Monumenta Legalia extra libros Juris Romani sparsa." Berolini, 1830, 8vo.

[3] J. P. de Ludewig Vita Justiniani atque Theodoræ Augustorum, nec non Triboniani. Halæ Salicæ, 1731, 4to.

December 530, he had been appointed, along with sixteen associates, to prepare a general Digest of legal
science, not from the edicts and rescripts of the emperors, but from the writings of those lawyers who enjoyed
the highest reputation in the forum.[4] The work which
they thus compiled contains a very copious collection of
legal principles and legal discussions, exhibiting one of
the most remarkable specimens of ancient genius and
ancient wisdom. It is divided into fifty books. Dr.
Blume has with much labour and ingenuity attempted to
ascertain the general principle of arrangement in the
titles of which the different books are composed; and his
theory has obtained the approbation of Hugo, and other
most competent judges. He supposes that the commissioners appointed by Justinian were divided into three
sections, and that to each section was assigned the task
of extracting the proper materials from a particular series
of works. We are thus to expect a triple series in each
title: the deviations from this general plan he conceives
to be but inconsiderable; and for particular modifications
he discovers an obvious and intelligible reason. The
first series commences with the commentaries on Sa-
binus, the second with those on the *Edictum Perpetuum*,
and the third with the works of Papinian. He has pursued his enquiries through many minute details, in which
we cannot at present accompany him, but must content
ourselves with referring to his elaborate *Ordnung der
Fragmente in den Pandectentiteln.*[5]

[4] Guil. Grotii Vitæ Jurisconsultorum quorum in Pandectis extant Nomina. Lugd. Bat. 1690, 4to.

[5] Zeitschrift für geschichtliche Rechtswissenschaft, herausgegeben von
Savigny, Eichhorn und Göschen, Bd. iv. S. 257. See likewise an article
by Hugo, in the Thémis, ou Bibliothèque du Jurisconsulte, tom. iii. p.

After the completion, but before the publication of the Digest or Pandects, the emperor employed Tribonian, Theophilus, and Dorotheus, to prepare a short and elementary work as a standard introduction to the study of the law. This work is professedly compiled from more ancient treatises of the same nature, and particularly from the Institutions of Caius, whom Justinian styles " Caius noster." The discovery of this latter work is of great importance in illustrating the text of the imperial Institutions, which have for so many centuries retained their place in the schools of jurisprudence, and have so generally served as models to those who in modern times have undertaken to write elementary treatises of law. " This little work," says Dr. Bever, " is so truly admirable, both for its method and conciseness, as well as for the elegance of its composition, that it has been imitated by almost every nation in Europe, that hath ever made any attempt to reduce its own laws to a regular and scientific form." [6] It is worthy of remark, that those who are unacquainted with the Institutions and Pandects, are unacquainted with the full compass of the Latin language.[7] The terse and appropriate phraseology

---

278.   Blume's speculations have not obtained the same approbation from Dr. Tigerström, De Ordine et Historia Digestorum libri duo, p. 481. Berolini, 1829, 8vo.—For the literature of the Pandects, I may further refer the reader to the prolegomena of Haubold's " Doctrinæ Pandectarum Lineamenta, cum Locis classicis Juris, in primis Justinianei, et selecta Litteratura maxime forensi." Lipsiæ, 1820, 8vo.

[6] Bever's Hist. of the Legal Polity of the Roman State, p. 480. Lond. 1781, 4to.

[7] Opuscula varia de Latinitate Jurisconsultorum veterum. Junctim edidit, et animadversiones adjecit Carolus Andreas Dukerus. Lugd. Bat. 1711, 8vo. Ge. Casp. Kirchmaieri Opuscula VI. rarissima de Latinitate Digestorum et Institutionum. Halæ, 1722, 8vo.

with which they so frequently abound, was transfused from the productions of a purer age; nor is it wonderful that they should occasionally be debased by a grosser mixture. " It is remarkable," as Mr. Hume has observed, "that in the decline of Roman learning, when the philosophers were universally infected with superstition and sophistry, and the poets and historians with barbarism, the lawyers, who in other countries are seldom models of science or politeness, were yet able, by the constant study and close imitation of their predecessors, to maintain the same good sense in their decisions and reasonings, and the same purity in their language and expression." [8]

The Institutions were sanctioned on the 21st of November 533; and on the 16th of December, the emperor issued two constitutions, the one in Latin and the other in Greek, by which he confirmed the Institutions, Code, and Pandects, and imparted to them the force and validity of law in the forum, and commanded them to be taught in the schools of Rome, Constantinople, and Berytus. Justinian survived till the year 565, and during that long interval he promulgated many new laws. [9] A

[8] Hume's Hist. of England, vol. iii. p. 300.—" Niuno autore de' bassi secoli," says Denina, " si può trovare che tanto si assomigli agli autori del secolo d'oro, quanto i giureconsulti, che fiorirono cento e cinquant' anni dopo Cicerone, si avvicinano all' eleganza e proprietà di quelli che scrissero sotto Augusto." (Discorso sopra le Vicende della Letteratura, p. 58, ed. Glasgua, 1763, 8vo).

[9] Justinian has found a most zealous defender in an English divine of the seventeenth century, Richard Crakanthorp, D.D. whose work bears the title of *Iustinian the Emperor defended, against Cardinal Baronius.* Lond. 1616, 4to. Here I may likewise mention one of his Spanish admirers, who published a work scarcely known to civilians. " El Principe en la Gverra, y en la Paz: copiado de la Vida del Emperador Iustiniano. Por Don Vicente Mut, Sargento Mayor de Mallorca. Madrid, 1640, 4to.

collection was at length formed of his Novels, or new Constitutions, to the number of one hundred and sixty-eight. The greatest part of them appear to have been originally written in Greek; some were however written in Latin, and others were at the same time exhibited in both languages.[1] These are followed by thirteen Greek edicts of Justinian, which properly conclude the *Corpus Juris Civilis,* although the common editions comprehend various Novels of Leo,[2] and some other emperors, toge-ther with other ancient documents, all of which are only to be considered as appendages.

We have now reached the era of the Greek jurispru-dence, of which the history is very obscurely known in this country; insomuch that there are probably many eminent lawyers who, in the whole course of their study and practice, never heard of such a book as the *Basilica.* A certain learned member of Lincoln's Inn has a copy of this voluminous repertory of ancient jurisprudence, which long adorned the library of a celebrated bibliomaniac, under the title of SANCTI BASILII OPERA, or the Works of St. Basil. Provided it was a fine copy with an ample margin, the contents of the book might be of little or no consequence to the possessor. This disin-terested collector of books was not perhaps trained to the legal profession; but what shall be said of Mr. Pinkerton, who was educated as a lawyer, who advanced such high claims to general erudition, and who treated other men's errors with such merciless severity? "There is," as he

---

[1] F. A. Biener's Geschichte der Novellen Justinian's. Berlin, 1824, 8vo.

[2] C. A. Beck de Novellis Leonis Augusti et Philosophi, earumque Usu et Auctoritate liber singularis: edidit C. F. Zepernick. Halæ, 1779, 8vo.

is pleased to remark, "an originality in the Greek writers which forms and nurtures genius; the Latin only foster imitation. A divine or a physician ought to be grounded in Greek; a lawyer requires Latin, for there is not one Greek writer on law."[3] These are the remarks of a person who was indeed sufficiently rash in many of his assertions, but who had however acquired a large fund of information; and I refer to such instances, not with the mere view of exposing ignorance, but in order to demonstrate that the field which we have now entered has been almost entirely neglected by our countrymen. Of the Greek writers on the Roman law, it is remote from my present design to attempt any thing approaching to a complete enumeration; I am however anxious to trace such an outline as may be calculated to direct the views of those students who possess sufficient ardour of curiosity to extend their enquiries beyond the vulgar limits.[4]

Some of the more ancient civilians wrote Greek treatises on particular portions of the Roman law: thus, for example, Herennius Modestinus, who flourished during the third century, composed in that language *Excusationum libri sex;* but of this denomination no entire work of so early a date has descended to our times. The first name which now arrests our attention, is that of Theophilus, the author of a Greek paraphrase of the Institutions. The task of compiling the original work, Justinian had committed to three individuals learned in the

---

[3] Pinkerton's Enquiry into the History of Scotland, vol. i. p. xii. Lond. 1789, 2 vols. 8vo.

[4] " Intelligitur autem ex iis quæ supra scripta sunt, parum esse juris Romani studioso, si Latine tantum, non etiam Græce doctus sit, nec præter Gallorum sermonem alias recentiores linguas didicerit." (Holtii Hist. Juris Romani, p. 8.)

law, namely, to Tribonian, Theophilus, and Dorotheus,
of whom the two latter are described as *antecessores*, or
public professors of law.   Whether this professor was the
same Theophilus who wrote the paraphrase, has been
long and much disputed among civilians : to recapitulate
all the arguments which have been urged on both sides
of the question, would require a very ample space, and I
shall therefore content myself with stating that I am
strongly inclined to adopt the opinion of those writers
who maintain their identity, and with referring the inquisitive reader to the copious discussions of Mylius and
Reitz.[5]   Theophilus was a professor at Constantinople,
and Dorotheus at Berytus.   During the reign of Justinian, the two imperial cities and Berytus were the only
places, within the limits of the empire, where public
schools of law were established, or indeed where law was
permitted to be publicly taught.[6]   Berytus, which that
emperor describes as a most beautiful city, was situate on
the coast of Syria : here a school of jurisprudence was
founded during the third century, and it was long fre-
quented by a numerous train of students, but its prosperity was first interrupted, and was finally subverted by

[5] Jo. Henrici Mylji, J. U. D. Theophilus; sive de Græcarum Juris Institutionum earundemque Auctoris Historia, Ætate, Auctoritate, Fatis,
Dotibus, Nævis, liber singularis.   Lugd. Bat. 1761, 8vo.   Reizii præf.
in Theophilum, p. xxv.   Of this work of Mylius, the first edition
appeared at Leipzig in 1730.   The entire tract may be found in Reitz's
Theophilus, tom. ii. p. 1034.

[6] Const. *omnem reip.* § 7, ad Antecessores.   Savigny has remarked that
we cannot suppose the Greek emperor to have exercised any direct legislative authority in Rome before the Gothic war; and that every thing
practical in this constitution is expressly limited to Constantinople and
Berytus. (Geschichte des Römischen Rechts im Mittelalter. Bd. i.
S. 398).

some of the great convulsions of nature. In the year
384 the town was greatly injured by an earthquake, and
in 554 it was visited by another earthquake, which left it
a heap of ruins. Some professors and a multitude of
students perished in this common calamity: the surviving
professors transferred their school to Sidon, and the surviving inhabitants made a vigorous effort to raise a new
city from the ruins of the old; but another calamity
awaited them, and this famous seat of jurisprudence was
totally consumed by fire.⁷ After a long interval another
town, which retains the name of Beirout or Baruti, was
founded by the Druses near the ancient site, and was
possessed by the Emirs as their capital and as their only
seaport, till they were expelled from it by Djezzar Pasha
of Acre.⁸ The name of Berytus, that celebrated "nurse
of tranquil life," is so conspicuous in the history of the
Roman law, that it has for a moment drawn us aside
from the more immediate subject of our investigation.

$$Bηρυτὸς\ βιότοιο\ γαληναίοιο\ τιθήνη.\ ^{9}$$

⁷ Heineccii Hist. Juris Civilis, p. 472. edit. Ritter. Lugd. Bat. 1748,
8vo. But see more particularly " Johannis Strauchii Jcti Berytus, seu ad
tit. Cod. de Metropoli Beryto Dissertatio publica." Brunsvigæ, 1662, 4to.

⁸ Frankland's Travels to and from Constantinople, vol. i. p. 328. Lond.
1829, 2 vols. 8vo.—" This town," says Mr. Carne, " the ancient Berytus, contains six thousand inhabitants: the situation is the most beautiful
of all the Syrian towns; the environs are laid out in plantations of mul-
berry trees, and a quantity of silk is produced and exported." (Letters
from the East, p. 239. Lond. 1826, 8vo.) Another recent writer has
stated that the population is variously "estimated at from 3000 or 4000
to 14,000;" and, in his opinion, the smallest number approaches nearest
the truth. (Bond's Memoir of the Rev. Pliny Fisk, A. M. p. 291, edit.
Edinb. 1828, 12mo.) See likewise Mr. Jowett's Christian Researches in
Syria and the Holy Land, p. 117. Lond. 1825, 8vo.

⁹ Nonni Dionysiaca, lib. xli. p. 708. edit. Falkenburgii. Antv.
1569, 4to.

The paraphrase of Theophilus is of great utility and importance in explaining the text of the Institutions.[1] He has not servilely confined himself to the original, and his work in a great measure supplies the place of a perpetual commentary.   It is a book indispensably necessary for every more learned and inquisitive student of the civil law.   This paraphrase is not indeed entirely free from errors: Reitz conjectures, and not without a considerable degree of probability, that Theophilus had dictated it to the students of Constantinople in the exercise of his functions as a public expounder of the law; and that for its transmission to posterity we are solely indebted to copies taken by his auditors, and uncorrected by himself.[2]   To this valuable relique the attention of modern lawyers was first directed by Angelo Poliziano. The earliest editions, containing the Greek text without a Latin version, were published by Viglius Zuichemus, a native of Friesland, who, after having been a professor of law in the universities of Padua and Ingolstadt, entered into holy orders, and became provost of the cathedral of Ghent.[3]   His two editions, which both appeared in 1534, were followed by many others; and among these we

---

[1] Cujacius was not very consistent in his opinion as to the age and merits of Theophilus. His variations are carefully indicated by Merillius, Ex Cujacio libri tres, p. 239. Paris. 1638, 4to.

[2] This paraphrase contains innumerable barbarisms; which are partly to be ascribed to the necessity of expressing in Greek the technical phrases of the Roman law. We meet with such expressions as these: κομφεσσορίως, νεγατορίως, ὀφφικίου, κουράτωρ, περσονάλιαι, πραειουδικιαλίαι, σάγκτα πράγματα, κουάσι κοντράκτον, φαμιλίας ἐρκισκοῦνδαι. Theophilus exhibits various instances of that departure from the quantity of Latin words which is so customary with the Greek writers. Thus Lentulus is expressed by Λεντοῦλος, and decretum by δέκρετον.

[3] Foppens Bibliotheca Belgica, tom. ii. p. 1153.

must distinguish two different editions by Fabrot[4], a very celebrated expounder of the Greek texts of the Roman law; but the fame of all former editors was totally eclipsed by Willem Otto Reitz, who published a splendid and most complete edition of Theophilus about the mid-dle of last century.[5] This learned and judicious man, whose name we shall more than once have occasion to mention, was born in the year 1702, was appointed rector of the Gymnasium of Middelburg in Zeeland in 1741, and died in 1769. In the title-pages of different publications, he is described as *Jurisconsultus*: he had taken the degree of doctor of laws, but although eminently skilled in jurisprudence, his ordinary occupa-tion was that of a classical instructor; and in the Dutch seminaries of learning, such attainments have very fre-quently been united in the same individuals. He be-longed to a family which produced several scholars, and one of his brothers was the editor of Lucian, and the author of a work which is well known to philologers.[6] Reitz's edition of Theophilus is so elaborate and satisfac-tory, that, in the opinion of Haubold, it is unequalled by any similar publication, except Ritter's edition of the Theodosian Code.[7]

Of the Pandects of Justinian, different Greek versions have been mentioned by different writers. One version

---

[4] Paris. 1638, 4to. Paris. 1657, 4to. Of the latter edition some copies have a new title, with the date of 1679.

[5] Hagæ Comitis, 1751, 2 tom. 4to.

[6] Joan. Freder. Reitzius de Ambiguis, Mediis et Contrariis; sive de Significatione Verborum ac Phrasium ambigua. Traj. ad Rhen. 1752, 8vo.

[7] Hauboldi Institutiones Juris Romani Litterariæ, p. 205. Lipsiæ, 1809, 8vo.

has been ascribed to Thalelæus, who was an antecessor
in the time of that emperor; but Pohl and Heimbach
have shewn, that there are no sufficient grounds for
believing that he undertook such a task.[s]　Another
translation is mentioned by Matthæus Blastares as having been executed by Stephanus, an advocate of Constantinople, who had been conjoined with Tribonian in
the commission for compiling the Pandects.　The same
individual appears to have illustrated the other parts of
Justinian's compilation; and some fragments of the works
of Thalelæus and Stephanus have been published by
Ruhnkenius.　The Code was likewise translated into
Greek : the translator is supposed to be the person who,
in the scholia of the Basilica, is repeatedly described as
$Κωδικεύτης$.　To many of the judges, as well as the
suitors, in the eastern empire, Latin must evidently have
been an unknown tongue.　When the seat of empire was
transferred from Rome to Byzantium, the first emperors
were anxious to transfer the use of the Roman language,
and for a considerable period this continued to be at
least the language of the court.　Teachers of Roman
eloquence were established in the second metropolis, and
they doubtless found many pupils among the youth who
aimed at a fashionable education, or were ambitious
of preferment; but it was not to be expected that the
great body of the people should be induced to unlearn
one language, and to acquire another.

During the interval which elapsed between the reign
of Justinian and that of Basilius, there were many Greek
writers on the Roman Law; and not a few names have
been recovered from the wreck of time by Lambecius,

---

[s] Suaresii Notitia Basilicorum, recensuit C. F. Pohlius, p. 66.　Heimbach de Basilicorum Origine, p. 25.

Suarés, Assemani,[9] and other learned enquirers, and many accurate notices have more recently been added by Heimbach. Basilius, who has obtained a conspicuous place among the legislators of the empire, derived his lineage from Armenia, but was himself born in Macedonia, and is commonly known by the name of Basilius the Macedonian. He rose from an origin sufficiently humble, and after having been a groom, he became sovereign of the east. In the year 866, Michael the Third associated him in the government, under the title of Cæsar. His benefactor was a weak and dissolute prince; and when Basilius endeavoured to give a better direction to his conduct, he was exposed to suspicions and snares, against which he opposed the dagger of the assassin, and thus became sole emperor in the course of the ensuing year. Among candidates for empire, it is utterly vain to look for rigid principles of piety or virtue: Basilius however appears to have been a person of no ordinary character; of his taste for literature he has left a specimen in his exhortations to his son Leo;[1] but his chief distinction arose from his attempt to form a complete body of law for the government of his dominions. The eastern empire, in which the Greek language was vernacular, was governed by a collection of laws chiefly written in Latin; and the different versions which had been executed, were without the sanction of public authority. It was therefore his object to select such enactments as were still in force, and having digested them into the form of a regular code, to invest them with the imperial sanction.

[9] Assemani Bibliotheca Juris Orientalis Canonici et Civilis. Romæ, 1762-6, 5 tom. 4to.

[1] Basilii Romanorum Imp. Exhortationum capita lxvi. ad Leonem filium, cognomento Philosophum. Lutetiæ, apud Federicum Morellum, 1584, 4to.

This great undertaking he did not live to complete. He died in the year 886, and was succeeded by his son Leo, who, in consequence of his studious propensity, obtained the surname of the Philosopher. His treatise on tactics was published by Meursius, and some of his other works are preserved in manuscript.[2] The body of Greek laws was completed under his direction: the date of its promulgation has not been ascertained; but as the student is referred to it in Leo's Ecloga, which was written in the year 910, the Basilica must have been in circulation before that period. Leo the Philosopher ended his reign and his life in the year 911, and was succeeded by his son Constantinus Porphyrogennetus, when only seven years of age. This learned prince likewise belongs to the catalogue of royal authors,[3] and from him the Basilica appear to have received their final revision. The revised edition Theodorus Balsamon, in his commentary on the Nomocanon of Photius, describes as $\tau\grave{\eta}\nu$ $\tau\epsilon\lambda\epsilon\upsilon\tau\alpha\acute{\iota}\alpha\nu$ $\mathring{\alpha}\nu\alpha\kappa\acute{\alpha}\theta\alpha\rho\sigma\iota\nu$;[4] and, according to the opinion of Heimbach, it was not divulged before the year 945. Whether the work has descended to our times as it was completed by Leo, or as it was afterwards reformed by Constantinus, has been disputed among the historians of the Roman jurisprudence. Brunquell avers that we now possess the Basilica in their revised form;[5] but Hoffmann considers this opinion as extremely doubtful,[6] and his suggestions seem to be confirmed by the subsequent investigations of Heimbach.[7]

[2] Fabricii Bibliotheca Græca, tom. vi. p. 367. edit. Harles.
[3] Fabricii Bibliotheca Græca, tom. vii. p. 681.
[4] Voelli Bibliotheca Juris Canonici veteris, tom. ii. p. 814.
[5] Brunquelli Hist. Juris Romani, p. 309.
[6] Hoffmanni Hist. Juris Romani, tom. i. p. 654.
[7] Heimbach de Basilicorum Origine, p. 16.

This great digest of the law received the title of the Basilica, τῶν Βασιλικῶν, derived, according to some writers, from the name of the emperor Basilius, or, according to others, from the circumstance of its containing βασιλικὰς διατάξεις, or imperial constitutions. In the West it never obtained the force of law; and its utility therefore consists in the illustration which it furnishes to the Justinian body of law, from which it is chiefly compiled. Its utility in this respect has long been understood and acknowledged. The advantages to be derived from a careful examination of the Basilica, were first exhibited in the writings, and more particularly in the *Observationes*, of Cujacius, who left no source of information unexplored; and they have been formally enumerated by more recent writers.[8] A portion of the work was first committed to the press by Gentian Hervet, who published at Paris in the year 1557 a Latin version of the forty-fifth, forty-sixth, forty-seventh, and forty-eighth books, and of certain fragments of the twenty-eighth and twenty-ninth books. Of the sixtieth book, which is of great length, Cujacius published a Latin version at Lyon in the year 1566, and this version was reprinted at Hanau in 1596.[9] The different portions which had thus been edited, were combined together by Dionysius Gothofredus, and printed at Hanau in

[8] Eckhardi Hermeneutica Juris, p. 587. edit. Walchii. Lipsiæ, 1802, 8vo.

[9] In the *Themis, ou Bibliothèque du Jurisconsulte*, tom. vii. p. 165, tom. ix. p. 321, the reader will find an elaborate dissertation by Professor Biener of Berlin, " Sur l'usage que Cujas a fait des Basiliques, et sur les manuscrits de ce recueil qui existent dans les bibliothèques de Paris; " and in tom. x. p. 161, he will find " Observations sur la Dissertation de M. Biener relative à l'usage que Cujas a fait des Basiliques," by Professor Berriat St. Prix of Paris.

1598, and again in 1606.[1] Cujacius had been occupied
in preparing some other portions for the press; and after
his death, which took place in 1590, Charles Labbé
published his version of the thirty-eighth and thirty-ninth
books, together with the Greek scholia. The book was
printed at Paris in the year 1609. But the most meritorious labourer in this department of literature and jurisprudence was Charles Annibal Fabrot, whose services
entitle him to a more particular commemoration. He
was born at Aix in Provence in the year 1580, and after
having made great progress in his classical studies,
he addicted himself to the study of law, and took his
doctor's degree in the year 1606. He afterwards became
an advocate in the parliament of Aix, and his merit procured him the friendship of several individuals of influence.
In 1609 he was appointed a professor of law in the
university of Aix, where he became second professor in
1632, and first professor, or dean of the faculty of law, in
1638. It was at this latter period that he published his
valuable edition of Theophilus. This work he dedicated
to the chancellor Seguier, who induced him to fix his
residence in Paris, and, on the condition of his undertaking the formidable task of preparing an edition of the
Basilica, procured him an annual pension of 2000 livres.
Fabrot, who appears to have been a man of great application, published the Basilica in Greek and Latin, after
an interval of nine years, having in the mean time been
engaged in several other works.[2] He has retained Cuja-

---

[1] See however Hugo's *Civilistisches Magazin*, Bd. ii. S. 414. Here the
reader will find a valuable contribution to the history of the Basilica.

[2] Τῶν Βασιλικῶν βιβλία Ξ'. Βασιλικῶν libri lx. in vii. tomos divisi.
Carolus Annibal Fabrotus, Antecessorum Aquisextiensium Decanus, Latine vertit, et Græce edidit ex Bibliotheca Regis Christianissimi. Parisiis,
1647, 7 tom. fol.

cius's version of the three books already specified, and
has himself translated the remaining books. He has
added the Greek scholia, which are likewise translated
into Latin. Of the sixty books which composed this
great work, he supposes that he has exhibited forty-one
in an entire form, though Meerman, Reitz, and other
writers are of opinion that this number admits of some
abatement; and those portions which are manifestly
defective, he has endeavoured to supply from the *Synopsis Basilicorum*, from Harmenopulus, and from other
sources. His edition is almost entirely without annotations, and is otherwise deficient in what may be considered
as necessary illustration. A dedication to his patron
Seguier, consisting of twelve pages, is followed by a
preface, extending only to the fourth page, and this again
is succeeded by Suarés's *Notitia Basilicorum;* but with
respect to the history of the ample compilation itself, or
of any other portion of the Greek jurisprudence, he furnishes his readers with no further information. His work
appears to have been urged with a degree of rapidity approaching to precipitation; for, as he informs us in the
preface, he sometimes laboured to supply two different
presses. He is the author or editor of many other works:
his labours contributed to illustrate the history as well as
the laws of the Greek empire; he was the editor of
several of the Byzantine historians, and the author of various publications on the civil and the canon law. He
was involved in the controversy which Salmasius maintained with equal learning and pertinacity, on the doctrines of the Roman law respecting usury.[3] One of his

---

[3] Epistola Car. Ann. Fabroti, Antecessoris Aquisextiensis, de Mutuo:
cum Responsione Cl. Salmasii ad Ægidium Menagium. Lugd. Bat.
1645, 8vo.

last labours was his edition of the works of Cujacius,
which he published in the year 1658, in ten volumes
folio: he thus performed a very important service to the
more learned students of jurisprudence; but his intense
application to this undertaking produced a malady which
terminated his life on the 16th of January 1659. He
died at Paris, leaving a son named Guillaume Fabrot,
who was a counsellor in the Cour des Monnoyes.[4]

After an interval of more than a century from the date
of Fabrot's edition, four entire books of the Basilica,
namely, the forty-ninth, fiftieth, fifty-first, and fifty-
second, were published by Reitz, of whose meritorious
labours I have already had occasion to speak. They
were first inserted in the fifth volume of Meerman's
Thesaurus Juris Civilis et Canonici, and thirteen years
afterwards they appeared in a separate form.[5] The
editor has added a Latin version, together with notes.
The separate volume contains Ruhnkenius's edition of
the commentaries of Thalelæus, Theodorus, Stephanus,
Cyrillus, Gobidas, and other Greek lawyers, on the titles
of the Pandects and Code, " *de Postulando* sive *de Advocatis*, nec non *de Procuratoribus et Defensoribus*." These
commentaries were first inserted in the third and fifth
volumes of Meerman's extensive collection. Ruhnkenius,

---

[4] Terrasson, Hist. de la Jurisprudence Romaine, p. 480. Niceron,
Memoires pour servir à l'Histoire des Hommes illustres dans la Repub-
lique des Lettres, tom. xxix. p. 355.

[5] Operis Basilici Fabrotiani Supplementum, continens libros quatuor
Basilicorum, IL. L. LI. & LII. nunc primum ex Codice manuscripto Regiæ Bibliothecæ Parisiensis integre editos. Latine vertit, variantes Lectiones collegit, Notasque criticas ac juridicas, tam aliorum quam suas,
addidit Gul. Otto Reitz, JCtus. Accedunt Thalelæi, Theodori, Stephani,
Cyrilli, aliorumque JCtorum Græcorum Commentarii in Tit. D. & Cod.
de Postulando sive *de Advocatis*, nec non *de Procuratoribus et Defensoribus*.
Novissime ex Codice MS. Bibliothecæ Lugduno-Batavæ edidit, Latine
vertit, et castigavit David Ruhnkenius. Lugduni Batavorum, 1765, fol.

who was so great a master of Grecian literature, and who had studied the civil law in the excellent school of Ritter, has translated them into Latin, and has illustrated them with annotations. At the suggestion of Hemsterhusius, he had resumed his juridical studies with the view of preparing himself for a law professorship;[6] but after having exhibited this very adequate specimen of his proficiency, he returned to those elegant pursuits of classical philology which have rendered his name so justly celebrated.

In the year 1825 a new edition of the Basilica was announced by Dr. Heimbach, professor of law in the university of Jena. In this formidable undertaking he is assisted by his brother, who spent nearly four years in searching for and collecting manuscripts in the libraries of France and Italy; and his labours have not only been of the utmost consequence to the work, but have been attended with the incidental advantage of leading to the discovery of many valuable reliques of Greek jurisprudence, not immediately connected with the professed object of his researches. He is preparing to publish the work of Athanasius Scholasticus, with other *anecdota;* and this will be followed by an edition of the Greek text of the Novels. Of the Basilica the first volume is already completed,[7] and a very favourable opinion is entertained of the editor's competency for the difficult task which he has undertaken.

[6] Wyttenbachii Vita Davidis Ruhnkenii : Opuscula, tom. i. p. 564. Lugd. Bat. 1821, 2 tom. 8vo.

[7] Basilicorum libri LX. Post Annibalis Fabroti curas ope Codd. MSS. a Gustavo Ernesto Heimbachio aliisque collatorum, integriores cum scholiis edidit, editos denuo recensuit, deperditos restituit, translationem Latinam et adnotationem criticam adjecit D. Carolus Guilielmus Ernestus Heimbach, Antecessor Jenensis. Tom. I. lib. I.-XII. continens. Lipsiæ, 1833, fol.

In this sketch of the history of the Basilica, we must not overlook the ancient *Glossæ*, which are not without their value. They were first published by Labbé, who ranks among the more learned cultivators of Greek jurisprudence, and were afterwards illustrated by Schulting and by Röver.[8]

Basilius and his family followed the example of Justinian, by preparing different elementary works for the benefit of those entering upon the study of the law. One of these, which in an imperfect form occurs in the collection of Leunclavius,[9] appears to have been promulgated in the name of this emperor, and of his two sons Constantinus and Leo, each of whom had been invested with the title of Augustus. This work has frequently been confounded with another Ἐκλογὴ τῶν Νόμων, prepared under the auspices of Leo and his son Constantinus Porphyrogennetus. The latter production remains in manuscript, but an edition of it was meditated by the learned Mascou, and a few pages have been published as a specimen.[1] It is however necessary to remark, that the history of these two works is involved in no small de-

---

[8] Caroli Labbæi Observationes et Emendationes in Synopsin Basilicωn, &c. cum veteribus Glossis Verborum Juris, quæ passim in Basilicis reperiuntur. Paris. 1606, 8vo.—These *Glossæ* were afterwards printed with " Cyrilli, Philoxeni, aliorumque veterum Glossaria Latino-Græca et Græco-Latina, a Carolo Labbæo collecta, et in duplicem alphabeticum ordinem redacta." Lutet. Paris. 1679, fol. They are to be found, with the emendations of Joseph Scaliger and other learned men, and the notes of Schulting, in Otto's *Thesaurus Juris Romani*, tom. iii. col. 1697. Röver's " Specimen Observationum et Emendationum ad Glossas veteres Verborum Juris," is subjoined to his edition of the " Fragmentum veteris Jurisconsulti de Juris Speciebus et de Manumissionibus, quod servavit Dositheus Magister." Lugd. Bat. 1739, 8vo.

[9] Leunclavii Jus Græco-Romanum, tom. ii. p. 79.

[1] Püttmanni Memoria Gottfridi Mascovii, p. 119. Lipsiæ, 1771, 8vo.

gree of obscurity. Different manuscripts exhibit different titles; the preface belonging to the one compendium is sometimes transferred to the other; and Constantinus, the son of Leo, is occasionally confounded with his own uncle of the same name.[2]

Long before the publication of the Basilica themselves, the *Synopsis Basilicorum* had been committed to the press by Joannes Leunclavius, or Loewenklau, a learned Westphalian, distinguished as a scholar and a civilian. He was the editor and translator of many Greek works, and the merit of his versions has been admitted by Huet, the most erudite bishop of Avranches.[3] One historian of the Roman law has, without any apparent ground, ascribed this abridgment to Romanus Junior Lacapenus:[4] the name of the author remains altogether unknown. It was published from a manuscript which Sambucus had found at Tarento, a place within the limits of the district formerly called Magna Græcia, where the Greek language long continued to be vernacular. In the manuscript, the different subjects are digested according to the order of the alphabet; but the editor has arranged them in the order of the sixty original books. The text is accompanied with a Latin version, and a series of annotations occurs at the end of the volume.[5] With re-

---

[2] Wæchtleri Opuscula juridico-philologica, p. 588. Lugd. Bat. 1733, 8vo.—"Inde factum est," says Pohl, p. 6, "ut in universa juris Byzantini postjustinianei historia nihil fere difficilius sit, quam harum Eclogarum ætatem et auctores definire." See likewise Heimbach, p. 93.

[3] Huetius de Interpretatione, p. 171. Paris. 1661, 4to.

[4] Struvii Historia Juris, p. 340.

[5] LX. Librorum Βασιλικῶν, id est, Universi Juris Romani, auctoritate Principum Rom. Græcam in linguam traducti, Ecloga sive Synopsis, hactenus desiderata, nunc edita per Joan. Leunclaium, ex Joan. Sambuci, v.

spect to the translation, a charge of plagiarism was brought against him by Freigius, a professor of law in the university of Altdorf.[6] A manuscript translation, executed by this professor, appears to have been communicated to him; but his knowledge of the Greek language and of the Roman law, and his skill as a translator, were such as to leave him little or no inducement to avail himself of this clandestine aid. The Synopsis was afterwards illustrated by Labbé, who published an ample collection of observations and emendations. Another *Synopsis Basilicorum*, which has never been printed, is preserved in different libraries. It is of smaller extent, and is commonly described by the Greeks as μικρὸν κατὰ στοιχεῖον. Michael Attaliata is the author of a third Synopsis, which has been inserted in the collection of Leunclavius,[7] under the title of Ποίημα νομικὸν, ἤτοι Πραγματική. From an epigram prefixed, it appears to have been composed in the third year of the emperor Michael Ducas, that is, in the year 1073. The author, who describes himself as a proconsul and judge, has not digested his little work in alphabetical order.

About the same period, a Σύνοψις τῶν Νόμων, or Synopsis of the Laws, was composed by the younger Michael Psellus, who had been preceptor to Michael

c. Bibliotheca. Item Novellarum antehac non publicatarum Liber. Adjunctæ et Adnotationes interpretis, quibus multæ leges multaque loca juris civilis restituuntur et emendantur. Basileæ, 1575, fol.

6 Wæchtleri Opuscula, p. 589.

7 Juris Græco-Romani, tam Canonici quam Civilis, tomi duo; Johannis Leunclavii Amelburnii, v. cl. studio ex variis Europæ Asiæque bibliothecis eruti, Latineque redditi : nunc primum editi cura Marquardi Freheri, J. C. cum ejusdem Auctario, Chronologia Juris ab excessu Justiniani ad amissam Constantinopolin, et Præfatione, &c. Francofurti, 1596, fol.

Ducas. It is addressed to this emperor, and is written
in verse. As it only consists of 1406 verses, it necessarily
contains a very scanty outline of legal science: its value
is not highly estimated by Augustinus,[8] and other competent judges; but as a literary curiosity it is not entirely
without its attractions. The lines of which it is composed
are πολιτικοὶ στίχοι, or popular verses;[9] a mode of
writing which, in many instances, had begun to supersede
the more classical structure of Greek as well as Latin
poetry. Accent or emphasis being substituted for quantity, lines were formed of a number of syllables corresponding with some particular species of verse; and some
original defects in this mode of composition might possibly be supplied by a peculiar adaptation of the voice.
The modern Greeks, who speak a language which can
scarcely be considered as different from that of their
classical ancestors, retain or have adopted a pronunciation
which appears to set at open defiance all the known and
acknowledged rules of prosody: while they profess to regulate the voice by accent, they make long syllables
short, and short syllables long; so that in their manner
of reading an ancient poet, it is utterly impossible for
our ears to recognize the melody of verse. They indeed
tell us, what may be sufficiently true, that our ears are
too obtuse to discover the delicacy with which they com-
bine accent with quantity; but, at all events, it is very
hard to imagine that their general system of pronunciation has been legitimately transmitted from the times of

---

[8] Augustini Emendationes et Opiniones, lib. iv. cap. iii. p. 175. edit.
Lugd. 1559, 8vo.

[9] Ilgen ad Carmina Homerica, p. 656. Gaisford ad Hephæstionem, p.
247. Maltby, Lexicon Græco-Prosodiacum, p. lxiv.

Homer, Pindar, and Sophocles. Psellus employs a verse of fifteen syllables, which seems intended to represent the iambic tetrameter catalectic. In the subsequent passage, he commences a general account of the *Corpus Juris Civilis:*

Πρῶτον δ' ἑρμηνευτέον σοι, πόσα τοῦ νόμου μέρη.
Τὸ μὲν γὰρ τούτων Κώδικος οὕτως ὠνομασμένον,
Πτυχίον δωδεκάβιβλον, ὅ φασὶ διατάξεις·
Ἔχει δὲ τοῦτο δόγματα, Δέσποτα, βασιλέων,
Ἀντιγραφάς τε νομικὰς, καὶ δικῶν ἀποφάσεις·
Τὸ δὲ καλοῦσι Δίγεστα, Ῥωμαικὴ δ' ἡ κλῆσις.
Ὑπάρχει δὲ τὸ Δίγεστα, Ἑλληνικῶς Πανδέκτης,
Ὅτι καὶ νόμων πέφυκε παντοδαπῶν δοχεῖον,
Καὶ πλεῖστοι συνεγράψαντο τοὺς νόμους τοῦ Πανδέκτου.
Τῶν δὲ Διγέστων, Δέσποτα, παντοδαπὰ τὰ μέρη·
Τὰ μὲν γὰρ πρῶτα λέγουσι περὶ συναλλαγμάτων,
Τετράβιβλος δ' ἡ σύνταξις, κλῆσις τῶν Πρώτων, πρώτη·
Τὸ μετὰ ταῦτα πέφυκεν ἑπτάβιβλον πτυχίον,
Ῥωμαικῶς λεγόμενον οὕτω, δὲ ἰουδίκης,
Ἤτοι περὶ τῶν κρίσεων, κ. τ. λ.[1]

I shall only transcribe other two verses, in which this juridical versifier states the maxim, that ignorance of fact, τοῦ φάκτου, but not of law, admits of a legal excuse:

Τοῦ νόμου μὲν ἡ ἄγνοια συγγνώμην οὐ λαμβάνει,
Τοῦ φάκτου συγγινώσκεται τοῖς νόμοις προσηκόντως.[2]

One of the latest Greek civilians of much note was Constantinus Harmenopulus, a judge of Thessalonica,

---

[1] Michaelis Pselli Synopsis Legum, versibus iambis et politicis, cum Latina interpretatione et notis Francisci Bosqueti, selectisque observationibus Cornelii Siebenii, emendatius edidit Ludovicus Henricus Teucherus, p. 10. Lipsiæ, 1789, 8vo.—This work of Psellus may likewise be found in Meerman's *Thesaurus Juris Civilis et Canonici*, tom. i. p. 37.

[2] P. 118. This rule is taken from the Basilica, lib. ii. tit. iv. § 9.

whom Suarés,[3] Jac. Gothofredus,[4] and other learned
writers have erroneously placed in the twelfth century.
He was born about the year 1320, and he appears to
have died about the year 1380.[5] He was a native of
Constantinople, and having been trained in the best
learning of that age, he gradually arrived at different
stages of preferment, and was eminent for his knowledge
of the canon as well as of the civil law.[6] In 1345 he
composed his Πρόχειρον Νόμων, or Manual of the Laws,
a work of considerable extent, and of considerable value.[7]
Harmenopulus was better acquainted with the principles
than with the history of the Roman law; and it may
perhaps be sufficient to mention his strange averment
that Justinian promulgated three different codes, namely,
the Gregorian, Hermogenian, and Theodosian. He is
said to have been initiated in Latin literature by As-
pasius, a Calabrian monk, whom his father had attracted
from Italy by the promise of an ample salary; but we
must apparently suppose him to have derived his knowledge of the Roman law from Greek compilations. He
makes a nearer approach to truth when he speaks of Caius
as the first of lawyers. His work has however been
found of importance in elucidating various points of law;
and many learned men have bestowed no inconsiderable
labour in illustrating it as one of the last reliques of
ancient jurisprudence. The Greek text was first published by T. A. Suallemberg,[8] and after a short interval

[3] Suaresii Notitia Basilicorum, p. 16.
[4] Gothofredi Hist. Juris Civilis, p. 19.
[5] Fabricii Bibliotheca Græca, tom. xi. p. 260. edit. Harles.
[6] Mastricht Hist. Juris Ecclesiastici, p. 318.
[7] Bachii Hist. Jurisprudentiæ Romanæ, p. 686.
[8] Parisiis, 1540, 4to.

a Latin version was added by Bern. a Rey.[9]   Another
version was executed by Jo. Mercerus.[1]   He was succeeded by Dionysius Gothofredus, who published at Geneva an edition including paratitla, various readings, and
a *Nomenclator Græcarum Dictionum Juris, ad Harmeno-
pulum.*[2]   This editor has professedly adopted the translation of Mercerus; but, as Reitz has remarked, most of
the notes are derived from the same source, and without
any form of acknowledgment.   An edition of Harmenopulus was for some time meditated by Ruhnkenius;[3]
but he finally abandoned the design, and it was afterwards adopted by Reitz, whose learned labours have so
greatly contributed to facilitate the study of this branch
of literature and jurisprudence.   He lived to prepare
his edition for the press, but died before its publication;
and the late Baron Meerman inserted it in the supplement to his father's Thesaurus.[4]   The text, adjusted by
a collation of various manuscripts, is printed without ac-
cents: it is accompanied with a new version, with notes
of the editor himself, and of several other civilians; and
besides other appendages, he has subjoined the Nomenclator of Gothofredus, corrected and enlarged.

Besides the works which have already been enumerated, several others of the same denomination have
been printed,[5] and many more are still preserved in

---

[9] Coloniæ, 1547, 8vo.

[1] Lugduni, 1556, 4to.

[2] Apud Guillelmum Læmarium, 1587, 4to.

[3] Bergmanni Præf. in Ruhnkenii Opuscula, p. xii.   Lugd. Bat. 1823,
2 tom. 8vo.

[4] Hagæ Comitum, 1780, fol.

[5] Here we must not entirely overlook a publication which bears the
following title: Τοῦ ᾿Ανατολικοῦ Νομίμου βιβλία γ΄.   Juris Orientalis
libri iii. ab Enimundo Bonefidio, J. C. digesti ac notis illustrati, et nunc
primum in lucem editi.   Cum Latina interpretatione.   *Excudebat Henr.*

manuscript, particularly in the Vatican, and in the Imperial Library at Vienna. What has hitherto been stated may perhaps be sufficient to excite, though not to gratify, the curiosity of those who are capable of being interested in such disquisitions; and if any reader is disposed to prosecute his enquiries to a greater extent, I beg leave to refer him to the respective publications of Suarés, Haubold, and Heimbach. [6]

Stephanus, 1573, 8vo. The first book contains imperial constitutions; the second, pontifical sanctions of the archbishops and patriarchs of Constantinople; and the third, rescripts of other ecclesiastical dignitaries.

[6] 1. Josephi Mariæ Suaresii, Episcopi Vasionensis, Notitia Basilicorum. Recensuit et observationibus auxit D. Christianus Fridericus Pohlius, Civitatis Lipsiensis Senator et Syndicus. Lipsiæ, 1804, 8vo.— Suarés was a native of Avignon, and became bishop of Vaison in the year 1633. This preferment he resigned in favour of his brother in 1666: he afterwards retired to Rome, where he was appointed vicar of St. Peter's, and keeper of the Vatican Library ; and in this city he terminated his career, on the 8th of December 1677. He was evidently a man of learning, and was the author of various works. His Notitia was prefixed to Fabrot's edition of the Basilica, was reprinted by Van Leeuwen, at the beginning of his edition of the Corpus Juris Civilis, and by Fabricius, in his Bibliotheca Græca, tom. xii., where it is accompanied with valuable annotations. Still however the work was not to be found in an accessible form ; and Dr. Pohl, syndic of Leipzig, has performed an important service by publishing a separate edition. The notes of Fabricius are retained, and those which he has himself added are numerous and able.

2. Manuale Basilicorum, exhibens Collationem Juris Justinianei cum Jure Græco Postjustinianeo, Indicem Auctorum recentiorum qui Libros Juris Romani e Græcis Subsidiis vel emendaverunt vel interpretati sunt, ac Titulos Basilicorum cum Jure Justinianeo et reliquis Monumentis Juris Græci Postjustinianei comparatos. Digessit D. Christ. Gottl. Haubold, Eques Ordinis Sax. Virtutis Civicæ, et Juris Professor Publ. Ord. in Academia Lipsiensi. Lipsiæ, 1819, 4to.—The collation which the reader must here expect is not that of passages actually quoted, and confronted with each other ; it consists in enumerating the succession of books and titles, and in adding perpetual references to the parallel passages. We also find a very laborious series of references to the works of

It has long been a current opinion that, in the western empire, all knowledge of the civil law became extinct, and was not revived till after the lapse of several centuries. "All the world knows," says Lord Kames, "that the Roman law, after being buried in oblivion for ages, came to be restored in Italy by an accident. The very books of that law were understood to be lost past recovery, till a copy of the Pandects was found in the town of Amalphi *anno* 1127,[7] by Lotharius the emperor when he took that town, in the war he carried on against Rodger king of Sicily and Naples. The knowledge of it increased so fast, that it was taught publicly by Vacarius at Oxford about the year 1150, during the reign of king Stephen.[8] This was as swift a progress as

modern civilians, who have illustrated the Justinian law from the Greek jurisprudence ; and the author has prefixed an " Index chronologicus Interpretum recentiorum e quorum Observationibus Manuale Basilicorum est digestum."

3. De Basilicorum Origine, Fontibus, Scholiis, atque nova Editione adornanda. Scripsit D. Carol. Guilielm. Ernest. Heimbach. Lipsiæ, 1825, 8vo.—Of the plan of his edition, this volume contains a learned and copious explanation, and is itself a valuable contribution to the history of the Greek jurisprudence. He has carefully traced the history of the Basilica, and of the sources from which they are derived ; and has added notices, not only of the editions, but likewise of the various manuscripts preserved in various libraries. His account of Greek works on the civil law he prosecutes to a period much more recent than that of the promulgation of the Basilica. A few notices may be found in the prolegomena to the " Fragmenta Versionis Græcæ Legum Rotharis Longobardorum Regis. Ex codice Paris. Gr. 1384, primus edidit Carolus Eduardus Zachariæ, J. U. D." Heidelbergæ, 1835, 8vo.

[7] In the date of this grand discovery there seems to be an error of ten years, for the siege of Amalfi is commonly referred to the year 1137. See however Brenkman's Historia Pandectarum, p. 25, 43.

[8] See Wenck's Magister Vacarius, primus Juris Romani in Anglia Professor. Lipsiæ, 1820, 8vo.

any science can be supposed to make."[9] A more recent writer has added something to the old stock of
speculation. "The fortunate, or perhaps unfortunate,
discovery of the Roman *Code*, at Amalfi in Italy, produced a great change in the institutions of almost every
country in Europe. The dignified clergy of that day immediately perceived how advantageous the adoption of
the regulations of Justinian would prove to them; and
the popes, who then pretended to dispose of the throne
of the Cæsars, were eager to support the arbitrary edicts
of emperors, who, like themselves, affected to think that
both their persons and their rescripts were inviolable.
The neighbouring countries cheerfully submitted to the
change, and thus engrafted slavery and the civil law on
that even-handed Gothic jurisprudence, which had en-
sured freedom to all the northern nations."[1] This philo-
sophic speculator, who thus attempts to twist a rope of
sand, has not even arrived at the point of distinction between the Pandects and the Code. So true it is that
when an English writer ventures to speak of the Pandects,
he generally finds his way to be dark and slippery.
This assertion may be further confirmed by the following examples, taken from writers of no mean talents;
one of whom was bred to the profession of the law, and
the other was " Juris utriusque Doctor."[2] Mr. Roscoe
shall supply was with the first example: " The system
of jurisprudence which in the fifteenth century prevailed

[9] Kames's Essays upon several Subjects concerning British Antiquities, p. 15. Edinb. 1747, 8vo.

[1] Stephens's Memoirs of John Horne Tooke, vol. ii. p. 16. Lond. 1813,
2 vols. 8vo.

[2] The following curious epitaph is quoted in Lord Orrery's *Letters
from Italy*, p. 174. Lond. 1773, 8vo. "Jo. Martinus Mairacca, *I. V.
Doctor* et Eques, nolens discretioni hæredum stare, vivus posuit." His

throughout the greatest part of Europe, was that of the Roman or civil law, which was principally founded on the Pandects or constitutions of Justinian." [3]—From these expressions it may be inferred, that this very elegant and accomplished writer was not aware of the existence of the Code, not to mention the other books which contribute to form the body of the Justinian law. Nor is it easy to discover how the Pandects answer to the description of the " constitutions of Justinian." Dr. Thomson speaks of the *Corpus Juris Civilis,* the Code, and the Pandects, as one and the same book. He informs us that Cunningham was solicited to " publish an accurate edition of Justinian's Corpus Juris :" in reference to the same project, he afterwards speaks of the "intended publication of Justinian's Code;" and again, of the " intended edition of Justinian's Pandect." [4] It is sufficiently evident that he supposes all these three appellations to be applicable to the same work.

lordship's editor, the Rev. John Duncombe, A. M., apparently supposes the initials I. V. to denote "justus vir," instead of "juris utriusque;" for his translation runs thus : " an honest man, doctor and knight."

[3] Roscoe's Life of Lorenzo de' Medici, vol. ii. p. 93.—The elegant Fabroni, alluding to a plan of translating his *Vita Laurentii Medicei,* expresses himself in the following terms : " Quod consilium quoque fuisse hominis Britanni audivi, ad quod abjiciendum fortasse valuere, quæ de eodem Laurentio historiæ monumentis mandavit ex illa ipsa natione doctus vir Guilelmus Roscoe, cujus opus sermonis elegantia, et rerum, quæ ad litterariam historiam sæculi XV. pertinent, copia maxime omnium judicio commendatur." (Vitæ Italorum Doctrina excellentium, vol. xx. p. 46).

[4] See Dr. Thomson's Introd. to Cunningham's Hist. of Great Britain. Lond. 1787, 2 vols. 4to.—" Renunciantur indies," says Otto, " utriusque juris doctores, quorum plerique in jure canonico adeo hospites sunt et peregrini, ut ne prima ejus principia degustaverint, nec omnino quid sit jus illud, quod profitentur . . . intelligere videantur." (Papinianus, sive de Vita, Studiis, Scriptis, Honoribus et Morte Æmilii Papiniani, Juris-

It was maintained by Taurellus, Augustinus, Brenk-man, and other learned civilians, that all the copies of the Pandects known to be extant are derived from the famous manuscript, which was first deposited at Pisa, and afterwards removed to Florence.[5] This opinion was zealously opposed by the Abate Grandi, professor of mathematics in the university of Pisa, whose *Epistola de Pandectis* was first printed in the year 1726.[6] The course of his enquiries also led him to call in question the traditionary tale respecting the marvellous resuscitation of the Roman law after the siege of Amalfi. Various writers had incidentally maintained the opinion which he adopts; and it had recently been maintained

consultorum Coryphæi, Diatriba, p. 256. edit. sec. Bremæ, 1743, 8vo.) Might we not very safely subjoin, *et in jure civili?* With respect to juridical knowledge, Dr. Thomson may fairly be described in the words of Lyndewode as "inter utriusque juris doctores minimus." Mr. Henry, a member of the English bar, and the senior Commissioner of Legal Inquiry into the Administration of Justice in the West Indian and South American Colonies, has recently published a translation of Van der Linden, in which he communicates to his readers this piece of information : "The Digest, or that part of the Pandects containing the selected opinions of the most celebrated Roman lawyers, on cases submitted to them, and which form fifty books of the Justinian Code." He afterwards states that the abbreviation L. denotes "the Liber, or Book of the Pandects." (Institutes of the Laws of Holland, by Johannes van der Linden, LL. D., translated by J. Henry, Esq. Lond. 1828, 8vo).

[5] Brenkmanni Historia Pandectarum, seu Fatum Exemplaris Florentini : accedit gemina Dissertatio de Amalphi. Traj. ad Rhen. 1722, 4to. Flaminio dal Borgo, Dissertazione sopra l'Istoria de' Codici Pisani delle Pandette di Giustiniano Imperatore. Lucca, 1764, 4to.

[6] Grandi Epistola de Pandectis ad cl. virum Josephum Averanium. Editio altera, notis variis, et appendice veterum monumentorum ab auctore locupletata. Florentiæ, 1727, 4to. The first edition was published at Pisa during the preceding year. His endeavours were seconded by a learned professor of divinity at Pisa, whose work was published at Florence n 1727 : " D. Virginii Valsechii Epistola de veteribus Pisanæ Civitatis

G

in a separate work by D'Asti.[7] The story of the manuscript seized as a warlike booty, he treats as a mere
fiction ; and Muratori has remarked, that the earliest
authority for this anecdote of the siege is Raynerius de
Grancis, a writer of the fourteenth century.   To Grandi's work, which attracted no small degree of attention,
an answer was published by Bernardo Tanucci, professor
of the civil law at Pisa;[8] nor was the mathematician
tardy in replying.[9] Tanucci soon prepared a copious
rejoinder.[1]   Grandi continued the controversy, under
the assumed name of Bartolo Luccaberti ;[2] and his antagonist concluded his exertions, by enlarging his first
epistle, and translating his second defence into Latin.[3]

Constitutis, ad clariss. et reverendiss. Patrem D. Guidonem Grandi."
This epistle has been reprinted by Hoffmann, *Hist. Juris Romano-Justinianei*, vol. i. app. p. 185. Lipsiæ, 1726-34, 2 tom. 4to.

[7] D'Asti dell' Uso e Autorità della Ragion Civile nelle Provincie dell'
Imperio Occidentale dal dì che furono inondate da' Barbari sino a Lotario
II. Napoli, 1720-2, 2 tom. 8vo.

[8] Lucæ, 1728, 4to.

[9] Grandi Vindiciæ pro sua Epistola de Pandectis, adversus inanes
Querelas et Oppugnationes Bernardi Tanuccii. Pisis, 1728, 4to.

[1] Tanucci, Difesa seconda dell' Uso antico delle Pandette, e del
Ritrovamento del famoso Manoscritto di esse in Amalfi, contra le Vindicie del P. D. Guido Grandi, Abate Camaldolense, e Lettore di Matte-
matica nello Studio di Pisa, libri due. Firenze, 1729, 4to.

[2] Nuova Disamina della Storia delle Pandette Pisane, e di chi prima le
rammentasse, come ancora d' altre incidenti Questioni, collo Scioglimento
delle Difficoltà, opposte all' *Epistola de Pandectis*, ed alle Vindicie del Rmo.
P. Abate Grandi da Bernardo Tanucci, Dottore da Stia. Opera di Bartolo
Luccaberti, divisa in parti iv. Faenza, 1730, 4to.—Fabroni informs us
that Grandi was himself the author of this work. (Vitæ Italorum Doctrina excellentium, tom. viii. p. 249). Some writers have however supposed Luccaberti to be a real person. See Eckhardi *Hermeneutica Juris*,
p. 76.

[3] Tanusii Epistola de Pandectis Pisanis, in Amalphitana Direptione
inventis, ad Academicos Etruscos, in qua confutantur quæ Guido Gran-

In these disquisitions, they were succeeded by Schwartz, a learned German, who rejected the notion that all the modern copies of the Pandects are derived from the Florentine manuscript.[4] Brenkman, who had devoted so much time and attention to this manuscript,[5] and had formerly maintained the opposite opinion, endeavoured to refute the arguments of Schwartz as well as Grandi;[6] and the same cause was, after a short interval, defended by Guadagni, professor of the civil law at Pisa.[7] But the history of the Roman law during the middle ages has recently been investigated with so much ability, and with such perseverance of research, that on this subject the labours of all previous writers appear to be of little comparative value: Savigny's work is indeed one of the most remarkable productions of the age in which we

dius, Cremonensis Abbas, et Antecessor in Pisano Gymnasio, opposuit Francisco Taurellio et Henrico Brencmanno. Florentiæ, 1731, 4to.—The same volume, which extends to 557 pages, includes the Latin translation of his *Defesa seconda.*

[4] Schwartz published a disquisition, " An omnia Pandectarum Exemplaria, quæ adhuc extant, e Florentinis manaverint." Altorfii, 1733, 4to.

[5] Gebaveri Narratio de Henrico Brenkmanno, de Manuscriptis Brenkmannianis, et suis in Corpore Juris Civilis Conatibus et Laboribus. Accedunt Mantissa de libro longe rarissimo, *Bibliotheca Antonii Augustini,* et Vita Henrici Newtoni. Gottingæ, 1764, 4to.

[6] Brenkmanni Epistola ad v. c. Franciscum Hesselium, qua examinantur præcipua Capita Epistolæ v. c. D. Guidonis Grandi de Pandectis, nec non Dissertationis similis argumenti, auctore v. c. Christiano Gotlib. Schwarzio. Traj. ad Rhen. 1735, 4to.

[7] Guadagni de Florentino Pandectarum Exemplari, an sit Imperat. Justiniani Archetypum, et an ex eo ceteri, qui supersunt, Pandectarum libri manaverint, Dissertatio. Romæ, 1752, 8vo.—This dissertation was inserted in Gori's *Symbolæ Litterariæ,* dec. ii. vol. iv.; and some copies were published in a separate form. Guadagni is likewise the author of a work entitled *Ad Græca Pandectarum Dissertationes.* Pisis, 1786, 4to.

live.[8]   The extinction of the Roman law with the western empire, and its accidental revival after the lapse of
six hundred years, will henceforth be viewed as one of
the numerous romances of history; but the researches
of this very able man, we are sorry to add, are little
known or appreciated in England, where the legend of
Amalfi is permitted to retain much of its original fresh-
ness, and where historical jurisprudence is more imperfectly understood than in any other learned country
of Europe.

In England the civil law was publicly taught at a very
early period.   The first professor was Vacarius; whose
history has recently been illustrated in a separate volume
by Dr. Wenck, a very learned civilian of the university
of Leipzig.[9]   Such a book could only have proceeded
from a German university : such is the proficiency, and
such the assiduity of the German civilians, that they are
capable of deriving instruction, or of finding entertainment, when those of most other nations could perceive
nothing but a barren waste.   The name of Vacarius is
not unknown to those who are acquainted with the writ-

---

[8] Savigny's Geschichte des Römischen Rechts im Mittelalter.   Heidelberg, 1815-31, 6 Bde. 8vo.—How far the English lawyers are disposed
to avail themselves of his researches, may partly be inferred from the following erudite passage, which occurs in a very recent publication : "The
Pandects were discovered at Amalphi, 2d Stephen. 3 Black. Com. 66."
(Merewether and Stephens's History of the Boroughs and Municipal
Corporations of the United Kingdom, vol. i. p. 6.   Lond. 1835, 3 vols.
8vo).

[9] Magister Vacarius, primus Juris Romani in Anglia Professor, ex
Annalium Monumentis et Opere accurate descripto illustratus, Juris
Romani in Bononiensis Scholæ Initiis Fortunam illustrans, Emenda-
tionem, Interpretationem hodiernam juvans, studiis Caroli Friderici Christiani Wenck, Jur. Doct. et Prof. Lips.   Lipsiæ, 1820, 8vo.

ings of Selden and Duck; and his services are stated in
the following terms by an author of considerable note,
Dr. Hurd, the late bishop of Worcester: " Matters continued on this footing during the three first of the Norman reigns.   The prince did his utmost to elude the
authority of the English laws; and the nation, on the
other hand, laboured hard to confirm it.   But a new
scene was opened under king Stephen, by means of the
Justinian laws; which had lately been recovered in
Italy, and became at once the fashionable study over all
Europe.   It is certain that the Pandects were first
brought amongst us in that reign; and that the reading
of them was much favoured by Archbishop Theobald,
under whose encouragement they were publicly read in
England by Vacarius, within a short time after the
famous Irnerius had opened his school at Bologna.   There
is something singular in the readiness with which this
new system of law was embraced in these western parts
of Europe... Vacarius had continued to teach it for some
time, in the archbishop's palace at Lambeth,[1] to great
numbers, whom first the novelty of the study, and then
the fashion of the age, had drawn about him.   The fame
of the teacher was high, and the new science had made
a great progress, when on a sudden it received a severe
check, and from a quarter whence one should not naturally expect it.   In short, the king himself interdicted
the study of it.   Some have imagined that this in-
hibition was owing to the spite he bore to Archbishop
Theobald.   But the truer reason seems to be, that the
canon law was first read by Vacarius at the same time,
and under colour of the imperial.   I think we may col-

---

[1] Vacarius, as the reader will afterwards perceive, did not teach the
civil law in the palace of Lambeth, but in the university of Oxford.

lect thus much very clearly from John of Salisbury, who acquaints us with this edict. For he considers it as an offence against the church, and expressly calls the prohibition an impiety." [2]

Of this early professor of the civil law, a very curious notice occurs in an ancient Norman chronicle, published by Duchesne: " Obiit Bechardus, VI. Abbas Becci, cui successit Rogerius Magister Vuacarius gente Longobardus, vir honestus et jurisperitus, cum leges Romanas anno ab incarnatione Domini MCXLIX. in Anglia discipulos doceret, et multi tam divites quam pauperes ad eum causa discendi confluerent. Suggestione pauperum de Codice et Digesta exceptos IX. libros composuit, qui sufficiunt ad omnes legum lites que in scolis frequentari solent decidendas, si quis eas perfecte noverit." [3] Selden has shewn that the name of the sixth abbot of Bec was not Bechardus, but Lethardus;[4] and in a manuscript, the one name might easily be mistaken for the other. But this very learned man did not perceive that the sense of the passage is completely obscured by the punctuation. I readily accede to the opinion of Wenck, for which he is partly indebted to Dr. Duck,[5] that the subsequent

[2] Hurd's Moral and Political Dialogues, vol. ii. p. 178. 6th edit. Lond. 1788, 3 vols. 8vo.—See likewise Dr. Sullivan's Lectures on the Feudal and English Laws, p. 199. Lond. 1772, 4to.

[3] Historiæ Normannorum Scriptores antiqui, edidit And. Duchesne, p. 983. Lut. Paris. 1619, fol.

[4] Seldeni Dissertatio Historica ad Fletam, cap. vii.

[5] Duck de Usu et Authoritate Juris Civilis, f. 139.—See likewise D'Asti dell' Uso e Autorità della Ragion Civile nelle Provincie dell' Imperio Occidentale, tom. i. p. 174, and Sarti de claris Archigymnasii Bononiensis Professoribus, part. i. p. 49. 54. 57. Bononiæ, 1769-72, 2 part. fol. This publication of Sarti, a work of uncommon research, did not extend beyond the first volume, which consists of two parts.

words form the first sentence, which is thus complete in itself: " Obiit Lethardus, VI. Abbas Becci, cui successit Rogerius." The remainder of the passage here quoted forms another sentence; and after the word *confluerent* we must place a comma, instead of a period. The expression, "cum leges Romanas," &c. is manifestly a preparative for some other statement:—when Vacarius read public lectures on the Roman law, and was attended by many students, poor as well as rich, he composed at the suggestion of the poor, that is, the poorer class of his own pupils, a compendious treatise in nine books, extracted from the Code and Pandects. At that period, books were commodities of a very high price, and it required an ample fortune to procure even a small library: the invention of printing had not rendered books common and cheap by multiplying copies in an easy and rapid manner ; nor could any considerable collection of manuscripts be formed without great expense or great labour. A private scholar with a very slender income may now collect a library, of which an abbot or even an archbishop could not then hope to rival the extent. Vacarius must therefore have performed a very acceptable service by providing those students, who could not afford to purchase copies of the Code and Pandects, with a short view of the leading doctrines which they contain. The grammar and sense of the passage are thus clear and consistent. Such an unprecedented combination of name and title as Rogerius Magister Vacarius, ought to have convinced Selden that the passage was completely mangled. He has first of all confounded Vacarius with Roger the seventh abbot of Bec; who was a person of so much consideration, that after the death of Theobald, he had it in his power to decline the splendid offer of the archbishopric of Canterbury. Having thus transformed the abbot into an Italian civilian, his next step is to identify him with Rogerius Beneventanus, author of a *Summa Codicis*, a treatise *De Præscriptionibus*, and of a work, which in our time is much better known, *De Dissensionibus Dominorum*. But this one individual must again be resolved into three. It is a very material fact, and sufficiently ascertained, that the name of the abbot was Roger de Bailleul; a name which clearly indicates a French lineage. If this ecclesiastic was a Frenchman, he could not be the same individual with Vacarius, who was an Italian; and when the civilian is thus deprived of the name of Rogerius, he cannot be identified with Rogerius Beneventanus.

Another important contribution to the history of Vacarius we find in Gervase of Canterbury's lives of the archbishops of that see. " Theodbaldus ad Romanum pontificem pro pallio profectus est. Quo suscepto a Romano pontifice Innocentio secundo, Theodbaldus in Angliam rediit, et a Cantauritis honorifice susceptus est. Erat autem in diebus istis apostolicæ sedis legatus Henricus Wintoniensis episcopus, qui erat frater regis. Hic cum de jure legati licet privilegium suum plus quam deceret extenderet in immensum, suumque archiepiscopum et episcopos Angliæ, ut sibi occurrerent, quolibet evocaret, indignatus Theodbaldus, et Thomæ clerici Londoniensis industria fretus, egit apud Celestinum papam, qui Innocentio successit, ut amoto Henrico Theodbaldus in Anglia legatione fungeretur. Oriuntur hinc inde discordiæ graves, lites et appellationes antea inauditæ. Tunc leges et causidici in Angliam primo vocati sunt, quorum primus erat Magister Vacarius. Hic in Oxonefordia legem docuit: apud Romam Magister

Gracianus et Alexander, qui et Rodlandus, in proximo papa futurus, canones compilavit."[6] The Thomas here mentioned as a clerk of London, was Thomas Becket, afterwards archbishop of Canterbury; who was a skilful lawyer, and a doctor of laws of the university of Oxford.[7] The testimony of this ancient biographer is important, as it ascertains the connexion of Vacarius with the same university; for the Norman chronicle only informs us that he taught the Roman law in England.

John of Salisbury, a remarkable writer for the age in which he lived,[8] has likewise furnished us with a short but valuable notice of Vacarius. " Tempore regis Stephani a regno jussæ sunt leges Romanæ, quas in Britanniam domus venerabilis patris Theobaldi, Britanniarum primatis, asciverat. Ne quis etiam libros retineret, edicto regio prohibitum est, et Vacario nostro indictum silentium: sed Deo faciente, eo magis virtus legis invaluit, quo eam amplius nitebatur impietas infirmare."[9]

Bishop Hurd, as we have already seen, supposes the study of the Roman law to have been prohibited, because " the canon law was first read by Vacarius at the same time, and under colour of the imperial." He afterwards subjoins, " it is true, the Decretals of Gratian were not yet published. But Ivo had made a collection of them in the reign of Henry I.; and we may be sure that some code of this sort would privately go about amongst the

----

[6] Historiæ Anglicanæ Scriptores x. p. 1665. Lond. 1652, fol.

[7] One of his biographers has stated that " for the decyding of weighty causes and instructing of the people, hee gaue himselfe to the study of the ciuil and cannon lawe." (The Life or the Ecclesiasticall Historie of S. Thomas, Archbishope of Canterbvry, p. 4. Colloniæ, 1639, 8vo.)

[8] See Harris's Philosophical Arrangements, p. 45

[9] Joannes Sarisberiensis de Nugis Curialium, lib. viii. cap. xxii. p. 672. edit. Lugd. Bat. 1639, 8vo.

clergy, from what was before observed of the pains taken
by Innocent II. to propagate the Decretals." In describing the compilation of Gratian as the Decretals, this
learned prelate is chargeable with considerable inaccu-
racy; it has long been currently known by the title of
Decretum, but is better described as " Decretorum Collectanea." The opinion of Bishop Hurd appears less
probable than that of Dr. Wenck; who supposes Vacarius to have read no lectures on the canon law, but only
to have borrowed from it some illustrations for his lectures on the civil law.

The learned professor has collected other notices of
Vacarius, and has corrected the errors of many previous
writers; and, with reference to a subject of this nature,
his work may be considered as a model of patient and
accurate research. He has however left a scanty glean-
ing for Savigny.[1] Having completed his elaborate account of the author, he proceeds to describe the work
which Vacarius compiled for the use of the poor students
of Oxford; and, in this part of his task, Wenck had not
been anticipated by any other writer. Of this epitome
he mentions four different manuscripts: the first belonged to Augustinus, the illustrious archbishop of Tarragona;[2] the second was in the library of the monastery
of Bec; the third is at present in the library of the chapter at Prague; and the fourth belonged to the professor
himself. He likewise refers to a mutilated copy in the
public library at Könisberg, and of which a particular
description is given by Dr. Dirksen, an eminent civilian

---

[1] Savigny's Geschichte des Römischen Rechts im Mittelalter, Bd. iv.
S. 350.

[2] See Gebaveri Narratio de Henrico Brenkmanno, p. 197.

of that university, who has recently been removed to Berlin.[3] It may not be improper to add, that several copies of the same epitome have more recently been discovered by Dr. Hänel, in his very extensive researches in the libraries of the continent. Wenck's manuscript is a small folio, written on vellum; and, according to his conjecture, it cannot be referred to a period more recent than the thirteenth century. Each page is divided into two columns; copious glosses, both interlinear and marginal, are added in a very small hand. The general doctrines of the law are embodied in the text, while the illustrations are consigned to the margin. Various glosses appear to have been added to those of the author himself. As a specimen of the performance, Wenck has inserted the prologue,[4] which extends to a considerable length, including digested extracts from the constitution prefixed to the Code, " De Justinianeo Codice confirmando," and from the title " De veteri Jure enucleando," as well as from the titles of the Pandects, " De Justitia et Jure," and " De Origine Juris." To this extract he has subjoined a copious and elaborate description of the work, together with an able estimate of its critical and historical value. Of the nine books of Vacarius, consisting of 485 chapters, he afterwards exhibits all the rubrics, and illustrates them with copious annotations.

The academical study of the civil law seems thus to have commenced in England under auspices sufficiently favourable. That it made some progress at this early

---

[3] Dirksen's Civilistische Abhandlungen, Bd. i. S. 319.

[4] " Quem quidem prologum," says Wenck, " tanto libentius nunc exhibeo, quanto firmius ex eo apparet, Vacarium et honestissimæ voluntatis hominem, et pro ætatis suæ conditione, minime infacundum, sed Latini sermonis satis gnarum fuisse." (Magister Vacarius, p. 65).

period, is sufficiently apparent from the treatise on the
laws and customs of England, which is commonly ascribed to Ranulph Glanville, chief justice during the
reign of Henry the Second.   Sir Matthew Hale has remarked, that although it perhaps was not written by
him, yet it seems to have been wholly written at that
time.[5]   According to the title of the book, it was composed in the time of Henry the Second, "justiciæ
gubernacula tenente illustri viro Ranulpho de Glanvilla;" an inscription which by no means describes the
chief justice as the author.   From these words, says
Lord Lyttelton, I infer that the book was not written
by Glanville himself, "but by some clergyman, under
his direction and care; I say clergyman, because it is
written in Latin, which could hardly be done by a layman
of that age."[6]   This treatise, to whatever author it may
be ascribed, is the most ancient book now extant on the
law of England.   It is not without considerable obligations to the civil law; and the beginning of the prologue is little more than a transcript from the procemium
of Justinian's Institutions.   For the benefit of those
readers who are not very familiar with either treatise, I
shall here insert the parallel passages :

" Imperatoriam Majestatem non
solum armis decoratam, sed etiam
legibus oportet esse armatam, ut
utrumque tempus, et bellorum et
pacis, recte possit gubernari, et
Princeps Romanus victor existat
non solum in hostilibus præliis,
sed etiam per legitimos tramites
calumniantium iniquitates expel-

" Regiam Potestatem non solum armis contra rebelles, et
gentes sibi regnoque insurgentes,
oportet esse decoratam, sed et legibus, ad subditos et populos pacifice
regendos, decet esse ornatam, ut
utraque tempora, pacis et belli,
gloriosus Rex noster ita feliciter
transigat, ut effrenatorum et indo-

[5] Hale's Hist. of the Common Law of England, p. 138.
[6] Lyttelton's Hist. of Hen. II. vol. ii. p. 267.

lens, et fiat tam juris religiosis-
simus, quam victis hostibus tri-
umphator."

mitorum dextra fortitudinis eli-
dendo superbiam, et humilium et
mansuetorum eqนitatis virga mo-
derando justitiam, tam in hostibus
debellandis semper victoriosus existat, quam in subditis tractandis
æqualis jugiter appareat." [7]

Glanville has servilely copied Justinian, and the author
of Fleta has servilely copied Glanville.[8] It is well
known that the treatise ascribed to the chief justice was
at a very early period adopted in Scotland, with a few
changes and modifications; and that, under this new
form, it bears the title of *Regiam Majestatem,* from the
initial words of the prologue. Having incidentally referred to the history of Scotish jurisprudence, I am induced to transcribe a very curious preamble, which is to
be found prefixed to different collections of ancient laws.
It is manifestly destitute of all authentic information, but
it affords an amusing proof of the admiration in which
the civil law was then held: from the story of the famous
embassy to Greece, as preparatory to the compilation of
the twelve Tables, this old Scotish writer has fabricated

[7] Tractatus de Legibus et Consuetudinibus Regni Angliæ, tempore
Regis Henrici Secundi compositus, Justiciæ Gubernacula tenente illustri
viro Ranulpho de Glanvilla, juris regni et antiquarum consuetudinum eo
tempore peritissimo. Londini, in ædibus Richardi Totteli, 8vo.—Glanville, Regiam Majestatem, and Fleta may be found in Houard's *Traités
sur les Coutumes Anglo-Normandes.* Paris, 1776, 4 tom. 4to.

[8] Fleta, seu Commentarius Juris Anglicani, liber primus, antiqua
Placita Coronæ continens. Lond. 1735, fol. In Houard's edition of the
entire work, consisting of six books, the prologue is omitted. Nor is
Bracton without his obligations to Justinian. His treatise commences in
the following manner : " In rege qui recte regit, necessaria sunt duo hæc,
arma videlicet et leges, quibus utrumque tempus, bellorum et pacis, recte
possit gubernari." (Henrici de Bracton de Legibus et Consuetudinibus
Angliæ libri quinque. Londini, apud Richardum Tottellum, 1569, fol.)

a more complicated story of twenty-four barons travelling in pairs, and collecting the laws of all Christian countries. " Because thar wes in that tyme sa mony sundry maner of men in Scotland, of divers naciouns, and divers conditions, the quilks held ilkan sundry maner of lauwis and consuetuds, that na man stud aw off an uther; and that tyme wes the noble abbay of Dunfermlyn be the said Saint Davy fundit and byggit in the honour of St. Mergarite his moder; in the quilk tym he mad mony castell, and abbays, and chanounryis, with sundry nouneris, and mayson Dieuwis,[9] that is to say, almis housses, in the honour of God and our Lady suet Saint Mary, and began throu a visioun he met in his slep at Dunfermlyn ; than send he efter his baronnis, and chesit out xxiiii. of the wissast and most hable men to . . ., and gert tham be sworn, that thay suld passe twa and twa in company togidder over all Cristyin kynriks, and wryt up all the lauwis of ilke land, bath in burcht and in land, and geff tham twa yers space to do this, and cum again til hym ; and quhen thay come agayn, thay fand the kyng at the New-castale upon Tyne, makand and biggand the castalle, and uthir syndry abbays of blak monks and of quhyt, and of quhyt chanounis, and nownerys, and maison Diewes; and thar he mad and stablest all his lauwis of Scotland, bath in bourch and in land, be hale assent of all his prelatis, lordis, baronis, burgisses, and commouns."[1]

<hr>

[9] *Mayson Dieuwis* is evidently a corruption of *Maisons de Dieu*, signifying hospitals. The phrase occurs in other Scotish writers. In the Frieris of Berwick, we meet with the following line. (Dunbar's Poems, vol. ii. p. 2. Laing's edit. Edinb. 1834, 2 vols. 8vo.)

The grit Croce kirk, and eik the Maison Dew.

[1] Hailes's Examination of some of the Arguments for the high Antiquity of *Regiam Majestatem*, p. 31. Edinb. 1769, 4to.

The influence of the Roman law on the law of England has been much more considerable than most lawyers
are aware. Of the nature and extent of this influence,
we cannot expect any sound estimate from individuals
who are almost totally ignorant of the laws of every
country but their own ;[2] and as with ignorance prejudice
is apt to march hand in hand, we cannot expect such
individuals to be very willing to admit the probability of
this opinion, to which they are incapable of applying the
proper test. I do not venture to interpose any decision
of my own; but it may here be proper and seasonable to
produce the opinion of several competent judges. " In-
asmuch as the laws of all nations," said the Lord Chief
Justice Holt, " are doubtless raised out of the ruins of
the civil law, as all governments are sprung out of the
Roman empire, it must be owned that the principles of
our law are borrowed from the civil law, and therefore
grounded upon the same reason in many things."[3] A
similar opinion is delivered by Dr. Wood: " Upon a review, I think it may be maintained that a great part of
the civil law is part of the law of England, and interwoven with it throughout."[4] According to Dr. Cowell,
the common law of England is nothing else but a mixture of the feudal and the Roman law.[5] And in refer-

[2] " Il me semble," says Dr. Jourdan, " que les Anglais commencent à
revenir de leur anciens préjugés contre le droit Romain ; mais il est encore bien difficile et bien rare de trouver un exemplaire du *Corpus Juris*
dans la bibliothèque d'un avocat de Londres." (Thémis, ou Bibliothèque du Jurisconsulte, tom. vii. p. 27.)

[3] Modern Reports, vol. xii. p. 482.

[4] Wood's Institute of the Civil Law, p. xi. edit. Lond. 1721, 8vo.

[5] Cowelli Institutiones Juris Anglicani, ad methodum et seriem Institutionum Imperialium compositæ et digestæ, epist. ded. Cantab. 1605,
8vo.—John Cowell, LL.D. master of Trinity Hall, and professor of the

ence to the Pandects, Sir William Jones has hazarded the subsequent opinion: " With all its imperfections,[6] it is a most valuable mine of judicial knowledge; it gives law at this hour to the greatest part of Europe, and, though few English lawyers dare make such an acknowment, it is the true source of nearly all our English laws that are not of a feudal origin." [7]   Many other testimonies might easily be added; but we already seem entitled to conclude, that to an English lawyer some knowledge of the civil law is by no means a superfluous

civil law in the university of Cambridge, published another work, entitled *The Interpreter, or Book containing the Signification of Words* (Camb. 1607, 4to.), which exposed him to the severe animadversion of the house of commons : he was himself committed to custody, and his book was suppressed by the king's proclamation. (Biographia Britannica, vol. iv. p. 364). In England the common lawyers were always jealous of the civilians; and some of Cowell's positions were too favourable to the prerogative of the crown. See Dr. Vaughan's Memorials of the Stuart Dynasty, vol. i. p. 183.   Lond. 1831, 2 vols. 8vo.

[6] A disquisition of 400 pages appeared under the title of " Jacobi Mæstertii, J. C. de Justitia Romanarum Legum libri duo repetitæ prælectionis." Lugd. Bat. 1647, 4to.   The first edition must have appeared several years before; for an answer to the work had been published with this title: " Cypriani Regneri de Injustitia quorundam Legum Romanarum libri duo, contra Jacobum Mæstertium, JCtum.   Adjecta est ad caput 19. libri 1. brevis Apologia pro Manibus Petri Cunæi adversus Claudium Salmasium," &c.   Lugd. Bat. 1640, 12mo.   This interference in another controversy excited the violent indignation of Salmasius, who described the writer by the foul name of Coprianus.   (Disquisitio de Mutuo, qua probatur non esse Alienationem, p. 5.   Lugd. Bat. 1645 8vo.)

[9] See Lord Teignmouth's Memoirs of Sir William Jones, vol. ii. p. 168 The reader may likewise consult the subsequent authorities.   Duck de Authoritate Juris Civilis, lib. ii. cap. viii.   Seldeni Dissertatio ad Fletam, cap. ix.   Ayliffe's New Pandect of the Civil Law, p. 40.   Lond. 1734, fol Barrington's Observations on the Statutes, p. 76.   Bever's Discourse on the Study of Jurisprudence and the Civil Law, p. 25, 31.

or useless acquisition. Of this study I venture to extend
my recommendation somewhat further than has been
done by Roger North. "Besides history," he remarks,
"there are other sorts of learning most reasonable for a
lawyer to have some knowledge of, though even superficial, as of the civil law. A man of the law would not
be willing to stand mute to the question, what is the difference between the civil and the common law, what is the
imperial law, what the canon, what the Pandects, Codes,
&c.? It is not at all needful to study questions in these
laws; but the rise and progress of them in gross is but
a necessary knowledge, and so far taking up but little
time, and had by mere inspection of some books, and
perusing their introductions." [8] For this recommendation, faint as it certainly is, I am inclined to give the
writer some degree of credit.[9] But of the importance of
acquiring a knowledge of the civil law, a much higher
estimate has been formed by several English lawyers of
greater name; and at present I shall content myself with
referring to the opinion and the example of Sir Matthew
Hale. We are informed by his biographer, Bishop Bur-

[8] North's Discourse on the Study of the Laws, p. 8. Lond. 1824, 8vo.
[9] Fulbeck is of opinion that "hee that frameth himselfe to the studie of
the ciuil law, may very profitably imploy his paines in reading of the
Code, Nouellaes, and Pandectes, which are necessary for the profession."
After mentioning various writers, he pronounces a very high encomium on
Gentili. "And amonge these, yea aboue these, him whom I lately named,
Albericus Gentilis, who by his great industrie hath quickned the dead
bodie of the ciuill law written by the auncient ciuilians, and hath in his
learned labours expressed the iudgement of a great state-man, the sound-
nesse of a deepe phylosopher, and the skil of a cunning ciuilian: learning
in him hath shewed all her force, and he is therefore admirable, because
he is absolute." (A Direction or Preparatiue to the Study of the Law,
f. 26. b. Lond. 1620, 8vo.)

H

net, that "he set himself much to the study of the
Roman law, and though he liked the way of judicature
in England by juries much better than that of the civil
law, where so much was trusted to the judge,[1] yet he
often said, that the true grounds and reasons of law were
so well delivered in the Digests, that a man could never
understand law as a science so well as by seeking it there,
and therefore lamented much that it was so little studied
in England."[2]

The statute law of England respecting the distribution
of the estates of intestates "is in a great measure borrowed from the 118th Novel of Justinian;"[3] and the
statute of distributions is known to have been prepared by a professional civilian, Sir Leoline Jenkins,
judge of the high court of admiralty.[4]   It may therefore

[1] See however Dr. Pettingal's Enquiry into the Use and Practice of
Juries among the Greeks and Romans. Lond. 1769, 4to. And on the
same subject I have met with a more recent work, published under the
following title: " De Judicio Juratorum apud Græcos et Romanos
Dissertatio, auctore G. F. A. Comite a Blankensee, Jur. utr. Doctore."
Gœttingæ, 1812, 4to.

[2] Burnet's Life of Sir Matthew Hale, p. 15. Lond. 1682, 8vo.

[3] Reports of all the Cases decided by Sir John Holt, p. 259.—Dr.
Harris has remarked, that " the three first chapters of this novel constitution deserve the attentive consideration of the reader, not only because
they contain the latest policy of the civil law in regard to the disposition
of the estates of intestates, but because they are the foundation of our
statute law in this respect. Vid. Holt's Cases, p. 259. Peere Williams's
Rep. p. 27. Prec. in Chanc. p. 593. Sir Thomas Raymond's Rep.
p. 496. And they are still almost of continual use, by being the general
guide of the courts in England, which hold cognizance of distributions,
in all those cases concerning which our laws have either been silent, or
not sufficiently express." (Justinian's Institutions, translated into
English, p. 364, edit. Oxford, 1811, 4to.)

[4] Wynne's Life of Sir Leoline Jenkins, vol. i. p. liii. Lond. 1724, 2 vols.
fol. The book so described is chiefly composed of letters relative to his

be presumed that a familiar acquaintance with the original text must be of no small importance to a practical lawyer.

Voet has attempted to prove that by the civil law the brother of an intestate excluded the grandfather;[5] and since the publication of his commentary on the Pandects, the same principle has been recognized in the law of England. This question was thrice discussed in the English courts during the last century: the latest decision was in the case of Evelyn v. Evelyn, pronounced in the year 1754 by the lord chancellor Hardwicke, who decreed in favour of the brother to the exclusion of the grandfather. "It was declared to be the opinion of the court," says Dr. Harris, "that, if the point in question had been *res integra*, and solely determinable by the Roman law, the decree would still have been the same; which declaration, from so high an authority, must have great weight in ascertaining the meaning of the Novel, and must incline civilians in general to think more favourably for the future of Voet's arguments, which were particularly quoted and much relied upon by the court."[6] With great deference to so high an authority, I will venture to assert that the opinion adopted by the lord chancellor is completely erroneous; and, without taking notice of all the arguments advanced on the occasion, it may be possible to evince that this assertion is not lightly

negotiations. After having been employed as an ambassador, this learned civilian became secretary of state. Some notices of him occur in Roger North's Life of the Lord Keeper Guilford, vol. ii. p. 55. 62.

[5] Voet, Commentarius ad Pandectas, tom. ii. p. 588. edit. Hag. Com. 1716, 2 tom. fol.—See Mühlenbruch, *Doctrina Pandectarum*, vol. iii. p. 227. edit. 3tiæ. Halis Saxonum, 1830-1, 3 tom. 8vo.

[6] Justinian's Institutions, translated by Harris, p. 367.—See Dr. Burn's Ecclesiastical Law, vol. iv. p. 417, 6th edit.

hazarded.   It is proper to add that the interpretation of
the Dutch professor and the English chancellor is likewise adopted by Dr. Hallifax, professor of the civil law
at Cambridge, and afterwards successively bishop of
Gloucester and St. Asaph.[7]   But the reasoning of Voet
proceeds upon very fallacious grounds.   If it is true, he
remarks, that brothers and sisters so concurred with ascendants in the nearest degree that the estate was to be
equally divided according to the number of individuals,
it would necessarily happen that the nearer ascendants
were less injurious to the brothers and sisters than the
more remote; for if we suppose the deceased to have left
two full brothers, his father and mother would only take
two equal parts of the inheritance, and each of the brothers a fourth part: but if both his grandfathers and
grandmothers survived, each of the brothers would only be
entitled to a sixth part; and if they were admitted along
with great-grandfathers and great-grandmothers to the
number of eight, each would in that case be entitled to
only a tenth part.   The learned commentator evidently
supposes a case of very rare occurrence : when could an
estate ascend to eight different ancestors in the same
degree of proximity?   From what we know of the ordinary course of human life, we may be well assured that
it could rarely, very rarely, ascend to four; for the parents of the intestate must be previously dead, and both
his grandfathers and grandmothers must survive.   But,
in the other case, not only his parents, but likewise both
his grandfathers and grandmothers, must be previously
dead ;—and who then must survive?   The fathers and

---

[7] Hallifax's Analysis of the Civil Law, p. 67.—See also the late Dr.
Browne's View of the Civil Law, vol. i. p. 226, edit. Lond. 1802, 2 vols.
8vo.

mothers of his paternal grandfather and grandmother,
and the fathers and mothers of his maternal grandfather
and grandmother. I will venture to affirm that such a
case has but seldom occurred in the history of mankind
at any period subsequent to the general deluge: if it
did occur, it might with peculiar emphasis be termed
hæreditas luctuosa. Whether we ought to ascribe much
importance to the suggestion of such a case as this, it is
not very difficult to determine. Nor is the question to
be decided by considerations of this nature : when the
terms of a law are express and unequivocal, we must
receive that law with all its consequences. Voet however supposes his doctrine to be sufficiently established
by the words of the Novel; for, according to his averment, it is clearly provided that if full brothers and sisters survive, " eos cum proximis gradu ascendentibus
vocari, si *aut* pater aut mater fuerint." Whatever colour
this notion may derive from such a translation, every
doubt must vanish when we consult the Greek text;
where it is very unequivocally stated that if full brothers
or sisters are found along with ascendants, they shall be
called to the inheritance with those who are nearest in
degree, even if such ascendants should be a father and
mother. Brothers and sisters are called to the succession along with ascendants, εἰ καὶ, *although* those ascendants should be a father and mother ; they are called
to the succession with ascendants of every degree, and
are not even excluded by those who stand in the first
degree, that is, by parents.[8]

[8] Εἰ δὲ μετὰ τῶν ἀνιόντων εὑρεθῶσιν ἀδελφοὶ ἢ ἀδελφαὶ ἐξ ἑκατέρων
γονέων συναπτόμενοι τῷ τελευτήσαντι, μετὰ τῶν ἐγγυτέρων τῷ βαθμῷ
ἀνιόντων κληθήσονται, εἰ καὶ πατὴρ ἢ μήτηρ εἴησαν. (Novell. cxviii.
cap. ii. p. 469. edit. Spangenberg.) " Si vero cum ascendentibus invenian-
tur fratres aut sorores ex utrisque parentibus conjuncti defuncto, cum

The importance of some knowledge of the civil law may be illustrated by another notable case. A trial which took place at Lancaster a few years ago involved the validity of a marriage celebrated in Scotland, and a Scotish advocate was called as a witness by one of the parties. This witness was cross-examined by a leading counsel, one of the most conspicuous characters of the present age ; and some of the questions which he proposed cannot be read without a feeling of greater astonishment than I am at present willing to express. "Are you not aware that it is a principle in the civil law, that a contract is void *cui dolus dat locum ;* that there is a principle in the civil law which voids a contract of that sort?" [9]

proximis gradu ascendentibus vocabuntur, *si et pater aut mater fuerint.*" The last clause is more properly translated by Hombergk, "*licet* pater aut mater sint." But the quotation of Voet, "si *aut* pater aut mater fuerint," is neither warranted by the Greek text nor by the common version; and Lord Hardwicke was well entitled to remark, that "it is not fair in him to alter the words of the Novel, on purpose to favour his own interpretation."

[9] Trial of the Wakefields, p. 244. Lond. 1827, 8vo.—That the marriage of Wakefield with Miss Turner would have been sustained as valid by the law of Scotland, may be considered as extremely doubtful. The marriage law of this country is comprised in the brief rule of Ulpian, *Nuptias non concubitus, sed consensus facit.* (Digest. lib. l. tit. xvii. fr. 30.) But this consent must be real, and not merely apparent ; it must be free consent, and not produced by fear or delusion. Marriage is a civil contract, but it commonly derives some corroboration from the solemnities of religion. It is a general maxim of law, that contracts founded on fraud are null and void ; and it would certainly be a very gross anomaly if this maxim were not to be applied to the most important of all contracts. The consent of Miss Turner was extorted by fraud and circumvention; nor does the direct application of physical force afford a more competent plea of nullity than the internal influence of fear and delusion. If a marriage take place while one of the parties is in a state of intoxication, such as would incapacitate that party for entering into any other contract, it is clear that this apparent consent would not be sufficient. The point was decided

According to the newspaper report, which is thus amended in the separate publication, [1] he asked the witness if he remembered an edict of the prætor *De Dolo Malo* contained in a novel of Justinian, and declaring that every contract was void, "si dolus causam dedisset contractui." The Novels of Justinian, as the merest tyro is well aware, consist of the constitutions promulgated by that emperor subsequently to the publication of his Code: but this edict of the prætor is a relique of much remoter times, and the learned gentleman might with equal propriety have referred to some undescribed statute of George the Third, as containing the original record of an order in Chancery issued by Sir Thomas More. [2] Should it however be objected that this passage is not to

---

in the case of Brown *v.* Johnston, 1818. The marriage of the parties was clandestine and irregular; but in the case of Cameron *v.* Malcolm, 1756, and of Allen *v.* Young, 1773, which were both founded on the celebration of marriage by clergymen, and with most of the usual formalities, it was decided that there was a want of that full and free consent which is essential to the validity of the matrimonial contract. Nor is it possible to overlook the more remarkable case of Macneill or Jolly *v.* Macgregor, which, after a litigation of ten years, was determined by the House of Lords in 1828. (Wilson & Shaw's Appeal Cases, vol. iii. p. 85. Dow & Clark's Reports, vol. i. p. 208. Bligh's New Reports, vol. ii. p. 393. Fergusson's Treatise on the present State of the Consistorial Law in Scotland, app. p. 76. Edinb. 1829, 8vo.) Mr. Brodie, the very able editor of Stair, has arrived at a different conclusion; but the circumstance is in some measure to be imputed to his not having had the benefit of this last decision, so material in itself, and pronounced after such ample discussion. (Stair's Institutions of the Law of Scotland, p. 27.)

[1] Αἱ δεύτεραί πως φροντίδες σοφώτεραι.

[2] On the subject of the prætor's edicts there is a recent work of ample extent: "Libri tres Edicti, sive libri de Origine Fatisque Jurisprudentiæ Romanæ, præsertim Edictorum Prætoris, ac de Forma Edicti Perpetui, quos scripsit Carol. Guil. Ludov. de Weyhe, Doctor Juris." Cellis Luneburgicis, 1821, 4to.

be found in the authorized report of the trial, we are
still left in possession of ample materials. The question
as to the invalidity of a contract founded on fraud[3] is
sufficiently pertinent; but how the next interrogatory
was to be rendered available to his client, it seems very
hard to discover. "Are you not aware that there is also
a prætorian edict, very well known in the civil law,
'Pacta conventa, quæ neque dolo malo, neque adversus
leges, neque quo fraus cui earum fiat, facta erunt, servabo?'"[4] In this edict, the prætor promises to interpose
his authority in order to confirm such bargains as are fair
and legal, but cannot be enforced by any ordinary
action; by furnishing an action or an exception, he
undertakes to mitigate the rigour of the ancient law.[5]
But what concern has all this with the abduction and
marriage of Miss Turner? Proceeding to overwhelm
the witness with another shower of erudition, he pro-
pounds the following question : "Are you aware that by
the civil law, by one of the novels of Justinian, a person

[3] "Nondum enim," says Cicero, "Aquillius, collega et familiaris meus,
protulerat de dolo malo formulas : in quibus ipsis cum ex eo quæreretur,
quid esset dolus malus, respondebat, cum esset aliud simulatum, aliud ac-
tum. Hoc quidem sane luculenter, ut ab homine perito definiendi."
(De Officiis, lib. iii. § 14.) Labeo has defined "dolum malum esse omnem caliditatem, fallaciam, machinationem ad circumveniendum, fallen-
dum, decipiendum alterum adhibitam. Labeonis definitio vera est."
(Digest. lib. iv. tit. iii. fr. 1. § 2.)

[4] This text is not quoted with sufficient accuracy. "Pacta conventa,
quæ neque dolo malo, neque adversus leges, plebiscita, senatusconsulta,
edicta principum, neque quo fraus cui eorum fiat, facta erunt, servabo."
(Digest. lib. ii. tit. xiv. fr. 7. § 7.)

[5] "Mihi vero succurrit, prætori esse propositum hoc edicto, egredi an-
gustias legis duodecim Tabularum, tantum probantis pacta oratione, id
est, ut dixi, solemniter facta; cum prætor etiam servet non solemnia."
(Noodt de Pactis et Transactionibus, cap. i.)

by fraud taking away a young woman, and by fraud marrying her, is guilty of a capital offence?" Here he ought
to have referred, not to the Novels, but to the Code; which
treats at considerable length of the crime that he is thus
pleased to describe as the taking away a young woman.
The only novel of Justinian to which we can suppose
him to allude, is the hundred and forty-third, of which it
is however evident that he has acquired a very imperfect
knowledge. Of this novel the rubric is, *De Muliere
Raptum passa*. The constitution itself, which is explanatory of a former law contained in the Code, relates
to the *rape*, not of a young woman, but of a woman of
any age or condition, whether maid, wife, or widow.
This is certainly not the case of "a person by fraud
taking away a young woman, and by fraud marrying
her." The crime to which the law relates is not simple
abduction, but rape; and so remote is this law from any
analogy to the case then before the court, that the inter-
marriage of a woman with her ravisher is strictly prohibited; "ut nulla sit mulieri vel virgini raptæ licentia,
raptoris eligere matrimonium."[6] In order to illustrate a
case of fraudulent abduction, followed by marriage, he
quotes a law relating to rape, which, according to that

---

[6] Novell. cxliii.—"Nec sit facultas raptæ virgini vel viduæ, vel cuilibet
mulieri raptorem suum sibi maritum exposcere." (Cod. lib. ix. tit. xlii.
§ 1.) If the parents of the woman consented to such a union, they were
liable to the punishment of deportation. The eye of the legislator seems
to have been chiefly fixed on one point; and he evidently had less regard
to the reparation of injury than to the prevention or punishment of crime:
"quoniam nullo modo, nulloque tempore datur a nostra serenitate licentia
eis consentire qui hostili more in nostra republica matrimonia student
sibi conjungere."

law, could never be followed by marriage. This is the same individual who soon afterwards averred in the House of Commons that, "as to the civil law, there was no knowledge of it in Scotland;" and that " it had been proved at the recent trial at Lancaster that this was mere sham and farce." Where the imputation of "sham and farce" must ultimately rest, we may safely leave to the determination of any competent judge. [7]

To these illustrations many others might easily be added. There is one English court which presents the most ample prospects of honour and emolument, and in which a competent knowledge of the civil law is confessedly of no small importance to the judges and practitioners. The forms of administering justice in the Court of Chancery are in a great measure derived from the Roman jurisprudence. The chancellors were for many ages dignified ecclesiastics, eminent for their skill in the civil and canon laws ; and their assistants, the masters in chancery, were, till a much later period, doctors in the same faculties. [8] "And (to speak with all due deference) if the other practitioners in this honourable and important seat of justice would sometimes condescend to look back upon the real sources of their proceedings, and correct some of their redundancies by the first principles of their profession, the civil law would not appear in a less favourable light, nor would the suitors

---

[7] " Inconsultæ temeritatis nota aspersus est apud jurisperitos, qui quod non didicerat, carpere non erubuerit." (Wissenbach, Vindiciæ Diatribæ de Mutuo, esse Alienationem, p. 248. Franekeræ, 1645, 8vo.)

[8] "The sixe masters," says Sir Thomas Smith, "are assistants to the court, to shew what is the equitie of the ciuill law, and what is conscience." (Commonwealth of England, p. 121. edit. Lond. 1633, 12mo.)

be more burthened with delay and expence. One principal object of this court arises from testamentary causes ; in which it has in many instances an exclusive jurisdiction, in others, a concurrent one with the ecclesiastical courts. But as devises of lands were little known in the English constitution till the statutes of wills in the reign of Henry VIII., the professors of the common law were very poorly provided with the rules for determining such disputes as then began daily to arise, and to open an entire new scene of very lucrative business. The right of testation however being very free and unlimited in the Roman republic, they gladly resorted to that rich magazine of good sense ; from whence they have imported very large and valuable materials, wherewith they have enlivened their more modern juridical writings ; and have thereby much improved the system of public justice. Here therefore the civil law speaks with good effect, where the common law is silent or deficient ; and deserves to be studied with great care and precision. And the same may be said of several other objects of this high jurisdiction." [9]

Whatever opinion may be entertained by common lawyers, there is in England one class of individuals who are more particularly bound to prosecute the study of the civil law. On them we usually bestow the appellation of civilians ; and if we include all those who have taken a

---

[9] Bever's Discourse on the Study of Jurisprudence and the Civil Law, p. 30. Oxford, 1766, 4to.—" In more modern times," says the late Dr. Wooddeson, " since the business of the chancery has become so diffusive, the advocates and judges in that court have frequently and unreservedly resorted for arguments and illustrations both to the text and comment of the Roman civil law." (Elements of Jurisprudence, p. 86. Lond. 1783, 4to.)

doctor's degree in this faculty, the class is sufficiently numerous. If we may rely on the authority of Dr. Bever, this happy country, which so seldom betrays the weakness of discovering its own deficiencies, "has never yet failed to produce a succession of great and able civilians." He is however compelled to admit that those great and able civilians have not been much distinguished as authors; and his friendly, if not partial, commendation might therefore be more safely hazarded. "England," he is pleased to state, "though it has never yet failed to produce a succession of great and able civilians, who have done the highest honour to their profession, both as advocates and statesmen, has contributed but little to the cultivation and advancement of this branch of knowledge by its writers. The truth is, that the study of the Roman law has been so little countenanced by the public in general, that few men of learning have chosen to exercise their talents in a field, where the prospect either of reputation or riches is so very barren and unpromising."[1]—Great and able civilians? Excellence is always comparative. In Lapland, he that attains the height of five feet eight inches cannot fail to be regarded as a person of extraordinary stature; but if the same individual should emigrate to Britain, he would there find himself of a very common size. In the university of Oxford, the study is merely nominal. The chief defect of the present system of education seems to be this: the regulated plan of study is, in a great measure, confined to what may be considered as merely the foundation of academical learning. When the student has taken the degree of bachelor of

[1] Bever's Hist. of the Legal Polity of the Roman State, p. x.

arts, he is too much encouraged to believe that he has completed his studies. Many members of the university lay an excellent foundation of classical learning; and notwithstanding some modern speculations, our judgment or our prejudices lead us to attach a very high degree of importance to such a foundation;[2] but after they have received all the advantages of this training, we do not so often find, if they continue their residence, that they betake themselves with any visible ardour to the appropriate studies of any of the faculties.

According to the statutes of the university, a student of the civil law, if he has not taken the degree of master of arts, is bound to attend the professor's lectures for five years; and if he has previously taken his master's degree, he is bound to attend them for three years.[3] Several years of attendance are further enjoined before he is entitled to the degree of doctor. But at present

[2] "Neminem unquam vidi," says Grævius, "qui deplorarit tempus, quod in excolendis literarum studiis posuit, multos, qui graviter conquerantur, se illis animum non expoliisse, aut desidia, aut culpa magistrorum, qui aut veram ad solidam doctrinam perveniendi viam iis non ostenderint, cum ipsi eam ignorarint, aut ab ea illos abduxerint, amore sui ablati, ne colant et suspiciant alia, quam se, ac quibus ipsi sunt dediti. Qui severioribus disciplinis se manciparunt, cognorunt et ipsi, absque humanitatis studiis nihil posse memoriæ prodi, quod ferat ætatem, sed omnia brevi ad instar solstitialium herbarum exarescere." (Præf. in Bern. Ferrarium de Ritu Sacrarum Ecclesiæ veteris Concionum, p. iii. Ultraj. 1692, 8vo.)

[3] "Statutum est, quod, qui juri civili studet, antequam baccalaureatum in illa facultate consequatur, si sit magister artium, per tres annos integros (numerandos a die suæ admissionis ad regendum) audiat publicum juris civilis professorem. Si quis vero juri civili det operam, qui non sit magister artium; per quinquennium completum, publicum juris civilis prælectorem diligenter et attente audiat." (Corpus Statutorum Universitatis Oxoniensis, p. 40. Oxon. 1768, 4to.)

there are no teachers and no actual students in this
faculty; some ancient forms are still left, while the substance has completely evaporated. Degrees, called regular, are conferred in considerable abundance, and
degrees, called honorary, are scattered with a most un-
sparing profusion on rank and wealth, totally disunited
from learning. An attendance of many years on the
lectures of one professor might be much more burden-
some than advantageous; but, in endeavouring to mitigate the rigour of the ancient statutes, it certainly was
not absolutely necessary to confer on the professor and
students a perpetual exemption from all the duties of
teaching and learning. In the opinion of competent
judges, the study of the civil law is the best foundation
of all juridical knowledge; nor is it a useless pursuit for
a classical scholar. " It may perhaps seem strange,"
says Bishop Hallifax, " to assert the utility of the Roman
law to the divine. But when it is recollected that frequent allusions to this law, in the instances of adoption,

By the statutes of the university of Coimbra, compiled by order of the
king in 1772, the course of juridical study is reduced from eight to five
years. At the expiration of the fourth year, the student may take the
degree of bachelor of the civil or the canon law, or of both. This degree
may be followed by those of licentiate and doctor, which cannot be taken
during the same year in which the candidate has completed his bachelor's
degree. (Estatutos da Universidade de Coimbra, liv. ii. p. 277. 605. 612.
Lisboa, 1772, fol.) The requisite course of study is very minutely detailed, and in some respects the plan is entitled to much approbation,
particularly in its close combination of history with jurisprudence. In
order to conduct this laborious course, his Majesty declares his intention
of appointing sixteen professors. One chair, that of the law of nature
and nations, is to be common to both the law faculties : eight are destined
for the faculty of the laws, that is, of the civil and municipal laws ; and
seven for the faculty of the canons, that is, of the canon law.

the right of citizenship, slavery, &c., occur in the New Testament, and especially in the writings of St. Paul; when it is remembered, too, that many of this profession are often called to preside, either as judges or surrogates, in the spiritual courts; and when it is further considered, how great a proportion the civil law bears in composing the ecclesiastical law of England; it will appear that a competent skill in Roman jurisprudence is far from being foreign to the character of a divine; as it qualifies him to understand with accuracy the original records of his faith, to support the dignity of his character as a spiritual judge, and to defend and secure the possession of his legal dues."[4] For the study of the Roman law, the classical training of this university is an excellent prepa-

[4] Hallifax's Analysis of the Civil Law, p. xviii. Geldart's edit. Camb. 1836, 8vo.—The subsequent quotation relates to Dr. Dickens, another professor of the civil law at Cambridge. " His determinations upon some of the questions that came before him were so excellent, that they were much attended to and admired; and an eminent divine has been heard to declare more than once, there were some passages in St. Paul's epistles he could not comprehend, till he heard them explained by him, in the most satisfactory manner, from the Roman laws." (Masters's Memoirs of Thomas Baker, B.D. p. 110. Camb. 1784, 8vo.) Hallifax has remarked that the annotations of Grotius on the New Testament, particularly on the Acts of the Apostles, and the Epistles of St. Paul, are full of quotations from the civil law. Many other commentators on the sacred text have borrowed occasional illustrations from the same source ; and, among the rest, Dr. Ward of Gresham College, in his Dissertations upon several Passages of the Sacred Scriptures. Lond. 1761-74, 2 vols. 8vo. Bishop Hallifax himself, and Dr. Powell, another eminent member of the university of Cambridge, have each evinced that a knowledge of the civil law may sometimes be useful to a divine. (Hallifax's Twelve Sermons on the Prophecies, p. 341. Lond. 1776, 8vo. Powell's Discourses on various Subjects, p. 209. Lond. 1776, 8vo.) See likewise Dr. Jortin's Discourses concerning the Truth of the Christian Religion, p. 55. 150. 177. edit. Lond. 1752, 8vo.

rative ; and if the leading members were sufficiently impressed with an idea of its importance, the study might
without much difficulty be revived.   If they were to
provide an able and popular lecturer, deeply skilled in
the ancient languages, and familiarly acquainted with the
recent discoveries and speculations of the continent, he
might speedily attract a respectable auditory.   The candidates for degrees in law could be compelled to attend;
and as we are not merely to enumerate those who have a
view to Doctors Commons, but likewise those who aim
at law-fellowships, their number would not be so inconsiderable, if we are even to suppose other candidates to
be generally discouraged by the necessity of studying
law as a preparation for taking a law-degree.   There are
besides many fellows of colleges who betake themselves
to the profession of the common law ; and of these a very
great proportion might at length be induced to attend
lectures on the civil law, provided those lectures were
delivered by a man of talents and learning.   Young
men of rank and fashion, if they can be led or impelled
to any species of study, may feel no peculiar antipathy
to this : legislators and ambassadors seem to be under an
obligation of acquiring some general notions of jurisprudence ; nor could they perhaps derive their elementary
knowledge from a more invigorating fountain. " Nothing,"
says a French writer, " is more proper to form the mind
and manners, than the study of the Roman law.   Every
one, who is of any considerable rank in life, ought to have
perused with attention, once at least, the Institutions and
the Code of Justinian." [5]   Dr. Jortin subjoins, " I am of
the same opinion; and I add to these the Theodosian

[5] Vigneul-Marville, Mélanges d'Histoire et de Littérature, tom. ii. p. 51.

Code, for the light which it gives to ecclesiastical history."[6]

The professor of the civil law at Cambridge, Dr. Geldart, finds pupils, and reads lectures. In the year 1768, it was enacted by the senate that no candidate should be admitted to the degree of LL. B. without producing a certificate of his having attended the professor's lectures for three terms ; and what has been found practicable in the one university, may be worth attempting in the other. Under the present system at Oxford, a bachelor of laws is not better trained in juridical studies than a bachelor of arts. His name must continue seven years on the boards, but the necessary period of his residence is only about four years. He continues nominally, though in too many cases not really, a student for five years longer, before he can be admitted to his doctor's degree; but if he declares his intention of following the profession of a civilian, he is permitted to take that degree in four years instead of five. Having thus been engaged in pursuing a shadow for eleven years, he is qualified to present himself at Doctors Commons; and, after the expiration of his year of silence, may at length be qualified to plead in the ecclesiastical and admiralty courts.[7] If he has sufficiently imbibed the spirit of his

[6] Jortin's Tracts, vol. i. p. 437. Lond. 1790, 2 vols. 8vo.—" It has often occurred to the writer," says Mr. Butler, " that, for persons designed for parliament or the bar, the interval between studies merely classical and studies practically useful could not be employed better than in the perusal of the Institutes, in the edition of them by Dr. Harris, and the *Syntagma* of Heineccius, as a commentary." (Reminiscences of Charles Butler, Esq., vol. i. p. 121.)

[7] Gray has given the following account of his taking a bachelor's degree at Cambridge : " By my own indefatigable application for these ten years past, and by the care and vigilance of that worthy magistrate the

foster-mother, he is likewise prepared to view with supreme contempt the graduates of all other universities
except those of Oxford and Cambridge, doubtless with
good reason; for what is Cujacius's knowledge of the
civil law, or Van Espen's knowledge of the canon law,
when put in competition with the multifarious advantages
of keeping one's name for eleven long years on the books
of some college in the magnificent university of Oxford?[8]
A graduate of another denomination once endeavoured
to intrude himself into this learned society.   It is not
universally understood that the archbishop of Canterbury enjoys the privilege of conferring degrees in all the
faculties; nor do I think it superfluous to add that, so
far as my knowledge extends, this privilege has generally
been exercised with sufficient propriety and reserve.

man-in-blue, (who, I'll assure you, has not spared his labour, nor could
have done more for his own son), I am got half-way to the top of Jurisprudence, and bid as fair as another body to open a case of impotency with
all decency and circumspection." (Works, vol. ii. p. 141. Mitford's
edit.)

[8] " The professor of civil law," says a well-informed member of this
university, " reads no lectures, notwithstanding every thing connected
with Roman antiquities is so congenial to the spirit of the place.   But
since this inexhaustible field presents no topic of general interest, and
since, even if the students in civil law were required to attend, they are
not sufficiently numerous to constitute a class, why may not the professor
examine privately the different candidates, in Heineccius, or Sigonius,
or Taylor, or even in Dr. Adam's Roman Antiquities?   These are works
of which no scholar should be ignorant; and many others, not only in
civil law, but in antiquities, and the law of nature and nations, might,
with a proper liberality of interpretation, be admitted to the choice of the
candidate.   Even *Propria quæ maribus* would be a respectable substitute
for the syllogisms upon contracts." (Observations suggested by the
Strictures of the Edinburgh Review upon Oxford, and by the two Replies; containing some Account of the late Changes in that University.
By Henry Home Drummond, B.C.L. Advocate. Edinb. 1810, 8vo.)

Archbishop Herring having conferred the degree of doctor of laws on John Hawkesworth, a very distinguished English writer, the new graduate made an attempt to be admitted as an advocate ; but it was decided that a Lambeth degree did not impart the requisite qualification, nor are we aware that any similar question has since been moved. Dr. Kenrick has made the subsequent allusion to this unsuccessful attempt:

> Repeatedly engross'd you see
> The same by H—ks—th, LL.D.,
>   At Lambeth dubb'd a doctor!
> He who, so learned in the laws,
> Had practised, had he found a cause,
>   A client, or a proctor.[9]

To these anecdotes of the profession in England, I may add that no person in holy orders can be admitted a member of the College of Doctors of Law exercent in the Ecclesiastical and Admiralty Courts. This question was, within a recent period, decided in the case of Dr. Highmore, who, perhaps somewhat unluckily for himself, had successively directed his attention to the three learned professions. His objects and his pursuits appear to have been so various, that it may be worth while to mention that he had prosecuted his studies in at least four universities. Philology and divinity he studied at Göttingen, and he became a deacon of the church of England. He studied medicine at Leyden and Edinburgh, and in one of those universities he became a doctor of physic. The study of the civil law he prosecuted at Edinburgh and Cambridge, and in the latter uni-

---

[9] Kenrick's Poems, Ludicrous, Satirical, and Moral, p. 168. Lond. 1768, 8vo.

versity he took the degree of doctor of laws. Having at
length made his election to adhere to the legal profession, he applied in due form to the Dean of the Arches,
but was informed that, having taken deacon's orders, he
could not be admitted a member of the college, such admission being expressly forbidden by the canons of the
church. To this decision, which was confirmed by the
archbishop of Canterbury, he submitted with great re-
luctance; and he made a formal appeal to the public respecting a case in which the public could not be expected
to feel any very deep interest.[1] If he had first become
an advocate, and had afterwards entered into holy orders,
it is to be presumed that the two professions of divinity
and law would, in that case, have been declared equally
incompatible. Dr. Taylor, having taken orders, ceased
to be a member of the college, and consequently was no
longer qualified to practise in the courts at Doctors
Commons.

Instead of endeavouring to rival their continental
brethren in extent of erudition or depth of research,
those who in this self-satisfied country bear the name of
civilians, are sometimes more disposed to content themselves with assuming very ludicrous airs of superiority.
In order to render this observation perfectly intelligible,
I shall produce a notable example. " One should suppose that justice was one of the simplest ideas in nature,
but how complicated must it appear when we travel from
the *Tractatus Tractatuum* down to the latest publications
on all sorts of law ? Little ought to be our surprise,
when we find that German and Dutch *magnificent* pro-

fessors, as they call themselves, and who in general are only schoolmasters, are the numerous and principal writers on the laws ecclesiastical, civil, and of nature, and of nations. A Bynkershoek, a Huberus, a Vattel, a Hubner, a Schlegel, a Busch, a Heineccius, a Grotius, a Pufendorf, are men who have written to serve a particular private personal, or otherwise some public political purpose. Had the wife of Grotius published her opinions upon some certain subjects, said a reader of lectures upon the Roman and civil law in one of our universities, she would have been of a different opinion. It is well known that in the foreign universities that whosoever takes a degree (and degrees are mostly taken in law) print and publish theses, which they make or are made for them. Nothing can be more ridiculous, when it is notorious that a thesis may be bought, as well as burghers briefs and false passes, for one or a few rix-dollars, [2] than to see such things dressed up with all the professorial pedantry of learning, and the authors as theatrically an-

[2] Mr Dyer informs us that "the son of a gentleman very high in the law called on him in London, with a most earnest request, which was, to make a Latin law thesis for a friend of his, the son of a dignitary in the church, who was about to keep an act in the law schools, but who, without a law degree, could not hold two livings, which were offered him. The gentleman's importunities prevailed over all excuses and remonstrances: the writer had but three days to perform this task in; and, owing to shortness of time, and a slight knowledge of the subject, this law thesis was, it may be supposed, very imperfectly executed. But the degree was obtained. Transactions of this kind are considered private; and in giving publicity to this, the parties alluded to may be assured that their names never have passed the writer's lips, and never shall. But degrees in all the faculties are thus easily to be obtained, and frequently are; so that a solitary example would be no discredit, and could create no surprise." (Academic Unity, p. 137. Lond. 1827, 8vo.) The reader must bear in mind, that this transaction had no reference to a foreign university.

tiquated as if they appeared in trunk hose, jackboots, slashed doublets, great slouched hats and feathers, ruffs or bands." [3]

This egregious puerility did not proceed from some young and nameless individual, but from a personage who had attained to the highest honours of his profession; from Sir James Marriott, who had been master of Trinity Hall at Cambridge, and judge of the High Court of Admiralty. The " reader of lectures in one of our own universities" might perhaps have found some difficulty in explaining the difference between the Roman and the civil law, which in common parlance are understood to signify one and the same thing. This learned and facetious person may possibly have been the identical Dr. Marriott, while he was yet a fellow of Trinity Hall. The judge of the admiralty might however have been aware that the German and Dutch professors never call themselves *magnificent:* this is a style appropriated to the rectors of universities; and the office of rector, which is always considered as highly honourable, is in many cases an office of no small power and authority. Our gracious sovereign is perpetual rector of the university of Göttingen. Marriott's speculations on academical degrees are such as might have been expected from so great an author, the thoughts and the language being extremely well adapted to each other. But the proficiency of the candidates is not solely estimated from their dissertations, which he improperly describes as theses. It may indeed be true that dissertations are occasionally procured by the money, and not by the labour of the candidate; but, in the German and Dutch univer-

[3] Marriott's Decisions in the High Court of Admiralty, p. xxx. Lond. 1801, 8vo.

sities, they are in many, if not most, instances the actual productions of their reputed authors; many of them display a
great portion of learning and ingenuity; and those of the
third rate will easily bear a comparison with a certain Latin
lucubration which this English civilian has bequeathed
to posterity.[4] Well did it become such a twaddler as
this to speak in contemptuous terms of Grotius, Pufendorf, Bynkershoek, and Heineccius ; to describe many
able and distinguished professors of law as being "in
general only schoolmasters." Under such schoolmasters
as these, Sir James Marriott was not qualified to act as
an usher of the lowest form. Between two individuals
of the same training, and occupying the same situation,
a greater contrast could not well be conceived than the
contrast between this judge of the admiralty and his immediate successor Lord Stowell. The talents and judgment of the one need not be more particularly described.
The other has been regarded as the ablest judge who
sat in any British court for the lengthened period during
which he occupied the bench. It is impossible to read
his decisions, either in admiralty or consistorial cases,
without being deeply impressed, not merely with his extent and accuracy of knowledge, but still more with his

[4] Poems, written chiefly at the University of Cambridge; together with a
Latin Oration upon the History and Genius of the Roman and Canon
Laws, with a Comparison of the Laws of England, spoken in the Chapel
at Trinity Hall, Cambridge, December 21, 1756. Camb. 1760, 8vo. The
title is not graced with the author's name, but the poetical address to the
queen is subscribed "James Marriott, LL.D., Fellow of Trinity Hall, and
one of the Advocates of Doctors Commons." His Latin oration bears
the following title: "De Historia et Ingenio Juris Civilis et Canonici,
cum Comparatione Legum Angliæ, Oratio habita in Sacello Aulæ Trini-
tatis die Commemorationis 1756, ex testamento Thomæ Eden, LL. D."
It is proper to mention, that this elegant volume was privately printed.

sagacity and discrimination of mind.   Nor can we overlook, what is indeed of very inferior moment, the terse
and elegant language in which he generally embodies his
thoughts.   A remarkable proof of his talents is to be
found in his elaborate and masterly judgment in the case
of Dalrymple v. Dalrymple; in which the Scotish law
relative to marriage is delivered with a clearness, precision, and consistency, to which it would perhaps be difficult to find a parallel in the writings of any author who
has treated of the same subject.

On the utility of this study to the Scotish lawyer,
it may seem unnecessary to dilate.   The law of Scotland
has derived so many of its maxims and principles from
the civil law, that the study of the one is justly regarded
as the best introduction to the study of the other; and
no person can indeed be admitted a member of the
Faculty of Advocates without undergoing a previous examination in the civil as well as the municipal law.   Till
a recent period, the candidates were only examined in
the former branch of study.[5]   "Although," says a late

---

[5] The following passage occurs in the Answers for the Dean and Faculty
of Advocates, to the petition of Mr. Patrick Haldane, Advocate : "Your
lordships very well know that the sole trial in order to admission as an
advocate, is upon the Roman law; and that gentlemen of this nation in-
tending to qualify themselves to be advocates, confine their studies chiefly
to that law; so that till within these very few years, gentlemen always
studied in foreign universities, and having laid up a reasonable stock of
the civil law, were admitted advocates without knowing one title of the
municipal laws of their own country; which laid them under a necessity
of commencing students of our own law after they were admitted advocates, and tied them to attendance at your lordships bar, the best place in
the world for seeing rules illustrated by examples in practice." This
paper, which is dated in 1722, relates to the admission of Haldane as a
judge; and is signed by a committee of five advocates, one of whom is
Duncan Forbes.

professor of the municipal law, " we have thus collected
and adopted a law of our own, which is partly written,
partly consuetudinary, yet as in the infinite variety of
cases which daily emerge, some questions will often occur which by no rule in our law can well be decided, our
judges therefore have recourse to the civil law, and are
thereby so far governed, as they find the rule of decision
therein set forth, nowise disconform and inconsistent
with our own law and practick: and therein the judges
are well justified by several acts of parliament, whereby
it is declared, that the lieges shall be governed by the
king's own laws, (that is, our own peculiar laws and customs), and by the common laws of the realm, (that is, the
civil law) ; so that we consider the Roman laws, which
are not disconform to our own fixed laws and customs,
to be our law.   For in the reign of James V. we find the
king's advocate commencing an action of forfeiture
against an heir, for the high treason of his father, on no
other foundation but the civil law; which, though mur-
mured against by the generality of the nation as a
novelty, was yet justified by the parliament as legal ; and
for no other reason but because it was agreeable to the
Roman law.[6]   And in king James VI. his time, we find

---

[6] 6 Jac. V. c. 69. Acts of the Parliaments of Scotland, vol. ii. p. 356.
" Howbeit the commoun law directly providis the samin."—In reference to
this act, Sir George Mackenzie has remarked, "that the common or civil
law is a sufficient warrand to sustain actions in this kingdom, because of
its great equity, except where the same is over-ruled by a contrary law or
custom." (Observations on the Acts of Parliament, p. 136. Edinb. 1687,
fol.) By the *common law* our earlier writers generally mean the civil
law; and the term continued to bear this signification till a recent period.
See the Information subscribed by Robert Dundas, in the Trial of Car-
negie of Finhaven, in the year 1728, for the murder of the Earl of Strath-
more, p. 39, 52. edit. Edinb. 1762, 8vo.   He undertakes to prove that
killing in such circumstances "was not capital by the common law,
which we in great measure follow in matters of that kind."

the legislature, in the abrogating of some former laws, thought it necessary to give a *non obstante* to the civil law, as well as to our own particular laws and constitutions. From all which it manifestly appears that the civil law has all along been considered as our law, and is justly made the rule of judgment in all cases wherein our law is silent, and when such decisions will prove nowise derogatory to our own proper laws and customs." [7]

The opinion of Lord Stair has been considered as less favourable to the authority of the civil law: he remarks, that it is not acknowledged as a law binding for its authority, but, as a rule, is followed for its equity.[8] This opinion seems to be expressed with a higher degree of precision. It is evident that the civil law of the Romans, considered as an entire system of jurisprudence, has never been fully received by any nation of modern Europe: many parts of it, as, for example, whatever relates to the power of the father and to the condition of slaves, are utterly inapplicable to modern manners; and such portions of it as have been adopted in those countries where it has even the greatest influence, are for the most part modified by the peculiar habits or circumstances of the people. The civil law is not in any proper sense the law of the land in Holland, Germany, or Scotland;[9] but in each of those countries it is the

---

[7] Bayne's Discourse on the Rise and Progress of the Law of Scotland, p. 166. subjoined to Sir Thomas Hope's Minor Practicks. Edinb. 1726, 8vo.—See likewise Cragii Jus Feudale, lib. i. dieg. ii. § 14. Mackenzie's Institutions of the Law of Scotland, b. i. tit. i. § 7. Bankton's Institute of the Laws of Scotland, b. i. tit. i. and Erskine's Institute of the Law of Scotland, b. i. tit. i. § 41.

[8] Stair's Institutions of the Law of Scotland, b. i. tit. i. § 12.

[9] How far this observation is applicable to Holland, may be learned

source from which almost all their municipal laws, not of a feudal origin, have manifestly been drawn. Whatever is gradually admitted by the courts, or is formally acknowledged by the legislature, becomes part and parcel of the law of the land.

It is a maxim of the civilians, that as laws may be established by long and continued custom, so they may likewise be abrogated by desuetude, or, in other words, they may be annulled by contrary usage. " Ea vero quæ ipsa sibi quæque civitas constituit, sæpe mutari solent, vel tacito consensu populi, vel alia postea lege lata." [1] These are the words of the Institutions, and the same principle is distinctly stated in the Pandects. Inveterate custom, we are there informed, is not improperly observed as law; and this is that law which is said to be established by the habits and circumstances of a people. For, as laws are only binding from their being approved by the judgment of the people, so those which they have confirmed without any formal enactment, must deservedly be considered as of general obligation.[2] For of what importance is it, whether the people declare their will by their suffrages, or by facts themselves?[3] It is therefore very properly held, that laws may be abrogated, not only by the suffrage of a legislator, but also by the tacit con-

from the ample treatise of Groenewegen, Tractatus de Legibus abrogatis et inusitatis in Hollandia vicinisque Regionibus. Lugd. Bat. 1649, 4to.

[1] Institut. lib. i. tit. ii. § 11.

[2] "Quantum autem," says Noodt, "debeat esse tempus, ut longa sit consuetudo, quia in jure non est expressum, judicis arbitrio relinquendum est." (Commentarius ad Digesta, p. 15.)

[3] "Jura populorum," says Macieiowski, " ita nascuntur, propagantur, senescunt et cadunt, ut eorum mores consuetudinesque dilabi et interire solent : quare rectissime illud receptum est, ut leges non solum suffragio legislatoris, sed etiam tacito consensu omnium per desuetudinem abrogentur." (Historia Juris Romani, p. 4.)

sent of the community.[4] This is the doctrine of the
civil law; and this doctrine has to a great extent been
adopted by the law of Scotland. When this tacit mode
of abrogating laws was some years ago mentioned in the
House of Commons, it excited the utmost surprize and
even astonishment among the English members; and
some of them were very much disposed to deny that such
a maxim had ever been devised. But their astonishment
would have been less if their academical studies had embraced the first elements of the Roman jurisprudence;
and it admits of no controversy that this is the maxim
of the Scotish lawyers, who hold that a statute may fall
into desuetude, and thus lose the force and efficacy of
law. Lord Stair, the great oracle of their law, has
remarked that "acts of parliament in this are inferior to
our ancient law, that they are liable to desuetude, which
never encroaches on the other."[5] Thus we perceive
that a statute may be abrogated by the force of custom,
which cannot however be opposed to customary law. It
is indeed to be recollected, that, in all countries, the
common or customary law derives its vital strength from
the remotest ages of social union, and becomes so completely assimilated with the habits, the feelings, and the
prejudices of the people, that they might almost as soon
be expected to abandon the use of their mother tongue.

---

[4] " Inveterata consuetudo pro lege non immerito custoditur, et hoc est
jus quod dicitur moribus constitutum. Nam cum ipsæ leges nulla alia
ex causa nos teneant, quam quod judicio populi receptæ sunt, merito et
ea quæ sine ullo scripto populus probavit, tenebunt omnes : nam quid
interest, suffragio populus voluntatem suam declaret, an rebus ipsis et
factis ? Quare rectissime etiam illud receptum est, ut leges non solum
suffragio legislatoris, sed etiam tacito consensu omnium per desuetudinem
abrogentur." (Digest. lib. i. tit. iii. fr. 32, § 1.)

[5] Stair's Institutions of the Law of Scotland, b. i. tit. i. § 16.

There is a considerable variety of opinion with respect to
the application of a principle which they all admit; some
maintaining that sixty, and others that one hundred
years are required to constitute this state of desuetude.
A distinction has sometimes been made between statutes
which are partly obsolete, and those which are *in viridi
observantia*, or in fresh observance.—"Such," says Sir
George Mackenzie, "is the force of custom or consuetude, that if a statute, after long standing, has never
been in observance, or, having been, has run into desuetude, consuetude prevails over the statute, till it be renewed, either by a succeeding parliament, or by a proclamation from the council; for although the council
cannot make laws, yet they may revive them."[6]   With
respect to this arbitrary and dangerous power of the
privy council, the law remains unaltered; but there is
something so rotten in this state of administration, that
the power may perhaps be supposed to be sufficiently
controlled by the spirit of the age.   Among Scotish lawyers there is another rule of interpretation, on which it
is not superfluous to bestow a cursory notice.   "This
power in custom," says Erskine, "to derogate from prior
statutes, has been confined by most writers to those
concerning private right; and it hath been adjudged
once and again, that laws which regard the public policy
cannot fall into disuse by the longest contrary usage."[7]
By adhering to this rule, the crown lawyers of more fla-

[6] Mackenzie's Institutions of the Law of Scotland, b. i. tit. i. § 10.
Erskine has without hesitation delivered a similar doctrine: "Where
the usage contrary to a statute hath not yet acquired strength enough to
abrogate it, the king and council may by proclamation prohibit the further
observance of such usage, and thereby restore the statute to its first vigour."
[7] Erskine's Institute of the Law of Scotland, b. i. tit. i. § 45.

gitious times must have been better enabled to satisfy
their employers.

With respect to the abrogation of statutes, the law of
England follows a different, and, in the opinion of many,
a much safer maxim; namely, that every statute continues in force till repealed by another statute. A remarkable instance of the application of this maxim
occurred in an appeal of murder, heard at the bar of the
King's Bench in the year 1818.[8]   After the preliminary
proceedings in this case, namely, that of Ashford *v.*
Thornton, the appellee threw down his glove, and formally challenged the appellant to single combat. If any
analogous case had occurred in the Court of Justiciary,
the judges would have been very much inclined to decide
that the law now pleaded had fallen into desuetude;[9]
but the judges of the King's Bench were bound to decide, and did accordingly decide, that this law, being
unrepealed, was still the law of the land.—" However
averse I am myself to the trial by battle," said the chief
justice, Lord Ellenborough, "it is the mode of trial
which we, in our judicial character, are bound to award.
We are delivering the law as it is, and not as we wish it
to be; and we must pronounce our judgment, that the
battle shall take place, unless the other party reserves

[8] See Barnewall & Alderson's Reports, vol. i. p. 405, and Kendall's
Argument for construing largely the Right of an Appellee of Murder to
insist on Trial by Battle, 3d edit. Lond. 1818, 8vo.—The right of appeal
derived its origin from the common law, but had been regulated by
statute.

[9] It may be proper to state, in the words of Professor Erskine, that "no
statute can however be repealed by mere non-usage or neglect of the law,
though for the greatest length of time; for non-usage is but a negative,
which cannot constitute custom : there must be some positive act that
may discover the intention of the community to repeal it."

for our consideration, whether, under the circumstances of the case, the appellee is entitled to go without a day." The counsel for the appellant afterwards mentioned to the court, that, as their lordships had decided that the appellee Thornton was entitled to his wager of battle, it was his duty, on the part of the appellant Ashford, to state that, having duly considered that judgment, he had no further prayer to make. By consent of both parties, the court ordered that judgment be stayed on the appeal, and that the appellee be discharged. A bill was soon after brought into one of the houses of parliament to repeal the law respecting appeals of murder, as well as that respecting wager of battle. This is the competent remedy which the law of England has in such cases provided; and we may perhaps venture to affirm that, upon the whole, it is preferable to that adopted by the law of Scotland. The progress of society, and the gradual improvement of civil institutions, may doubtless render the principles of many laws completely obsolete; and, by slow and imperceptible degrees, it may become absurd or oppressive to enforce their execution. It has been remarked by Mr. Barrington, who was one of the Welsh judges, that "many acts of parliament fortunately, for the most part, lie buried in the statute-book, till the spleen and resentment of individuals call them forth, to the disgrace of the law, and the distress of the person prosecuted."[1] It may therefore be urged, that by means of the principle recognized in the law of Scotland, the court could frequently prevent old and disgraceful laws, such as the spirit of the age abhors, from being converted into instruments of oppression; and this seems to be the strongest argument that can be advanced in

[1] Barrington's Observations on the more ancient Statutes, p. 500.

favour of such a principle.   Many disgraceful laws long continued unrepealed in the statute-book; and the English legislators have a very strong propensity to revere whatever has been impressed with the stamp of antiquity. This however is a species of zeal that is not always according to knowledge : those who upon all occasions are ready to extol the wisdom of our ancestors, are seldom conspicuous for their own wisdom ; nor is it too rash to aver that the folly of our ancestors has at least been equally prominent.   *Nolumus leges Angliæ mutari,* is a sentiment perpetually repeated with unabated approbation.   It is a sentiment first uttered in a barbarous age, and altogether worthy of such an origin.   Let us ascend no higher than the reign of the amiable Queen Mary, or that of her gentle sire Henry the Eighth; let us then extol the wisdom of our ancestors, and consider whether it is not as well that the laws of England have been gradually subjected to a few changes and modifications. " Surely," says Bacon, "every medicine is an innovation, and he that will not apply new remedies must expect new evils; for time is the greatest innovator: and if time of course alter things to the worse, and wisdom and counsel shall not alter them to the better, what shall be the end ? It is true that what is settled by custom, though it be not good, yet at least it is fit; and those things which have long gone together, are, as it were, confederate within themselves : whereas new things piece not so well; but, though they help by their utility, yet they trouble by their inconformity: besides, they are like strangers, more admired, and less favoured.   All this is true, if time stood still; which, contrariwise, moveth so round, that a froward retention of custom is as turbulent a thing as an innovation; and they that reverence too much old times, are but a scorn to the new."[2] The nature of man himself is progressive; in his political institutions, as well as in his individual existence, he gradually passes from infancy to manhood: what was useful or pleasant in childhood, is not to be endured in a maturer age; and what was suitable in one stage of intellectual or political improvement, is altogether unsuitable in another. It is therefore evident, that in a country where laws cannot be allowed to fall into desuetude, they may often subside into the condition of a dead letter. But, on the other hand, the application, to particular cases, of this principle of a tacit abrogation, may be considered as of too delicate and dangerous a nature to be safely entrusted to every judge at every period; especially when we recollect that the precise interval required to class any statute with those which have fallen into desuetude has never been sufficiently defined. Those who chance to reside in Scotland, may easily ascertain how many years are necessary to complete their prescriptive right to an acre of land; while they are left in a state of some uncertainty how many are necessary to exempt them from the operation of a law which may award the punishment of death.

Notwithstanding its importance as a branch of professional study, the civil law has been too much neglected in the Scotish universities. Sir Thomas Craig, who died in the year 1608, expresses his regret that in his time there were no professors by whom it was publicly taught[3]; nor can we easily suppose him to have been en-

---

[2] Bacon's Essays, p. 131. *Of Innovations.*

[3] " In plerisque negotiis jus civile sequimur, non quidem edocti, et in eo instituti, quod nulli adhuc quod sciam apud nos juris fuerint profes-

K

tirely mistaken in the statement of such a fact. In relation to this subject, a late writer seems too rashly to have charged him with ignorance.[4] To prove that professorships have been founded, does not prove that lectures have been read by the professors: it is well known that there is a professorship of the civil law at Oxford; but when did Dr. Phillimore read a lecture on the civil law? In the Scotish universities, lectures on the civil as well as the canon law had certainly been read at an earlier period.   In what manner law was taught at St. Andrews in the year 1574, we learn from the very curious Diary of a student who then attended the professor's lectures. "In the thrid and fourt yeirs of my course, at the direction of my father, I hard the comissar, Mr. Wilyeam Skein, teatche Cicero de Legibus, and diuerss partes of the Institutiones of Justinian.   I was burdet in the houss of a man of law, a verie guid honest man, Andro Greine be nam, who louit me exceiding weill, whase wiff also was an of my mothers [freinds]; I am sure sche haid nocht sone nor bern sche loued better.   This lawier tuk me to the consistorie with him, whar the comissar wald tak pleasour to schaw ws the practise in judgment of that quhilk he teatched in the scholles.   He was a man of skill and guid conscience in his calling, lernit and diligent in his profession, and tuk delyt in na thing mair nor to repeat ower and ower again to anie schollar that wald ask him the things he haid bein teatching.   Likwayes my ost Andro acquentit me with the formes of summonds and lybelling, of contracts, obligatiounes, actes, &c.; but

sores qui jus publice docerent, quod sane dolendum est." (Cragii Jus Feudale, p. 14. edit. Baillie.   Edinb. 1732, fol.)

[4] Ross's Lectures on the Law of Scotland, vol. ii. p. 9.   Edinb. 1792, 2 vols. 4to.

my hart was nocht sett that way."[5]   Whether Craig
would regard this as a very efficient mode of teaching the
civil law, we need not stop to enquire.   The law professorship at St. Andrews was suppressed by the visitors
appointed in the year 1597; the last professor being
William Wellwood, a man of learning, and the author of
several works.[6]   After a short interval, we find a private
teacher of law, evidently the civil law, residing in Edinburgh.   This was Dr. Murdison, who had taken his
degree at Leyden, and had been a professor of natural
philosophy in that university.[7]   Robert Boyd, who had
long known him at Saumur, mentions his having died in
the year 1617.[8]

For several centuries, the Scotish youth have been
much accustomed to pursue their studies in the most celebrated schools of law on the continent.   Till the earlier
part of last century, this was the ordinary course of study
prosecuted by those who were destined for the legal profession; and a writer in the reign of Charles the First,
thought it not a little "strange to see ane man admitted
to teach the lawes, who was never out of the countrie

[5] Diary of James Melville, p. 23.   Edinb. 1829, 4to.

[6] Maccrie's Life of Andrew Melville, vol. ii. p. 119, 319-21.

[7] Vota et Gratulationes Amicorum, quum nobilissimus doctissimusque
vir Johannes Murdisonius Scotus, Naturalis Philosophiæ in illustri Batavorum Academia Professor, post Licentiam in utroque Jure summum in
eadem Facultate Gradum assumeret. Lugd. Bat. 1604, 4to. The poems
are three in number, written by three distinguished individuals, Domini-
cus Baudius, Daniel Heinsius, and Petrus Scriverius.

[8] Boyd's Obituary contains the following notice, under the date of
June 1617 : " En ce moy et an, j'ay ésté adverty de la mort de ces mes
bonnes amys; Mr. Murisoun, D. [ès] Loys, lequell il enseignoyt à Edinr.,
à moy longuement cognu à Saumure ; Mr. Thomson, pasteur de la
Chastaignoraye," &c. (Bannatyne Miscellany, vol. i. p. 289.)

K 2

studieing and learning the lawes."[9]   The law of Scotland is to a great extent founded on the principles of the civil law; and without a competent knowledge of the civil law, no man can attain to a complete and masterly knowledge of the law of Scotland.   At an early period, when the students of law were very few in number, the professors were without a sufficient incitement to exertion; and the Scotish youth were compelled to seek for able preceptors in other countries.[1]   The reputation of Cujacius, Donellus, Govea, Balduinus, Contius, Hotman, and many other great names, elevated the French schools of law beyond all competition: their celebrity however was at length eclipsed by the more modern universities of Holland;[2] and the students then repaired to Leyden and Utrecht, instead of Bourges and Toulouse.   So early as the year 1590, the judges, the magistrates, and the advocates and clerks to the signet, had raised a fund of 3000*l.*

---

[9] Spalding's Hist. of the Troubles in Scotland, vol. i. p. 179.   Edinb. 1828-9, 2 vols. 4to.   The individual to whom he alludes is James Sandilands, professor of the canon, and afterwards of the civil law in King's College, Aberdeen.

[1] "Ea enim ætate sapere, nisi Romano jure, homines non videbantur." (Gadendam, Hist. Juris Cimbrici, p. 54.   Hamb. 1770, 8vo.)

[2] "Interea autem in Belgii septentrionalis partibus et apud Batavos, publica libertate firmata, omnes disciplinæ et artes humaniores efflorescebant.   Quantum hic populus in medicina et scientiis naturalibus præstiterit, omnibus notum est ; quantumque auctorum veterum studium iis debeat, neminem fugit.   Nec minus autem apud illos erudita jurisprudentia colebatur, tantique nominis atque ponderis Batavorum sunt jurisconsulti, ut inter juris Romani interpretes primum locum obtinuerint. Servabat ad nostra usque tempora Batava juris schola Cujacianam in jure veteri tractando rationem, quæ in ipsa hujus viri immortalis patria neglecta erat.   Neque fortasse tam facile recentissimis temporibus cultior urisprudentia restituta fuisset, sine jurisconsultorum illorum studiis." (Warnkoenig, Commentarii Juris Romani Privati, tom. i. p. 100.)

for the endowment of a professorship of law in the university of Edinburgh; each of these three parties contributing an equal portion. Adam Newton, an advocate, was first appointed to the office; but having neglected to obtain the approbation of the magistrates, he was dismissed in the year 1594. He afterwards procured better employment, and successively became tutor and secretary to Henry, prince of Wales.[3] In the professorship he was succeeded by Hadrian Damman of Bysterveldt, who was born in the neighbourhood of Ghent, and there was for some time employed in teaching the classics.[4] His name occurs in the list of professors of philosophy and eloquence in the university of Leyden.[5] At Edinburgh

---

[3] Newton, though a layman, held the deanery of Durham from 1606 to 1620, when he resigned it ; and during the latter year he was created a baronet. He translated into Latin King James's book against Vorstius, and the first six books of Father Paolo Sarpi's history of the council of Trent. The last two were translated by Dr. Bedell. (Birch's Life of Prince Henry, p. 14. 218. Lond. 1760, 8vo.) "Sic se gessit," says Dempster, "ut moderatione summa cum maximum locum occuparit, majorem mereri censeretur." (Hist. Ecclesiast. Gentis Scotorum, p. 505.)

[4] Sanderus de Gandavensibus Eruditionis Fama claris, p. 13. Antv. 1624, 4to. Andreæ Bibliotheca Belgica, p. 9. edit. Lovan. 1643, 4to. According to these writers, Damman was invited to Scotland by Buchanan. In this country he appears to have acquired an estate ; for in his metaphrase of Du Bartas, he describes himself as *Dominus de Faire-hill.* The literary historians of Flanders mention some of his poems as having been printed on the continent ; and after his settlement in Scotland, he published the following works. Schediasmata. Edinb. 1590, 4to. Bartasias, qui de Mundi Creatione libri septem ; e Guilielmi Salustii Dn. de Bartas Septimana, poemate Francico, liberius tralati, et multis in locis aucti. Edinb. 1600, 8vo. Both these volumes were printed by Waldegrave. A letter from Damman to Lipsius, dated at Leith on the 10th of September, 1599, occurs in Burman's Sylloge Epistolarum, tom. i. p. 453.

[5] Meursii Athenæ Batavæ, p. 351.

he retained his chair for a few years, and was afterwards resident of the States General at the court of Scotland. In the year 1597, after his resignation, the interest of one-third of the sum formerly contributed was allotted for a professor of humanity, and the interest of the remainder for the maintenance of six exhibitioners. Newton and Damman had both taught humanity, without reading any public lectures on law.[5]   After an interval of a century, the Scotish parliament voted a salary of one hundred and fifty pounds sterling to Alexander Cunningham, as professor of the civil law.[6]   This act, passed in 1698, was to continue in force during the period of five years; and the same provision in his favour was, for the same period, renewed in 1704.[7]   Cunningham, who

[6] Crawford's Hist. of the University of Edinburgh, p. 34-40.

[7] Acts of the Parliaments of Scotland, vol. x. p. 176. vol. xi. p. 203. On the 19th of August 1698, a petition from Alexander Cunningham, " for encouraging a design for illustrating the civill law," had been remitted to the committee for the security of the kingdom.   Vol. x. p. 145.   About this period, several advocates began to read private lectures on the civil law.   One of these was Alexander Drummond, who, in the year 1699, inserted the following advertisement in an Edinburgh newspaper : " These are to give advertisement to all persons who are desireous to be instructed in the knowledge of the Institutions and Pandects of the civil law, and the laws of this kingdom, or either of the two, or both, that Mr. Alexander Drummond of East-field, Advocate, does profess to teach the same; and by reason of a singular method he uses in teaching of the civil law, he undertakes to perfite and accomplish any of a middle capacity, more in a years time, then others have been by being abroad and out of the country three years.   How profitable and advantagious this may tend to the kingdom in general, he leaves it to every one to judge.   He is to be spoke with at his lodging in the foot of Blackfrier Wind."   Another private lecturer on the civil and municipal laws, was John Spottiswoode; and their example was followed by John Cunningham, who published his inaugural lecture under the title of " Joannis Cuningamii, J. Cti. Oratio inauguralis, recitata Edinburgi cum primum Jus Civile docere coepit."

appears to have possessed an easy fortune, afterwards
settled in Holland, where he enjoyed a high reputation
as a civilian, and as a classical scholar: he chiefly distinguished himself by his edition of Horace, and his
formidable attack on Dr. Bentley; but he did not live
to complete his long-meditated edition of the Pandects.[8]
A professorship of the civil law was endowed by the
magistrates in the year 1710. The resort of Scotish
students to the foreign universities now became less frequent, but the practice was never entirely discontinued;
and of the present race of lawyers, several have studied
at Leyden, Utrecht, and Göttingen.

The university of Leyden, which was founded in the
year 1575,[9] became, and suddenly became, a renowned
seminary of learning. The civil law soon began to be
taught and studied with eminent ability and ardour: the
first impulse was given by Hugo Donellus, a French
protestant, who had been driven from his native country
by the direful spirit of persecution, and who has bequeathed some very learned works to posterity. At this
period the French schools of law stood unrivalled; and
to those schools students resorted from almost every
country of Europe. The curators of the university of
Leyden sought for learned men wherever they were to be
found: the chairs in the different faculties were in very
many instances filled by foreigners, and some of the greatest names in their academical annals are foreign names;

Edinb. 4to. This publication is without a date, but it probably appeared
about the same period with " A Discourse by Mr. John Cunninghame,
Advocate, at the Beginning of his Lessons upon the Scots Law." Edinb.
1705, 4to.

[8] Of Alexander Cunningham a more ample account may be found in
the seventh edition of the *Encyclopædia Britannica*, vol. vii. p. 544.

[9] Meursii Athenæ Batavæ, p. 16. Lugd. Bat. 1625, 4to.

Scaliger and Salmasius were Frenchmen, Vossius, Gronovius, and Ruhnkenius were Germans, and Wyttenbach
was a Swiss.   This university could soon boast of several
eminent professors of law.   The other Dutch universities,
those of Utrecht, Harderwyk, Groningen, and Franeker,
were of a more recent foundation : each of these had its
law professors, and the reputation of Utrecht was sometimes equal to that of Leyden.   If Holland had added
no other name to the annals of jurisprudence, the native
country of Hugo Grotius must still have commanded our
respect.   He was not only distinguished as a lawyer, but
likewise as a classical scholar, as a poet, as an historian,
and as a theologian.   With the civil law he was intimately
acquainted; and on this subject he has left a work, which
however professedly consists of philological illustrations.[1]
Grotius may justly be considered as the founder of a new
science, that of the law of nature and nations; for of his
great work the subject is much more extensive than the
title.   His treatise *De Jure Belli ac Pacis* will never
cease to be regarded as a singular monument of his
genius and learning.   The previous labours of Alberico
Gentili, and some other writers of inferior note, had but
little effect in smoothing his path; but the resources of
his own talents and erudition were not easily exhausted;
and if he has not produced a perfect work, he has at least
produced a work which in many respects is still unrivalled.
" Grotius," says Dr. Smith, " seems to have been the
first who attempted to give the world any thing like a
system of those principles which ought to run through
and be the foundation of the laws of all nations ; and his

---

[1] Hugonis Grotii Florum Sparsio ad Jus Justinianeum. Parisiis, 1642,
4to. In the course of the following year two editions appeared at Amsterdam in duodecimo.

treatise of the laws of war and peace, with all its imperfections, is perhaps at this day the most complete work
that has yet been given upon this subject."[2] The copious-
ness of his classical quotations cannot be supposed to be
equally relished by readers of every denomination, but
they certainly are not without their attraction to readers
of classical learning and taste; and it is necessary to
distinguish between such as are introduced to prove particular facts, and such as are merely introduced for the
purpose of illustration. "Of what stamp," it has been
asked by Bentham, "are the works of Grotius, Pufendorf, and Burlamaqui? Are they political or ethical,
historical or juridical, expository or censorial? Sometimes one thing, sometimes another: they seem hardly
to have settled the matter with themselves." In these
suggestions we perceive nothing very ingenious or original.
The principles of natural law are closely blended with
the principles of ethical science, nor is it easy to make
an entire separation between the general principles of
law and politics; and examples, drawn from the history
of mankind in various stages of society, may certainly
find a suitable place in a work intended to illustrate the
law of nature and nations.[3]

[2] Smith's Theory of Moral Sentiments, p. 610.

[3] "Morum disciplina," says Mosheim, "quam Christus ejusque legati
tradiderunt, meliorem formam, pluraque præsidia contra varii generis in-
commoda nacta est, postquam jus, quod natura seu recta ratio imperat,
diligentius quam antea indagatum, et clarius explanatum est. Ducem
se in hoc genere præbuit Hugo Grotius, vir incomparabilis, libris de
Jure Belli et Pacis; quem ut maxima quæque ingenia alacriter se-
querentur, ipsa rei dignitas et utilitas effecit. Quorum quidem labores
quanto illis auxilio fuerint, qui de vita et officiis hominis Christiani
disseruerunt, is demum videbit, cui libros hujus argumenti post eorum
ætatem exaratos, cum illis qui antea in honore fuerant, conferre pla-
cuerit." (Institutiones Historiæ Ecclesiasticæ, p. 851. Helmstadii,

His brother Guilielmus Grotius is the author of a learned and valuable biography of the ancient civilians.[4] Vinnius, a professor of Leyden, flourished about the same period: among other works, he published a copious and elaborate commentary on the Institutions, which still maintains its place among the best productions of this class.[5] Matthæus soon afterwards published his commentary on the two books of the Pandects which treat of crimes and punishments; nor has it been supplanted by any work of a more recent date. Many able civilians were from this time to be found in the universities and in the courts of Holland; but the brightest era of the history was perhaps the close of the seventeenth and the commencement of the eighteenth century; an era which was adorned by Huber, Voet, Westenberg, Schulting, Noodt, and Bynkershoek. All of them have written copiously on the Roman law, and their respective merits are very extensively known, even in Britain. Voet is regarded as the great oracle of the practising lawyers in Scotland. "With us now-a-days," says Professor Wilde, "the authority of this whole law seems, in Scotland, to be referred to Voet. It is not the *Corpus Juris* itself that is now held in estimation; and the authority of this Dutchman is now far beyond any authority of Paulus or Ulpian,

1755, 4to.) Of the life and character of Grotius, I have given a brief sketch in the seventh edition of the *Encyclopædia Britannica*, vol. xi. p. 1-8.

[4] Vitæ Jurisconsultorum quorum in Pandectis extant nomina, conscriptæ a Guilielmo Grotio Jurisconsulto Delph. Lugd. Bat. 1690, 4to. This work, which is posthumous, is reprinted in Frank's *Vitæ tripartitæ Jurisconsultorum veterum.* Halæ Magd. 1718, 4to.

[5] "Cujus ad Institutiones commentarius per longum tempus tanquam oraculum consulebatur, hodieque quibusdam in scholis solus consulitur." (Warnkoenig, tom. i. p. 102.)

or any decision of a Roman emperor, strengthened by the advice of all the lawyers in his states. In short, the commentaries of Voet are made our Roman law. But there can be no question that this law will never be known, nor a firm and settled jurisprudence be established upon its principles, unless by studying *itself;* and, when this has been gone through in the proper manner, by the after study of the commentators in modern times (and of Voet among the rest, for valuable he is without any question), comparing them all along with the knowledge of the classic originals, in the system itself, as already fully acquired, and throwing away, most especially, all their modern metaphysics, which have nothing to do with the civil law."[6]   The writings of Schulting have less reference to modern practice, and are therefore less known to mere practitioners; but they are replete with philological and historical illustrations of ancient jurisprudence.   In this point of view, his collection of the *Jus Antejustinianeum* is a publication of great value and importance.   The publication of his posthumous annotations on the Pandects has at length been completed, under the superintendence of a very competent editor, Professor Smallenburg of Leyden.[7]   Noodt, the relation of Schulting, was likewise a very able expounder of the Roman law, and enjoyed a high reputation as a lecturer and as an author.   They both finished their academical career at Leyden.   Bynkershoek, president of the supreme court

---

[6] Wilde's Preliminary Lecture to the Course of Lectures on the Institutions of Justinian, p. 58. Edinb. 1794, 8vo.

[7] Antonii Schultingii, quondam in Academia Lugduno-Batava Juris Antecessoris celeberrimi, Notæ ad Digesta seu Pandectas. Edidit atque animadversiones suas adjecit Nicolaus Smallenburg, in eadem Academia Jur. Prof. Ord. Lugd. Bat. 1804-35, 7 tom. 8vo.

of Holland, was another lawyer of great ability and
learning: his various works contain many interesting discussions, and still maintain their popularity at home and
abroad.   Nor must we here omit the name of Brenkman,
who is chiefly remembered for his "Historia Pandectarum, seu Fatum Exemplaris Florentini," published at
Utrecht in 1722.   With the view of consulting and
studying the Florentine manuscript, he made a journey
to Italy, and was enabled to obtain access to this precious
relique through the influence of a learned English envoy,
Dr. Newton, who was afterwards judge of the high court of
admiralty, and who was much connected with the scholars
of his time.[8]   To the study of this manuscript Brenkman devoted several years, but he only lived to execute a
part of his plans.   His papers afterwards came into the
possession of Gebauer, and by him were used in preparing the Göttingen edition of the *Corpus Juris Civilis.*
" Wieling, Otto's successor at Utrecht," says a recent
writer, " is known from the *Jurisprudentia Restituta,* the
too pompous title of a book in which he had but little
share."[9]   But this writer had apparently forgotten Wie-

---

[8] Sir Henry Newton, LL.D. is the author of a collection of *Epistolæ,
Orationes, et Carmina.* Lucæ, 1710, 4to. A supplement to this collection bears the imprint of Amsterdam, with the same date. An account
of his life is subjoined to Gebauer's *Narratio de Henrico Brenkmanno.*
Gottingæ, 1764, 4to. Some notices of Newton may be found in Mr.
Dunster's edition of "Cider, a poem in two books, by John Philips,"
p. 174. Lond. 1791, 8vo.

[9] The title of Wieling's publication is " Jurisprudentia Restituta; sive
Index Chronologicus in totum Juris Justinianæi Corpus, ad modum Jac.
Labitti, Ant. Augustini, et Wolfg. Freymonii, nova tamen et faciliore
methodo collectus. Accesserunt Opuscula IV." &c. Amst. 1727, 8vo.
The four tracts here mentioned were written by Labitte, Hahn, Brenk-
man, and Reinold.

ling's *Lectiones Juris Civilis,* in which he claims an undivided property, and which afford a very favourable specimen of his talents and erudition. W. O. Reitz is well known to the more philological students of the civil law for his elaborate and valuable editions of Theophilus and Harmenopulus. Meerman, an individual of rank and fortune, rendered a very important service to the cause of jurisprudence, by the publication of his great collection intitled *Thesaurus Juris Civilis et Canonici,* consisting of seven volumes in folio; and a supplementary volume was added by his son, whose princely library has recently attracted so much attention. The works of the elder Meerman are likewise worthy of being preserved. To the names of these learned civilians we must add those of Van Eck, Best, Vande Water, D'Arnaud, Idsinga, Rücker, the Cannegieters, the Voordas, and Bondam. It is not superfluous to mention that in the Dutch universities there have been many professors who, although not belonging to the law-faculty, have with uncommon erudition illustrated various branches of the civil law; and here it will be sufficient to recall to the reader's mind the names of Salmasius, [1] Gronovius, Perizonius, Burman, and Ruhnkenius.

When Holland was incorporated with the French

---

[1] " Non aliud studium profiteor nisi juris, ut in eo tantum me oblectem, et animum pascam, non ut τὰ δ'λφιτα inde mihi procurem. Non enim in foro causas elatro, nec e cathedra theses ventilo, sed eos qui hæc faciunt animi gratia aliquando defrico." (Salmasii Confutatio Diatribæ de Mutuo, tribus Disputationibus ventilatæ auctore et præside Jo. Jacobo Vissembachio, J. U. D. eodemque Professore in Academia Franekerana Frisiorum, p. 237. Lugd. Bat. 1645, 8vo.) He had been admitted an advocate of the parliament of Dijon, but he never followed the practice of the bar. This work, it may be proper to recollect, was published without the author's name.

empire, the universities of Leyden and Groningen were new-modelled, but it certainly cannot be supposed that they were improved by such visitors. The rest of the Dutch universities, and many other literary institutions of the country, were suppressed. Soon after the erection of the kingdom of the Netherlands, the attention of the government was directed to this important subject; and the number and site of the various universities and colleges were decided in the year 1815. The university of Utrecht was re-established; those of Leyden and Groningen were placed on their former footing; and it was determined to allot an equal number of universities to the southern provinces of the kingdom. Louvain became for the second time the seat of a university, and the other two were érected at Ghent and Liége. At a much earlier period, Louvain had been a flourishing seminary of learning : here Lipsius had taught humanity, and Perez the civil law; [2] and here, during the earlier part of last century, Van Espen had obtained the highest celebrity as a professor of the canon law.

In each of the universities of the Netherlands, as they were thus constituted, the law-faculty consisted of three or four professors, who were appointed by the king; and extraordinary professors were occasionally nominated, with the advice and concurrence of the curators. A regular course of study was prescribed to candidates for degrees. Those who aspired at the highest honours in the law line, must previously have taken a degree which

---

[2] Perez ranks among the ablest commentators on the Code. The following edition of his work, printed by D. Elzevir, is perhaps the best : " Ant. Perezii, J. C. S. C. & R. Majestatis Consiliarii, in Academia Lovaniensi Legum Antecessoris, Prælectiones in duodecim libros Codicis Justiniani Imp." &c. Amst. 1671, 4to.

corresponds to that of bachelor of arts, and must therefore have studied Greek and Latin literature, Roman antiquities, universal history, logic, and the elementary branches of mathematics. This seems to be an excellent regulation; and the course of law itself was extensive, including statistics and medical jurisprudence.[3]

From such wise and salutary arrangements, in conjunction with the acknowledged ability of many of the professors, we were naturally induced to expect the most favourable result; and in this expectation we are not prepared to say that we have experienced any material disappointment. A late writer has however given a more disadvantageous representation. " For many years past," he remarks, " the once flourishing republic of Holland has been on the decline. The political changes, the increased prosperity and maritime power of this country and of France, have deprived her of much of her ancient wealth and importance. At Leyden the university is still attended by between three and four hundred students; but the ancient zeal for learning has declined, and the alumni are generally content with a bare sufficiency of knowledge, to carry them through the every-day concerns of life. This change has been very rapid. That university in which, eighty years ago, many of our celebrated men received their education, and where so many foreigners were assembled, from every quarter of the globe, to enjoy the benefit of quiescent instruction, is now completely deserted by all strangers, except the sons of a few Westphalian proprietors, attracted thither by its vicinity to their homes." In most of these statements

---

[3] See an article of Warnkoenig, " De l'Enseignement du Droit dans les Universités du Royaume des Pays-Bas," Thémis, tom. i. p. 391. This article may likewise be found in his edition of Mackeldey, p. 23.

we are by no means disposed to acquiesce; though it is sufficiently evident that the unsettled state of public affairs must have had an unfavourable influence on all the ordinary pursuits of science and learning. That the ancient zeal for learning has thus declined, is not so easily to be taken for granted: Hemsterhusius, Valckenaer, Ruhnkenius, and Wyttenbach have indeed left no successors of equal erudition; but Holland still contains many able and accomplished scholars, and is in fact one of the most learned countries of Europe. We have likewise reason to believe that the university of Leyden is not so completely deserted by foreign students; and where law is taught by such professors as Smallenburg, the students can have no reason to complain of their defective opportunities of improvement. Many of the academical dissertations which proceed from this university are still very learned and elaborate, and they are not unfrequently distinguished by the terseness of their Latinity. Here philology is wedded to jurisprudence. And in all this the reader cannot fail to perceive that there is something more than "a bare sufficiency of knowledge, to carry them through the every-day concerns of life." It cannot be denied that historical jurisprudence is cultivated with more assiduity and success in the universities of Germany; it is at least certain that the Dutch civilians have not given so many public proofs of their familiarity with this important and interesting department.

On the establishment of the university of Liége, Dr. Warnkoenig, a native of Germany, and at that time a private teacher of law at Göttingen, was appointed professor of the civil law, and he pronounced his inaugural oration on the 4th of November 1817. He may now be considered as a naturalized subject of his majesty the king of the Netherlands;

Πατρὶς γάρ ἐστι πᾶσ', ἵν' ἂν πράττῃ τὶς εὖ.[4]

In the year 1827 he was removed to the university of Louvain, where he was associated with Holtius and Birnbaum. After a short interval, his adopted country was agitated by a sudden revolution, and his services were then transferred to the university of Ghent. Here he still resides, and he continues to labour in his vocation with the utmost assiduity. He has published various works of no small utility to his own pupils, and to other students of the Roman law. His publications are partly in Latin, partly in French. He is evidently a man of talents and judgment; and possessing a perfect knowledge of the Roman law, as it is now taught in his native country, he has greatly contributed by his writings to diffuse a more extensive intelligence of the discoveries and speculations of the German civilians. He has written many valuable articles for periodical works, and, among the rest, for the " Thémis, ou Bibliothèque du Jurisconsulte," of which he continued for several years to be one of the editors, being associated with Jourdan, Blondeau, Demante, and Du Caurroy. His improved edition of Mackeldey's introduction to the study of the Roman law,[5] his annotations on Gibbon's famous chapter,

[4] Aristophanis Plutus, v. 1151. edit. Brunck.

[5] Introduction à l'Etude du Droit Romain, traduite de l'Allemand de M. F. Mackeldey, Professeur à l'Université de Bonn, par M. L. Etienne, à Paris : revue, augmentée, précédée d'un Précis encyclopédique, et suivie d'une nouvelle restitution de la Loi des XII. Tables et de l'Edit Perpétuel, par M. L. A. Warnkoenig. Mons, 1826, 8vo. This introduction forms the first part of Mackeldey's very popular work, of which the eighth edition has since been published : " Lehrbuch des heutigen Römischen Rechts." Giessen, 1829, 2 Bde. 8vo.

and his analysis of Savigny's law of possession, are all valuable acquisitions to the student; but his principal works in this department are his *Institutiones* and his *Commentarii*, the one a text-book of moderate extent, and the other a more ample and elaborate treatise. Of the Institutions, the first edition was printed at Liége in the year 1819: it was prepared for the press in unavoidable haste, and of this haste it certainly bears some marks. The second edition, which appeared after an interval of six years, is in all respects greatly improved. The work has now reached a third edition, in which it has undergone many further changes and modifications; and, in its present form, it is to be numbered among the best text-books that have yet been published.[6] His Commentaries claim a higher rank.[7] The introduction, which is partly historical and partly literary, exhibits the history of the law in its more general lineaments, and includes notices of the principal civilians who have flourished in different countries, together with an enumeration of the most important works connected with the study. It is written with learning and discrimination, and is extremely well adapted to the purpose which the author has in view. The work itself is divided into six books, and the method is his own, neither servilely borrowed from Justinian, nor

[6] Institutiones Juris Romani Privati, in usum Prælectionum Academicarum vulgatæ, cum Introductione in universam Jurisprudentiam et in Studium Juris Romani; auctore L. A. Warnkoenig, Juris utriusque Doctore, in Universitate Belgica, quæ Gandavi est, Juris Professore Publico et Ordinario, &c.   Bonnæ, 1834, 8vo.

[7] Commentarii Juris Romani Privati, ad exemplum optimorum Compendiorum a celeberrimis Germaniæ Jurisconsultis compositorum adornati, in usum Academicarum Prælectionum et Studii privati; auctore L. A. Warnkoenig, Juris utriusque Doctore, &c.   Leodii, 1825-9, 3 tom. 8vo.

from any modern writer. This method is sufficiently distinct, and the author generally writes with clearness and precision. He has carefully refrained from expressing the notions of the ancient civilians in the phraseology of modern schoolmen : he has therefore refrained from a practice which is not merely exceptionable in point of taste, but which has a strong tendency to leave erroneous impressions in the mind of the student. Both works are evidently the productions of a learned and able man ; nor do we despair of seeing them admitted into the libraries of most of the English lawyers who do not utterly despise this branch of study. Those who shudder at the grim aspect of the German language, may derive a competent knowledge of the German discoveries and speculations from his French and Latin publications. The most inveterate admirers of Heineccius must admit that some important discoveries have been made, and that some material improvements have been introduced, during the lapse of an entire century; and we beg leave to submit to their consideration, more especially to the consideration of such of them as may be employed in teaching others, whether it would not at least be advisable to compare his Institutions with those of Warnkoenig.

As we can frequently judge of causes by their effects, so we can frequently estimate the learning of the preceptor by that of his pupils. Of their knowledge of the civil law, some of his students have given very satisfactory proofs. In confirmation of this remark, we could mention various names; but at present we shall content ourselves with mentioning the name of Dr. Dupont. Before he had completed his academical studies, he obtained the university prize for the best dissertation on the fourth book of Caius;[8] and this is certainly a masterly production for so young a writer. He encreased his celebrity by the publication of his inaugural dissertation,[9] and was soon appointed a lecturer on the civil law at Liège.

In the case of Dr. Warnkoenig, we have an instance of a foreign professor of the civil law introduced with eminent advantage into one of the new universities of the Netherlands. A rich old university is like a fat old gentlewoman, not easily brought within the influence of modern improvements; but it may deserve the consideration of those who are interested in the prosperity of the new university of London, whether they ought not to follow this example. A university without a professorship of the civil law, would in many countries be considered as a strange anomaly. Should such a chair be thought necessary, they may chance to place in it a true-born Englishman, who is unacquainted with the very elements of the science which it becomes his duty to teach; for such appointments are by no means unprecedented in the universities of the south, or in the universities of the north. The governors of the new institution ought to recollect, that their only hopes of ultimate success must rest on the favourable opinion of the

[8] Everardi Dupont, in Academia Leodiensi Juris Candidati, Disquisitiones in Commentarium IV. Institutionum Gaji, recenter repertarum. Lugd. Bat. 1822, 8vo. Pp. 227.

[9] Dissertatio inauguralis juridica, de Præscriptionibus secundum hodierni et Romani Juris Præcepta. Leodii, 1823, 4to. Pp. 63.—A more recent dissertation by Baron W. L. D. J. de Crassier deserves to be mentioned, as indicating the bent and direction of juridical studies in this university. It bears the title of "Dissertatio inauguralis juridica, de Confectione Codicis Theodosiani, præmissa brevi Disputatione de Causis crescentis et decrescentis Jurisprudentiæ Romanæ." Leodii, 1825, 4to. Pp. 32. See *Kritische Zeitschrift für Rechtswissenschaft*, Bd. i. S. 152.

public; and that this favourable opinion can only be secured by an enlightened and inflexible regard to the merit and qualifications of those upon whom they bestow their offices and emoluments. If they were to nominate as professor of the civil law a young man of talents and learning, a native of Germany, or educated in a German university, and possessing a complete knowledge of the science, as it is now taught in that country, they might thus confer an important benefit on the institution and on the public.

Germany, where law was long a barbarous science, or at least where the doctrines of the law were often conveyed in a very barbarous phraseology, has at length extricated itself from its ancient trammels, and has risen beyond all competition. Many of its earlier civilians were extremely prolix in their mode of discussion, and extremely diffuse and scholastic in their style; and exerting much industry in the accumulation of materials, they became, if not great authors, certainly authors of great books. As specimens of their persevering industry, it may at present be sufficient to mention the immense commentaries on the Institutions of Justinian, written by Schneidewin, Mynsinger, and Harpprecht. One of the first names that attract much notice is that of Gregorius Haloander, who, after having distinguished himself as a learned editor of the *Corpus Juris Civilis*, died at a premature age, in the year 1531.[1] During the latter part of this century, the chairs were occasionally filled by men of distinguished merit: Gipha-

---

[1] An account of the life of Haloander may be found in Conradi's Parergorum libri quatuor. Helmstadii, 1740, 8vo. As to the merits of his edition, see likewise Jauchii Meditationes Criticæ de Negationibus Pandectis Florentinis partim recte vel male jam adjectis, aut detractis, vel circumscriptis, p. 64. Amst. 1728, 8vo.

nius, Donellus, Scipione Gentili, and Rittershusius, were
all professors of law in the university of Altdorf;[2] but it
is to be recollected that only one of these four, Rittershusius, was a native of Germany.   Like Giphanius, he
was conspicuous for his classical learning; and all of them
enjoyed an extensive reputation, which time has not completely impaired.   About the same period, many other
foreigners of eminence occupied law-chairs in the German universities; and among this number we find Balduinus, and the elder Gothofredus.   But the ensuing
century exhibits degeneracy, rather than improvement.
We must not however omit the name of Bachov, an acute
and learned commentator on the Institutions; and
Conring, although he has written but little on the Roman
law, was too remarkable a person to be entirely overlooked on the present occasion.   He alternately taught
medicine and political science: he is the author of many
able works on a great variety of subjects;[3] and he seems
to have been the earliest writer who illustrated the history
of the German law with any considerable degree of accuracy and precision.   The German civilians of that
era have not left many productions of superior utility or
interest;[4] but the name of Samuel Pufendorf appears
with distinguished lustre in the history of a new science,

    [2] Zeidleri Vitæ Professorum Juris in Academia Altdorffina. Norim-
bergæ, 1770, 4to.
    [3] Hermanni Conringii Opera: curante commentariisque suis hæc opera
passim augente et illustrante Johanne Wilhelmo Goebelio.   Brunsvigæ,
1730, 6 tom. fol.
    [4] " Durante sæculo xvii, Germani jurisperiti pro forensi quoque usu
potius quam ad juris artem promovendam scripserunt, et in eo plurimam
operam collocarunt, ut patrium jus indagarent, et de eo cum juris Romani
usu conjungendo studerent ; unde illa librorum juris Romano-Germanici
multitudo, in dies crescens usque ad sæculi xviii finem." (Warnkoenig,
Commentarii Juris Romani, tom. i. p. 109.)

the law of nature and nations. He was a man of distinguished talents; but his general learning was greatly inferior to that of Grotius, and he was less familiar with the blandishments of polite literature. In his principal work, "De Jure Naturæ et Gentium," he has professedly many obligations to his illustrious predecessor, and likewise to another writer of a very different character, namely Thomas Hobbes, whom he greatly admired for his sagacity in investigating the structure of human society.[4] His earliest work, entitled "Elementa Jurisprudentiæ universalis," had appeared in 1660: in the course of the following year, the Elector Palatine nominated him professor of the law of nature and nations at Heidelberg; and this was the earliest foundation of such a professorship in any university.[5] Mr. Stewart has committed a material error in describing Gentili as a lecturer on the law of nature in the university of Oxford;[6] this is

[4] " Sic et Thomas Hobbes in operibus suis ad civilem scientiam spectantibus plurima habet quantivis pretii ; et nemo, cui rerum ejusmodi est intellectus, negaverit, tam profunde ipsum societatis humanæ et civilis compagem rimatum fuisse, ut pauci priorum cum ipso heic comparari queant. Et qua a vero aberrat, occasionem tamen ad talia meditanda suggerit, quæ fortasse alias nemini in mentem venissent." (Pufendorfius de Jure Naturæ et Gentium, præf.)

[5] This fact is distinctly stated by Pufendorf himself, in the preface to his great work, and by Barbeyrac, in the preface to his translation, *Droit de la Nature et des Gens*, tom. i. p. cvii., 5me edit. Amst. 1734, 2 tom. 4to.

[6] Stewart's Dissertation on the Progress of Metaphysical, Ethical, and Political Science, p. 38, first edit. " He sought an asylum at Oxford, where he published, in 1588, a book *De Jure Belli;* and where he appears to have read lectures on natural jurisprudence, under the sanction of the university."—His three books *De Jure Belli* appeared successively, in 1588 and 1589, and were first published together, Hanoviæ, 1598, 8vo. Gentili was appointed professor of the civil law in 1587, and this office he executed for about twenty-four years. (Wood's Athenæ Oxonienses, vol.

not a common error in chronology, but it proceeds upon
a total misconception of the state and progress of the
science. Alberico, the elder brother of Scipione Gentili,
belonged to a family of Italian protestants, who were
driven from their native country by the foul spirit of ecclesiastical persecution:[7] having found a place of refuge
in England, he was appointed, not professor of the law of
nature and nations, but professor of the civil law at Oxford, and he died about the year 1611.

The close of the seventeenth century cannot long
arrest our attention. Leibnitz, whose researches were so
profound and so multifarious, did not neglect the study
of jurisprudence; and if he had devoted a larger portion
of his time to that study, he would doubtless have produced some composition worthy of so great a name. " For
the variety of his genius, and the extent of his research,"
as Mr. Playfair has remarked, " Leibnitz is perhaps
altogether unrivalled." The juridical publications which
about this period appeared in Germany, are generally
written in barbarous Latin : their very titles are often
sufficient indications of the hopeless condition of the
authors taste ; such titles, for example, as " Usus
modernus Pandectarum," and many others cast in the
same classical mould.   This barbarism had become
inveterate and almost endemical : Ludewig relates that
when he had a conference respecting the publication of a
work on the Institutions, the bookseller made a condition
that it should be entitled "Usus modernus Institutionum."[8]
If the author had insisted on substituting hodiernus instead

ii. col. 90. Bliss's edition.)   He was a doctor of laws of the university of
Perugia, and was incorporated at Oxford.

    [7] See Dr. Maccrie's Hist. of the Reformation in Italy, p. 166, 2d edit.
Edinb. 1833, 8vo.

    [8] Ludewig Vita Justiniani, præf.   Halæ, 1731, 4to.

of *modernus*, it is to be presumed that the negotiation must have come to an abrupt termination. Thomasius, a professor in the university of Halle, introduced some changes in the mode of teaching jurisprudence, and, among others, that of lecturing in the German language. This new university rose to distinction, and attracted many students. Here Wolf, a philosopher and mathematician, wrote very copiously on the general principles of law: his *Jus Naturæ*, published from 1740 to 1748, extends to no fewer than eight volumes in quarto, and must at least be regarded as an adequate specimen of the author's perseverance. Böhmer, a professor of the same university, and afterwards chancellor of the duchy of Magdeburg, was eminent as a civilian and canonist: several of his original works are still regarded as useful and important, and he published one of the best editions that have yet appeared of the *Corpus Juris Canonici*. Here I may take the liberty of suggesting, that one of his works[9] would have supplied some valuable information to Bishop Kaye for his " Ecclesiastical History of the second and third Centuries, illustrated from the Writings of Tertullian." Reinold, who belongs to the same era, was likewise an acute and learned civilian: in all his discussions he aims at brevity and precision, and his Latinity is terse beyond the common standard of his age and nation.[1] Nor must we here omit the name of Everard Otto, who, though a professor in a Dutch university, was

---

[9] J. H. Böhmeri Dissertationes Juris Ecclesiastici antiqui ad Plinium Secundum et Tertullianum. Lipsiæ, 1711, 8vo. Halæ, 1729, 8vo. The first edition contains ten, and the second contains twelve dissertations.

[1] B. H. Reinoldi Opuscula Juridica. Lugd. Bat. 1755, 8vo.—To this volume Jugler has prefixed a dissertation " De insignibus Germanorum in Jurisprudentiam elegantiorem Meritis."

a native of Germany. He was an acute and subtle lawyer, possessed of no mean erudition: he is the author of various works, and, among the rest, of a well-known commentary on the Institutions; and he has performed a most important service by the publication of his great collection, entitled *Thesaurus Juris Romani*, consisting of five ample volumes in folio, and comprehending a large number of rare tracts on the civil law. Hoppe, who flourished somewhat earlier, wrote a commentary on the Institutions, which has been highly commended by an English civilian. " The turn and manner of his comments," says Dr. Taylor, " is such, that I think they might very successfully serve for an introduction to the more diffusive and comprehensive work of Vinnius, where we commonly set out. Above all, the *lemmata*, or axioms, which he is constantly gathering up, in the course of his notes, are the happiest, the clearest, and the most faithful compendium of law that I ever met with; and with the help of a small comment, would make a valuable system by themselves."[2]

But the most conspicuous among the German civilians of that age was Jo. Gottlieb Heineccius, who was born in the year 1681, and prosecuted the study of law at Halle. He was successively a professor in this university, and in those of Franeker and Frankfort: having resumed his chair at Halle, he died there in the year 1741, leaving behind him a very high reputation. He was unquestionably a man of talents, as well as learning; and possessing a clear and logical head, he commonly writes in a very distinct and intelligible manner. His works are numerous, and are not altogether confined to subjects of jurisprudence: he had taught philosophy as well as law, and

[2] Taylor's Elements of the Civil Law, p. ix.

was by no means unskilled in ancient erudition. Of the importance of conjoining the study of history with the study of jurisprudence, he was fully aware; and besides an able history of the civil law, he composed a work of great interest and utility, entitled "Antiquitatum Romanarum Jurisprudentiam illustrantium Syntagma," with which no similar publication has yet come into competition. The two works of Heineccius, the elements of the civil law according to the order of the Institutions, and according to the order of the Pandects, were long used as text-books in a great proportion of the universities of Europe: they contain a very methodical, and upon the whole a very able view of the principal doctrines of the Roman jurisprudence; and although in some countries it has become fashionable to depreciate the author and his works, I am far from being disposed to follow the example. " The works of Heineccius," says Dr. Reddie, " were certainly of use as compendiums; but his axiomatical method, the introduction of which was his principal merit, savoured too much of the scholastic logic; and though it may serve to help the memory, yet it does so too often at the expense of the judgment. His method, which, to a superficial observer, is apparently perspicuous, in reality frequently confuses the mind of the reader, by the absurdity of attempting to derive one axiom from another; and, by giving definitions of every thing, he renders obscure what stands in need of no illustration. In his zeal to deduce every thing from given premises, however fanciful, he would make it appear that the Roman jurists derived all their knowledge from the Stoics, as if the Stoics alone had been gifted with ordinary intellectual faculties; and, although a writer upon pure Latinity, his works are full of barbarous words and un-

Roman phraseology."[3]   A very different estimate of his
merits has been formed by Sir James Mackintosh, whose
opinion on a subject of this nature is also entitled to
attention.   "It is hardly necessary," he remarks, "to
take any notice of the text-book of Heineccius, the best
writer of elementary books with whom I am acquainted
on any subject."[4]   It must indeed be admitted that the
phraseology of Heineccius is often sufficiently scholastic,
and that he not unfrequently expresses the ideas of the
ancient civilians in terms of modern invention;[5] but if we
compare his style with that of Thomasius and many
other lawyers of the same era, it seems to exhibit a model
of classical purity and elegance.   The merit of his
axiomatical method of arranging the doctrines of the
law, may certainly be considered as doubtful.   It was
strenuously attacked by several of his contemporaries,
and, among the rest, by J. Wolfang Trier, who, under
the borrowed name of G. J. Schütz, published a tract
entitled " Examen Methodi Axiomaticæ, qua in Elementis Juris Civilis usus est jurisconsultus celeberrimus
Joh. Gottl. Heineccius."   Heineccius and his method

---

[3] Reddie's Historical Notices of the Roman Law, and of the recent
Progress of its Study in Germany, p. 82.   Edinb. 1826, 8vo.

[4] Mackintosh's Discourse on the Study of the Law of Nature and
Nations, p. 31.   Lond. 1799, 8vo.

[5] In this respect, he only followed the example of his predecessors, and
indeed is less faulty than most of their number.   "Hinc," says Böckelmann, "facile admitto vulgata illa, jus in re, jus ad rem, dominium utile,
dominium directum, conditio potestativa, casualis, contractus innomina-
tus, obligatio mixta, naturalis, civilis, testamentum privilegiatum, actio
nativa, dativa, judicium summarium, judicium reconventionale, possesso-
rium, summariissimum, rotulum testium, et similia plura, quæ vel prorsus
barbara, vel non eo quo nunc sensu Latine dicuntur : et tamen servanda
ob frequentissimum eorum usum hodiernum.   (Commentariorum in
Digesta Justiniani Imp. libri XIX. præf.   Lugd. Bat. 1678, 4to.)

found a zealous defender in Sellius, and they have found many admirers in various countries.[6]

The labours of Heineccius in the department of historical jurisprudence were preceded by those of Struve, Hoffmann, and Brunquell, who have each produced an elaborate history of the civil law. They were soon followed by Bach, a professor in the university of Leipzig, who published his " Historia Jurisprudentiæ Romanæ" in the year 1754.[7] This is an able and scholar-like per-

[6] Sellii Vindiciæ Methodi qua in Elementis Juris Civilis usus est vir illustris atque excellentissimus J. G. Heineccius, oppositæ G. J. Schutzii Examini ejusd. Methodi. Accedit in calce ipsum Examen Schutzianum. Traj. ad Rhen. 1724, 8vo.—" Cada qual de estos miembros," say the authors of another elementary work, " se trata alli en particular con orden y método geometrico, el qual nos ha parecido unico para hacer perceptibles los principios de nuestra jurisprudencia, y desengañar á los que han pretendido hacer á esta ciencia incapáz de demostracion mathematica." (Instituciones del Derecho Civil de Castilla, por los Doctores Don Ignacio Jordán de Asso y del Rio, y Don Miguél de Manuèl y Rodriguez. Madrid, 1771, 4to.)

The labours of Heineccius were not confined to the civil law. Among other books, he published *Fundamenta Stili Cultioris;* which were improved by Gesner, and continued to be held in considerable estimation till superseded by the more complete and useful work of Scheller, entitled *Præcepta Styli bene Latini,* of which the third edition was published at Leipzig in 1797, in 2 vols. 8vo. In reference to both works, see the Bibliotheca Critica, vol. i. part. iv. p. 118. Heineccius, who taught others the art of writing Latin, is not himself very nice or scrupulous in his language. He even ventures to use such expressions as these : " si professor dicat, *collegium prælegam* pro honorario." (Recitationes in Elementa Juris Civilis, p. 423. edit. Leovard. 1773, 8vo.) In order to understand this barbarous phraseology, it is necessary to recollect that in German, " ein Collegium lesen," signifies to read a course of lectures.

[7] An account of Jo. August Bach may be found in the collection of Harless, De Vitis Philologorum, vol. i. p. 68. vol. iii. p. 182. The author speaks very highly of his learning and talents. See likewise the Bibliotheca Critica, vol. ii. part. i. p. 88. Klotzii Acta Litteraria, vol. i. p. 129, the prolegomena to his Opuscula, and Stockmann's preface to Bachii Car-

formance, and in some respects it has not yet been surpassed. It has received considerable improvements from
Stockmann. There were various contemporary writers
who brought to the illustration of the civil law a competent stock of philological and historical learning; and
among these we may venture to class Conradi, Schwartz,
Mascou, Ritter, Hommel, and Gebauer. We have observed, or think we have observed, among the present
race of German lawyers, some disposition to undervalue
the character of their more immediate predecessors:
but the one class requires no adventitious aid, and the
other may be allowed to stand upon its own merits. It
must at the same time be admitted that the study of
jurisprudence has during our own age received a new direction and a new impulse; and this change is in no
small degree to be imputed to the exertions and to the
example of a very distinguished member of the university
of Göttingen.

Gustaf Hugo, the individual to whom I allude, was
born at Lörrach, in the duchy of Baden, in the year
1764. He belongs to a family of lawyers, and his father
had filled various civic or municipal offices. The son
prosecuted his juridical studies in the university of Göttingen, where he resided three years, and where his pro-
mising talents attracted the attention of some of the
most eminent professors. Here, at the age of twenty-
one, he had the honour of obtaining one of the annual
prizes awarded by the law-faculty of the university: the

mina. Dresd. et Lips. 1787, 8vo. "Habebat Ernestus," says Wyttenbach, "disciplinæ alumnum Bachium, elegantissimæ juvenem doctrinæ,
insigne decus jurisprudentiæ, veteres Cujacios et Gothofredos relaturum,
nisi longiorem ei vitam fata invidissent." (Vita Davidis Ruhnkenii, p. 47.
Lugd. Bat. et Amst. 1799, 8vo.)

subject of his essay is the foundation of succession in cases of intestacy, according to the more early and more recent principles of the civil law;[s] nor is it possible to read this juvenile composition without discovering a fair and full promise of that acute and philosophical spirit which pervades his more mature productions. He was afterwards employed in superintending the studies of a young prince at the court of Dessau, where he continued for two years; and at the age of twenty-four, he became a professor of law in the university of Göttingen. With all the ardour of a young and vigorous mind, he now prosecuted the study of what is denominated in Germany the pure Roman law; that is, the Roman, unblended with their own municipal law. From the commencement of his career, he felt himself dissatisfied with the usual routine of contemporary professors, and determined to pursue a different course. Their method, as well as their language, was frequently too scholastic; the doctrines of the ancient civilians were not always distinguished with sufficient care from the opinions or inferences of modern commentators; the objects of law were often subdivided with little regard to the order of nature, or the principles of sound logic; nor did the speculations of jurisprudence derive all the requisite illustration from the light of history and philosophy. Hugo was not only capable of perceiving these defects, but likewise of applying a remedy: his lectures were immediately distinguished for their lucid method, their philosophical precision, their original and masterly discussion; and although, like other innovators, he could not but expect to encounter opposi-

---

[s] Gustavi Hugo Badensis Commentatio de Fundamento Successionis ab Intestato ex Jure Romano antiquo et novo. Gottingæ, 1785, 4to.

tion and obloquy, he pursued his career with unabating vigour, and was encouraged by the attendance of very numerous auditories. He evidently derived considerable advantages from his familiarity with the English and French writers. It indeed appears that his education had been more French than German, and that a long residence in Alsace and at Montbelliard had rendered him perfectly familiar with the native language of Montesquieu.[9] French he speaks with great facility and correctness, and English in a very intelligible and characteristic manner. His earliest publication after his return to Göttingen, was a translation of Gibbon's long and remarkable chapter on the civil law: this chapter, illustrated with his notes, forms a little volume. He began, and has long continued, to read a separate course of lectures on the history of the Roman law, and in this department his general merits are very conspicuous. As a text-book for his students, he published a history of the Roman law, which has gradually received many additions and improvements. He has published several other works as text-books for his different courses of lectures; and they are combined in a series of octavo volumes, under the general title of *Lehrbuch eines civilistischen Cursus*, or Outlines of a Course of Study for a Civilian. He is besides the editor and principal author of a work in five volumes, entitled *Civilistiches Magazin*, which includes contributions from some of the first civilians of Germany. All these publications have passed through various editions, and are known wherever

[9] Hugo's Beyträge zur civilistischen Bücherkenntniss, Bd. i. S. 15. See an excellent article of Warnkoenig, "De l'Etat actuel de la Science du Droit en Allemagne, et de la Révolution qu'elle y a éprouvée dans le cours des trente dernières années." *Thémis*, tom. i. p. 11.

the civil law is studied with any degree of ardour. The author has bestowed unusual attention upon the fountains of the law, and is particularly conversant with the fragments of the ancient civilians. He has published separate editions of Ulpian[1] and Paulus,[2] and had some concern with the collection which appeared at Berlin in the year

[1] Domitii Ulpiani Fragmenta quæ nunc parum accurate dicuntur, in unico codice Tituli ex Corpore Ulpiani inscripta. Editionem et præfationem quintam, cui quartum annotatio, tertium integra codicis lectio, iterum ex Caii Institutionibus emendatio adjecta, curavit Gustavus Hugo, Eques Guelphicus, J. U. D. Britanniarum Hannoveræque Regi a Sanctioribus Just. Cons. Professor Goettingensis. Berolini, 1834, 8vo. Since the appearance of the first edition, several other learned men have illustrated the works of Ulpian. Among other publications, the following deserve to be mentioned : " Domitii Ulpiani quæ in primum Digestorum librum migrarunt Fragmenta. Textu ad codd. MSS. recognito edidit D. Carolus Bucher, augustissimo Bavariæ Regi ab Aulæ Consiliis, et Professor P. O. in Academia Friderico-Alexandrina Erlangensi." Erlangæ, 1819, 8vo. "Ueber Dominium. Ein Titel aus Ulpians Fragmenten, als Versuch einer Bearbeitung juristischer Classiker für Schulmänner, commentirt, übersetzt, und mit vier etymologischen Excursen herausgegeben von D. Fr. Ballhorn genannt Rosen, Director der F. L. Regierungs-Canzlei in Detmold." Lemgo, 1822, 8vo. " Dissertatio Critica de Ulpiani Fragmentis. Quam, illustris Jureconsultorum Ordinis auctoritate, ad Professionem Juris Ordinariam in Academia Vratislaviensi rite suscipiendam, die xxii. Julii a. MDCCCXXIV. hora ix. publice defendet auctor D. Freder. Adolphus Schillingus, assumto ad respondendum socio Carolo Schoenbornio, Sem. Phil. Sodali." Vratislaviæ, 8vo. "Animadversionum Criticarum ad Ulpiani Fragmenta Specimen I. II. Auctore D. Freder. Adolpho Schillingo, Professore Lipsiensi." Lipsiæ, 1830, 8vo. Schilling has published a third and a fourth specimen; and it is to be hoped that his different tracts on Ulpian will at length be combined in one volume.

[2] Julii Pauli Sententiarum Receptarum ad Filium libri quinque ex Breviario Alariciano. In usum prælectionum edidit, cum editione principe contulit, Indicem Editionum omnium Corporis Juris Civilis Fontium adjecit Gustavus Hugo. Berolini, 1795, 8vo.

M

1815.[3] To this collection he promised, and indeed the title-page announces, a preface, and a list of the editions of the different works; but he has not yet found it convenient to fulfil his engagement, nor is it very probable that he will now recur to this labour.

It is generally, if not universally, admitted that the labours of Hugo have produced a very powerful effect, and that the well-directed exertions of the present race of German civilians are to a very considerable extent to be imputed to his precepts and example. He is the founder of a school of historical jurisprudence, which is firmly established in Germany, and which is gradually extending itself in various other countries.[4] His reputation is too high to escape the glance of envy; and he has on some occasions experienced the zeal of his enemies as well as of his friends. Like many other individuals of quick perception and keen observation, he is naturally inclined to be satirical; and not unfrequently, when he finds an opportunity of mentioning his opponents, "naso suspendit adunco." A large portion of his resentment has fallen upon Thibaut, Dabelow, and Schweppe. He may not perhaps have given more provocation than he received; but he is now descending into the vale of years, and his quarrels and animosities are among the last sub-

---

[3] Jus Civile Antejustinianeum, codicum et optimarum editionum ope a Societate Jurisconsultorum curatum. Præfatus est et Indicem Editionum adjecit Gustavus Hugo. Berolini, 1815, 2 tom. 8vo.

[4] Dr. Reddie remarks that " a great zeal for the study has spread itself through all the continental universities; and the Roman law is historically inculcated in Upsala, Moscow, and Dorpat, as well as in Erlangen, Basel, and Tübingen." (Historical Notices of the Roman Law, p. 114.) This historical school seems to be firmly established in Poland; where Dr. Macieiowski, professor of law in the university of Warsaw, has lately published a second edition of an able work entitled *Historia Juris Romanani.* Varsaviæ, 1825, 8vo.

jects on which a good man can then reflect with satisfaction.

Hi motus animorum, atque hæc certamina tanta
Pulveris exigui jactu compressa quiescent.

Among the most distinguished of his friends and fellow-labourers we cannot fail to class Haubold and Savigny. Christian Gottlieb Haubold, whose personal history may perhaps be unknown to most of my readers, was born at Dresden on the 4th of November 1766. His father became professor of natural philosophy in the university of Leipzig, and died soon afterwards, leaving him in the sixth year of his age; but although he was thus deprived of a parent, his guardians gave him an excellent education. He entered the university in the year 1781, and pursued a liberal course of study, but was not slow in selecting jurisprudence as his proper department. His mother had married as her second husband a printer named Saalbach, who treated him with the kindness of a father, and who had induced him to give an occasional attendance in the office, with the view of preparing himself for continuing the business: he was however too eagerly bent upon other pursuits, and during his academical course he attended the lectures of no fewer than ten different professors of law. In 1784 he took the degree of master of arts, and in the following year that of bachelor of laws; in September 1786, he qualified himself as *Magister Legens*, and during the ensuing semester he read his first course of lectures, on the history of the Roman jurisprudence. Having taken his doctor's degree in 1788, he was next year appointed extraordinary professor of juridical antiquities, in 1796 ordinary professor of the law of Saxony, and he successively attained to all the usual honours belonging to the law-faculty.[5] He continued to read lectures on the Roman and the Saxon law, and he devoted a very uncommon degree of attention to their history and literature. The various works which he published, chiefly relate to the Roman law, and are almost all written in the Latin language; they are the result of indefatigable research, and are uniformly distinguished by extent of learning and solidity of judgment. In all that relates to what the Germans describe as the literature of the law, he was without a rival, and his works are of the greatest value in directing the researches of the curious enquirer. This most learned and estimable professor died at Leipzig in the year 1824, at the premature age of fifty-eight, leaving a family to bewail his loss. His very able successor Dr. Wenck, well known even in this country as the author of *Magister Vacarius*, has already followed him to the grave.

Friedrich Carl von Savigny is still a professor of law in the university of Berlin, and is equally remarkable for his ingenuity and for his research. His work on the law of possession contains an admirable discussion of a difficult and abstruse subject;[6] but the most durable monument of his talents and learning is his history of the Roman law during the middle ages. Of the former work an analysis has been published in the French language by Warnkoenig;[7] and an English translation of the latter was undertaken by a learned advocate, who

[5] Autobiographieen Leipziger Gelehrten, herausgegeben von M. Heinrich Gottlieb Kreussler, S. 39. Leipzig [1810] 4to.

[6] Das Recht des Besitzes ; eine civilistische Abhandlung von Friedrich Carl von Savigny. Giessen, 1818, 8vo. This is not the first edition.

[7] Analyse du Traité de la Possession, d'après les Principes du Droit Romain, par M. de Savigny; revue et corrigée sur la quatrième édition de l'ouvrage, par M. L. A. Warnkoenig. Liége, 1824, 8vo.

has not however been encouraged to proceed beyond the first volume.[8] Hugo, Haubold, and Savigny have, each in his own department, given a signal impulse to the juridical studies of the age, and they have been followed in the same career by many other distinguished civilians.

In Germany, the study of almost every branch of jurisprudence is prosecuted with surprizing ardour and success. Several of the great schools of law have already been mentioned, but the smaller universities of the protestant states have each contributed to support the national reputation in this department of science.— The smaller schools, such, for example, as those of Kiel and Greifswald, have been found valuable seminaries for the greater; and it frequently happens that the most eminent professors are invited from one place to another. Cramer, one of the most classical of the German civilians, lately closed a long and distinguished career at Kiel.[9] In some of the universities, the students

---

[8] The History of the Roman Law during the Middle Ages : translated from the original German of Carl von Savigny, by E. Cathcart, [LL. D. Advocate.] Vol. I. Edinb. 1829, 8vo. Of a French translation of the same work, two or three volumes have already appeared.

[9] Cramer published a singular account of his own life, under the title of "Haus-Chronik, meinen Anverwandten und Freunden zum Andenken gewidmet." Hamburg, 1822, 8vo. His professional works, generally written in Latin, are learned and able. Among other works, he published "Supplementi ad Barnabæ Brissonii Opus de Verborum quæ ad Jus Civile pertinent Significatione Specimen I." Kiliæ, 1813, 4to. From the excellence of this specimen, it is much to be regretted that the author was not induced to prosecute the undertaking. A previous publication bears the following title : "De Verborum Significatione Tituli Pandectarum et Codicis, cum variæ lectionis apparatu. Curavit Andr. Guil. Cramer, Jurisconsultus." Kiliæ, 1811, 8vo.

of law bear a very large proportion to those of all the other faculties. The first class of teachers are the ordinary professors, who form the law-faculty : next to them are the extraordinary professors, or professors *extra ordinem;* and these are followed by the *Privatdocenten,* or graduates who have a license to teach within the precincts of the university. Thus it happens in most cases that the student may make his election among several teachers of the same branch; and thus a lecturer possessing neither talents nor reputation has but little chance of finding auditors. The candidate who applies for permission to teach in this faculty, must previously have taken the degree of doctor of laws, not necessarily in the same university; and he must afterwards submit to the process of *habilitation,* by which he completes his right of exercising the functions of a teacher. In most of the universities, this process consists in publicly defending either a regular dissertation, or a series of *theses;* but at Berlin, a new university in which the regulations are particularly strict, he is besides obliged to lecture in Latin before the members of the faculty, and in German before the public. This is called a " Disputatio pro Facultate Legendi." Many of their academical dissertations are very able and elaborate. This class of individuals forms the great nursery of professors. What imparts to the law-faculties a degree of importance unknown in other countries, is the circumstance of their being, in various instances, courts of appeal; they are not merely consulted in difficult and intricate questions of law, but in certain cases, criminal as well as civil, they are empowered to receive appeals from courts of high jurisdiction. The consultations, which in some universities are very numerous, encrease the emoluments as well as the labours of the professors.[1]

Such is the present state of juridical science in those countries where of late it has chiefly flourished, and where the study of jurisprudence is so conspicuously combined with the study of history. "Perhaps," says Professor Wilde, "one of the great reasons of the civil law having fallen into such disrepute among us, has been an ignorance of its rise, progress, and authority, in this, and the other countries of modern Europe. The student is introduced, all at once, to the study of a system, in itself exceedingly deep and comprehensive, without any of that previous training which is necessary to give him proper ideas of the subject to which he is to apply his mind. It appears before him as a vast and confused object, of which his perceptions are exceedingly indistinct and uncertain. On the other hand, when he is led up to it through the avenue of historical knowledge, and when the prospect opens upon him easily and by degrees, his after acquaintance with it will be both more accurate and more lasting. Accordingly, this of itself is a great and a powerful reason for introducing the study of the principles of the civil law by the study of its history."[2] In order to promote, as far as lies within the narrow compass of my power, the historical study of the civil law, I shall here intro-

[1] An instance lately occurred of a reference from a British court to the law-faculty of a German university. In the case of Fischer *versus* the Earl of Seafield, the court of session submitted certain points of Saxon law to the faculty of Leipzig, and obtained a very elaborate opinion, which, in the translation printed by order of the court, extends to sixty-two pages in quarto.

Wilde's Preliminary Lecture to the Course of Lectures on the Institutions of Justinian, p. 64.

duce some critical notices of the most remarkable writers who have laboured in this interesting department.[3]

Modern civilians have divided the history of the Roman law into *external* and *internal*. The terms were first employed by Leibnitz, but with some difference in their application. The external history details the various sources of the law, and the labours of those who have digested, preserved, and cultivated it; while the internal history embraces the doctrines of the law themselves, with their principal changes and modifications. Many works published under the title of histories of the civil law, are almost entirely confined to its external history: books of this description are better adapted to the taste of those readers who have not devoted themselves to juridical studies; but a knowledge of the internal history of the Roman law is an essential part of the knowledge which ought to be acquired by every civilian, who is entitled to that appellation.

The lawyers of the middle ages, being unacquainted with philology, which is the handmaid of history, were grossly ignorant of the history and antiquities of the Ro-

---

[3] Meyer is a declared and decided opponent of the historical school of jurisprudence, and it must be admitted that he has discussed the doctrines of Savigny with much ability ; but his arguments, ingenious as they certainly are, I am inclined to consider as less solid than plausible. Among many other suggestions, he states that the Romans prescribed the historical method, partly as useless, "parcequ' il est impossible de rendre raison de toutes les lois ;" and in support of this allegation, he quotes the authority of Julianus : " Non omnium quæ a majoribus constituta sunt ratio reddi potest." (De la Codification en général, et de celle de l'Angleterre en particulier, en une Série de Lettres adressées à M. C. P. Cooper, Avocat Anglais, p. 48. Amst. et Lond. 1830, 8vo.) But if we cannot discover the reasons of all laws, is it a necessary inference that we must investigate the reasons of none ?

man law.[4]   On the revival of elegant letters, this branch
of study did not long continue to be entirely neglected.
Among the earliest scholars who applied the light of classical learning to the civil law, we must not fail to mention
Angelo Poliziano, who died at a premature age in the
year 1494.   He was a person of singular talents and
attainments, who only required a greater length of days
to have earned the highest reputation.   To the celebrity
of an Italian and Latin poet, and of a classical critic, he
was solicitous to add that of a civilian : he first directed
the attention of modern lawyers to the valuable paraphrase
of the Institutions by Theophilus;[5] and he was the first
who attempted a collation of the renowned Florentine
manuscript of the Pandects.[6]   In the course of the ensuing century, Italy could boast of Alciatus, and other
learned men who were capable of availing themselves of
the treasures of ancient erudition, and of applying them
to the illustration of ancient jurisprudence.   Portugal
produced Antonio Gouvea, better known by the name of
Goveanus, who was alike eminent as a critic and a lawyer ; and about the same period, Spain produced Antonio Agustin, or Augustinus, the illustrious archbishop
of Tarragona, whose indefatigable labours have reflected

---

[4] " The first attempts of this kind were pretty modest, only by explaining the text in short glosses, which was Accursius's method : but he not
having had the assistance of human learning, and particularly of the
Greek tongue, the want of these have betray'd him to gross and childish
mistakes; and it is a wretched gloss, where a sentence of Greek occurs in
the text, *Hæc Graica sunt, quæ nec legi nec intelligi possunt.*" (Baker's
Reflections upon Learning, p. 189, 5th edit.   Lond. 1714, 8vo.)

[5] Mylii Theophilus, p. 40.

[6] Brenkmanni Historia Pandectarum, p. 306. Traj. ad Rhen. 1772, 4to.
Bandini, Ragionamento Istorico sopra le Collazioni delle Fiorentine
Pandette fatte da Angelo Poliziano.   Livorno, 1762, 4to.

much light on various departments of history, antiquities, and law.[7]   He was alike eminent as a civilian and canonist.   In France, Budæus had previously begun to apply himself to the philological illustration of the Roman law ; and his eminent skill in the Greek as well as the Latin language enabled him to apply a strong and steady light to many subjects which were then viewed through a dim medium.[8]   In the career of erudition he was followed by Balduinus, Contius, Hotman, and many other French lawyers of great attainments ; but in this department of study the most illustrious of modern names is that of Cujacius, who conjoined a masterly knowledge of ancient literature with the most consummate knowledge of the law.[9]   He was born in 1522, and died in 1590.

[7] An account of his life has been written by another eminent civilian of the same nation, Don Gregorio Mayans y Siscar. This biography, extending to 183 pages, is appended to Agustin's *Dialogos de las Armas i Linages de la Nobleza de España*.   Madrid, 1734, 4to.   The archbishop was born in 1517, and died in 1586.

[8] " Probe hoc viderunt," says Rücker, " quibus prima instauratæ veræ jurisprudentiæ gloria debetur, viri egregii, Gulielmus Budæus et Andreas Alciatus : hanc enim ob causam insignes illi duumviri non aliunde primam obscuratæ penitus et conturbatæ juris arti lucem accendendam esse putarunt, quam a Latinitate et elegantia.   Novam igitur, prioribusque interpretibus plane incognitam ingressi viam, civilis prudentiæ studio Latinam feliciter junxerunt literaturam, eaque prælucente cum ipsi, tum alii deinceps jurisconsulti infinita veterum loca, quæ antea dubia, obscura, et difficilia habebantur, confirmarunt, illustrarunt, enodarunt."   See his Oratio de Superanda Studii Juris Civilis Difficultate (p. 270), subjoined to his Dissertatio de Civili et Naturali Temporis Computatione in Jure. Lugd. Bat. 1749, 8vo.

[9] " Horum ille Cujacius vestigiis insistens, linguarum, antiquitatum, et historiarum lautissima instructus supellectile, optimorumque in omni disciplinæ genere scriptorum veterum studiosissima lectione, ac pertinaci præstantissimorum, qui illic latebant, thesaurorum veluti effossione, universam hac eadem ratione jurisprudentiam illustrare aggressus est, non Romanam solam, cujus nihil reliquit intactum, verum jus quoque feudale

It was by the persevering and united efforts of such able men as these that the spirit and the history of the civil law were at length fully understood; and although none of them has undertaken a work strictly historical, their labours have smoothed the way for all succeeding historians of the Roman jurisprudence.

We cannot discover that a regular history of law was attempted by any ancient writer. The only relique which makes an approach to this description, is the extract from the *Enchiridion* of Pomponius inserted in the title of the Pandects,[1] "De Origine Juris et omnium Magistratuum, et Successione Prudentium." Sextus Pomponius, who appears to have survived till the reign of the Antonines, was a lawyer of eminence; but the historical notices which we thus derive from his work, have not been found accurate or satisfactory.[2] This fragment has been illustrated by many different commentators; and Byn-

---

et canonicum : ac de ipsis etiam patriæ suæ consuetudinibus idem aliquando consilium agitavit. Illaque universa tali modo effecta dedit, ut eadem opera nullum non genus scriptorum adjuvaret, exponeret, emendaret. Is quoque cuilibet rei sua propria adsignavit principia, singulasque jurium species accurate distinxit et separavit." (Schultingii Oratio de Jurisprudentia Historica : Jurisprudentia Ante-Justinianea, p. 928. Lugd. Bat. 1717, 4to.)

[1] "The civilians, who pretend that, if the Latin tongue were lost, it might be found in the book of Pandects, would take it ill to be thought mistaken in the word Pandect; which, altho' a masculine, is generally used by them in a feminine signification." (Baker's Reflections upon Learning, p. 182.) In confirmation of this remark, he refers to H. Stephanus de Abusu Linguæ Græcæ, p. 12. See likewise a short tract prefixed to the work of Augustinus de Nominibus Propriis τοῦ Πανδέκτου Florentini. Tarracone, 1579, fol.

[2] See Reinoldi Opuscula Juridica, p. 502, and the preface of Heineccius to Opuscula ad Historiam Juris, et maxime ad Pomponii Enchiridion illustrandum, pertinentia, collegit Jo. Ludovicus Uhlius. Halæ, 1735, 4to.

kershoek, one of the most able of their number, professes
to supply what his predecessors have left deficient.[3]

The earliest attempt at a history of the civil law, so
far as I have been able to ascertain, was that of Aymarus
Rivallius; whose "Historia Juris Civilis" is said to have
been first printed in the year 1515.[4] After some preliminary discussion, he exhibits an outline of the history
of the seven kings of Rome, and traces their supposed
influence on the legislation of the state. In the second
book, which occupies much more than one half of the
volume, he treats of the twelve Tables, and recites many
laws which he imagines them to have contained. He
afterwards proceeds to enumerate various laws of a more
recent origin. " Sed ut primam juris disciplinæ speciem
absolvamus, memorare consules et alios magistratus convenit, qui post XII. Tab. leges ad populum tulerunt.
Dicemus igitur post Livium, Nepotem, Gell. et Macro-
bium Satur. iii. Blondumque in Roma Triumphante, et

[3] Bynkershoek Prætermissa ad l. 2. D. de Origine Juris : Opera, tom.
iii. p. 1. See likewise Wæchtleri Opuscula juridico-philologica, p. 726.
Traj. ad Rhen. 1733, 8vo. The most copious, though not the most va-
luable, commentary was published by G. vander Muelen: In Historiam
Pomponii de Origine Juris et omnium Magistratuum, et Successione
Prudentium, Exercitationes. Trajecti ad Rhenum, 1691-3, 3 part. 8vo.

[4] Valentiæ, 1515, 8vo. Mogunt. 1527, 8vo. Ibid. 1530, 8vo. Ibid.
1533, 8vo. These editions are mentioned by Haubold, Institutionum
Juris Romani Privati historico-dogmaticarum Lineamenta, p. 26. edit.
Lips. 1826, 8vo. A copy in my possession bears the following title :
" Aymari Rivallii Allobrogis, Jure consulti eruditissimi eloquentissimi-
que, Civilis Historiæ Juris, sive in XII. Tab. Leges, Commentariorum
libri quinque, jam denuo diligenter recogniti. Historiæ item Juris Pont.
liber singularis." Lugduni, 1551, 8vo. Pp. 272. The running title of the
principal part of the volume is *Historia Juris Civilis.* The author's vernacular designation was Aymar du Rivail, Seigneur de la Rivaliere.—
See Savigny's Geschichte des Römischen Rechts im Mittelalter, Bd. vi.
S. 387.

jureconsultos, Philelphum et alios, quas leges post XII.
Tab. populus Ro. consule et alio magistratu interrogante
constituerit. Non omnes leges tamen enumerare propo-
nimus, sed eas tantum, quarum vetusti scriptores crebrius
meminerunt." The third book relates to *Senatusconsulta* and *Prœtorum Edicta*, the fourth to *Decreta Principum.* In the fifth book he treats of the *Responsa Prudentum,* and introduces slight notices of those lawyers,
"qui imperatorum autoritate responderunt, et juris scientiam in hac ultima reipub. specie professi sunt." The
volume concludes with a very brief "Historia Juris Pontificii," consisting of only seven pages. In such a production as this, it would be unreasonable to expect any
very profound research, or any great nicety of criticism;
but Rivallius had at least the merit of setting a good
example.

After an interval of several years, the conjunction of
history and jurisprudence was strenuously recommended
by Franciscus Balduinus, a man of a fervid spirit, and of
multifarious erudition. He did not himself undertake a
history of the civil law; but in a publication intended as
the precursor of a more extensive performance, he
strongly urges the necessity of its historical study.[5]
Nor must we overlook the eminent services of his contemporary Carolus Sigonius, who, although not a lawyer
by profession, has very ably illustrated various departments in the legal antiquities of Rome. His treatise

---

[5] De Institutione Historiæ universæ, et ejus cum Jurisprudentia Con-
junctione, Προλεγομένων libri II. Fr. Balduini. Parisiis, 1561, 4to.—
This work was reprinted in a curious collection, entitled, "Jo. Bodini
Methodus Historica, duodecim ejusdem argumenti Scriptorum, tam
veterum quam recentiorum, Commentariis adaucta." Basileæ, 1576,
8vo.

"De Senatu Romano," published under the name of
Joannes Sarius Zamoscius, is best known to classical
scholars; but his two books "De antiquo Jure Civium
Romanorum," his three books "De antiquo Jure Italiæ,"
his three books "De antiquo Jure Provinciarum," and
his three books "De Judiciis," are well known and much
esteemed among civilians.

Rivallius was followed by Valentinus Forsterus; of
whose history of the civil law it is more safe to commend
the design than the execution. His work is a folio
volume of 265 pages, and is but slight and unsatisfactory.[6] A considerable proportion of his pages he has
devoted to the succession of the ancient and modern lawyers; but his notices are too superficial to excite any
great degree of interest.[7]

The next history is that of Jacobus Gothofredus, entitled "Historia seu Progressus Juris Civilis Romani,"
and forming the first part of his "Manuale Juris."[8] This
historical sketch is of small extent, but is able and comprehensive. The author's works, as has already been
stated, are numerous, and are uniformly distinguished by

[6] Valentini Forsteri Jureconsulti de Historia Juris Civilis Romani
libri tres; in quibus traditur ortus Romani Imperii, subjiciuntur mutati-
ones insignes Magistratuum in Repub. Rom. et caussæ, initia et progressus Juris Civilis, &c. Basileæ, 1565, fol.

[7] "Superest historia prudentum, quam describere quidam agressi sunt,
sed parce ac timide. Post hos Forsterus idem ausus, sed infeliciter; ut
quemque hortari possim serio, caveat illum. Miseret sane Christophori
Besoldi, qui plus illi tribuit, quam fas erat." (C. A. Ruperti ad Enchiridion Pomponii de Origine Juris libri III. Animadversionum, tertia
elaborati cura, p. 301. Franequeræ, 1696, 12mo.)

[8] Of the Manuale Juris of Gothofredus, an edition was published by the
late Professor Berthelot. Paris. 1806, 8vo. There are many other
separate editions; and it is inserted in Trotz's collection of the author's
Opera Juridica minora. Lugd. Bat. 1733, fol.

a prodigious mass of learning; but his " Fontes quatuor Juris Civilis," and his commentary on the Theodosian Code, must again be particularly mentioned, for the strong light which they reflect on the history of the Roman jurisprudence.

Another writer whom it seems necessary to mention, is Dr. Duck, chancellor of the diocese of London, and one of the few English civilians who enjoy any share of continental reputation. He is the author of an elaborate treatise on the use and authority of the Roman law in the dominions of Christian princes.[9] Of the general history of that law he has introduced a brief outline, and has bestowed much patient investigation in tracing its progress in various portions of modern Europe. In his researches he was greatly aided by Dr. Langbaine, the learned provost of Queen's College, Oxford;[1] and his publication exhibits the peculiarity of each chapter bearing the signature of that very distinguished prelate Dr. Usher, archbishop of Armagh.[2] The utility of Duck's labours has been generally acknowledged. " In justice to the authority of this writer," says Barrington, " I can-

[9] De Usu et Authoritate Juris Civilis Romanorum, in Dominiis Principum Christianorum, libri duo, authore Arthuro Duck, LL.D. Lond. 1649, 8vo. Lond. 1653, 8vo. Lugd. Bat. 1654, 12mo. Lipsiæ, 1676, 12mo. Magdeburgi, 1676, 12mo. Leodii, 1679, 12mo. Lond. 1679, 8vo.—Camus or his editor Dupin mentions a French translation, published at Paris, 1689, 12mo. (Lettres sur la Profession d'Avocat, et Bibliothèque choisie des Livres de Droit, tom. ii. p. 293.) The Magdeburg and Liége editions of the original work are here enumerated on the same authority.

[1] Wood's Athenæ Oxonienses, vol. iii. col. 258. " In which book Dr. Gerard Langbaine's labours were so much, that he deserved the name of co-author."

[2] " Approbatio operis per D. Jacobum Armachanum Archiepiscopum, rogatu Authoris, ad finem singulorum capitum est apposita."

not but mention that Giannone and other the most celebrated civilians style him their coryphæus: we are too
apt in this country to defer to foreign authors, as the
Roman law is so little attended to, or practised in England."[3]   An able writer has mentioned as a presumption
of the real merit of his work, that it was reprinted at
Leyden and at Leipzig.[4]   No other English author, so
far as I recollect, had attempted any historical sketch of
the Roman jurisprudence; for Sir Thomas Ridley's
" View of the Civile and Ecclesiasticall Law," although it
includes an account of the different books which form
the body of the civil law, contains few or no historical
details.   The great object of the writer is to shew
" wherein the practice of the civil and the ecclesiastical
law is straitened, and may be relieved within this
land."[5]

    After a moderate interval followed the tract of Simon
van Leeuwen, or Leewius, entitled, " De Origine, Progressu, Usu, atque Authoritate Juris Civilis Romani,
ejusdemque varia Editione atque Emendatione, Historica
Narratio."[6]   The author, a practising lawyer, possessed

    [3] Barrington's Observations on the more ancient Statutes, p. 76. 3d
edit. Lond. 1769, 4to.
    [4] Remarks on the Study of the Civil Law ; occasioned by Mr. Brough-
am's late Attack on the Scottish Bar. By James Browne, LL. D. Advocate. Edinb. 1828, 8vo.
    [5] Ridley's View of the Civile and Ecclesiasticall Law, and wherein the
Practise of them is streitned and may be relieued within this Land.
Lond. 1607, 4to. Oxford, 1634, 4to. Oxford, 1662, 8vo. Oxford, 1675,
8vo. All these editions, except the first, contain notes by John Gregory,
A.M. of Christ Church.
    [6] De Origine et Progressu Juris Civilis Romani Authores et Frag-
menta veterum Jurisconsultorum, cum notis Arn. Vinnii, et variorum :
auctore et collectore S. Leewio, J. C. Lugd. Bat. 1672, 8vo. The historical tract occurs in p. 711 of this collection.

a great degree of industry, but was less remarkable for his critical discernment ; nor was he sufficiently skilled in the niceties of the Latin language. These observations may be verified by an examination of his well-known edition of the *Corpus Juris Civilis,* published in folio in the year 1663. The historical sketch of the Roman law consists of only thirty-seven pages. A more ample narration was soon afterwards published by Doujat, a professor in the university of Paris, who has likewise written a history of the canon law.[7] About this period, the historical study of the Roman law began to make some progress in Germany; and one of the attempts to promote it was the publication of Schubart, a professor at Jena, " De Fatis Jurisprudentiæ Romanæ." This work made its appearance in the year 1696;[8] and the efforts of the author were seconded by Christian Thomasius, a professor in the newly founded university of Halle. Thomasius, who was born in 1655, and died in 1728, was a person of a shrewd intellect, and was much disposed to think for himself ; but he was deficient in philological learning, and greatly deficient in elegance of taste. He published a short compendium under the following title, which is sufficiently barbarous : " Delineatio Historiæ Juris: accedit in fine accuratior Formatio Status Controversiæ de Usu moderno Juris Romani in Germania.[9] This work merely consists of

[7] Doujat's history of the civil law was published in Latin, under the title of Historia Juris Civilis Romanorum. Paris. 1678, 12mo.

[8] The latest edition of Schubart's work was published under the superintendence of Tilling. Lipsiæ, 1797, 8vo.

[9] This work of Thomasius is reprinted in Hoffmann's Hist. Juris Romani, tom. i. Among other works, he published " Nævorum Jurisprudentiæ Romanæ Antejustinianeæ libri duo," &c. Halæ Magdeburg. 1707, 4to. This is the second edition.

N

a scanty outline; but the example and the lectures of the author seem to have produced a very beneficial effect in 'the German universities.[1] He was the preceptor of Heineccius, who, possessing a more classical taste, and a greater extent of erudition, had no small influence in recommending this branch of study.

Contemporary with Thomasius was Gianvincenzo Gravina, who has been considered as the most elegant of all the more recent civilians. This distinguished person, a poet and a critic, as well as a lawyer, was a native of Calabria, and professor of the civil law in the university of Rome.[2] He was born in 1664, and died in 1718.

[1] Hugo's Lehrbuch der juristischen gelehrten Geschichte, S. 481.

[2] Carafa de Gymnasio Romano, et de ejus Professoribus, lib. ii. p. 432. Romæ, 1751, 4to. See likewise Fabronii Vitæ Italorum Doctrina excellentium, tom. x. p. 1. There is an elegant account of Gravina, published under the title of " J. Andreæ Serrai de Vita et Scriptis Jani Vincentii Gravinæ Commentarius." Romæ, 1758, 4to. A collective edition of his works, Latin and Italian, was published at Naples by Sergio, 1756-8, 3 vols. 4to. All his Latin works are not to be found in the edition of Mascou. Lipsiæ, 1737, 4to. A collection of his Opuscula was published by Dr. Burgess, the late bishop of Salisbury. Oxon. 1792, 8vo. The critical writings of Gravina are highly commended by Salfi. Referring to the treatise Della Ragion Poetica, he remarks, " Nous croyons que depuis Castelvetro, Gravina est le seul qui ait raisonné sur cette matière avec autant de profondeur que d'originalité." (Histoire Littéraire d'Italie, tom. xiii. p. 457.) Dr. Warton is of opinion that Blackwell " has taken many observations from this valuable book, particularly in his twelfth section." (Essay on Pope, vol. i. p. 136.) He alludes to Dr. Blackwell's " Enquiry into the Life and Writings of Homer." Lond. 1735, 8vo. The treatise Della Tragedia has likewise been much commended. He is himself the author of five tragedies, and the hero of one of these is the famous lawyer Papinian. (Di Vincenzo Gravina, Giurisconsulto, Tragedie cinque. Napoli, 1717, 8vo.) Gravina's learned repose was not a little disturbed by a series of very bitter, and certainly very ingenious satires, published under the name of Q. Sectanus, the real author of which was at length discovered to be L. Sergardi.

His generous patronage of Metastasio is well known to many individuals, who feel no particular interest in the history of the civil law.[3] His "Origines Juris Civilis," which first appeared in 1701, embrace a very elegant and classical account of the history, internal as well as external, of the Roman jurisprudence: it is a work of various learning, and is eminently adapted to the taste of liberal scholars, who have not made the law their particular study. It has frequently been remarked that Gravina is greatly indebted to the previous labours of Sigonius, Cujacius, Gothofredus, and other writers; but if he has borrowed with some degree of freedom, he has at least employed their materials with much taste and judgment. His work was received with peculiar favour in Germany, where it passed through several editions, and was illustrated by the able annotations of Mascou.[4]

In these compositions the civilian is most cruelly vilified under the name of Philodemus. The works of Sergardi may be found in a collective form. Lucæ, 1783, 4 tom. 8vo.

[3] See Dr. Burney's Memoirs of the Life and Writings of Metastasio, vol. i. p. 3-14.

[4] Mascou is himself the author of a very learned and ingenious contribution to the history of the Roman law. It bears the title of "Gotfridi Mascovii de Sectis Sabinianorum et Proculianorum in Jure Civili Diatriba. Inserta est Disquisitio de Herciscundis." Lipsiæ, 1728, 8vo. Many able disquisitions may likewise be found in his "Opuscula Juridica et Philologica. Recensuit, præfatus est, et animadversiones nonnullas adspersit J. L. E. Püttmannus." Lipsiæ, 1776, 8vo. Püttmann has published a separate account of his life, under the title of "Memoria Gottfridi Mascovii." Lipsiæ, 1771, 8vo. Dr. Douglas, the late bishop of Salisbury, who attended his lectures at Leipzig, has mentioned him in the following terms. "Mascou has a brother, who is professor of the law of nature and nations; a very singular man, of great learning indeed, but I fear much learning has made him mad. He lives for months without stirring from his lodging; and in the intervals of his lectures amuses himself with translating Latin epigrams into Greek. He is an excellent

Another history of the civil law was about this period produced by Ferriere, dean of the law-faculty in the university of Paris.[5] The work, a duodecimo volume of considerable extent, was probably of some use to the French students of that era: it was more than once re-printed; and an edition of it appeared so lately as the year 1788. It was translated into the English language by John Beaver. But such a history, we may venture to assert, would not be found altogether satisfactory by the pupils of Blondeau. The history of the Roman law, written by Struve, a professor in the university of Jena, was published during the very same year with that of Ferriere, and is a work of more research and value.[6] The author is entitled to the praise of an industrious compiler; and notwithstanding the augmented number

classical scholar, and a great civilian, especially in the antiquities of the Roman law, but unfortunately he has not a happy talent of communicating his knowledge to others." (Douglas's Select Works, p. 35. Salisbury, 1820, 4to.)

[5] Histoire du Droit Romain, contenant son origine, ses progrès, &c. par M. Claude-Joseph de Ferriere, Doyen des Docteurs-Régens de la Faculté des Droits de Paris, et ancien Avocat au Parlement. Paris, 1718, 12mo. Paris, 1760, 12mo. Paris, 1788, 12mo. The History of the Roman or Civil Law, shewing its origin and progress, &c., written originally in French by M. Claude-Joseph de Ferriere: to which is added, Dr. Duck's Treatise of the Use and Authority of the Civil Law in England. Translated into English by J. B., Esq. Lond. 1724, 8vo. The dedication is signed John Beaver. Dr. Cooper, who describes the translator as Dr. Beaver, has perhaps confounded him with Dr. Thomas Bever. See the preface to "The Institutes of Justinian, with notes by Thomas Cooper, Esq." Philadelphia, 1812, 8vo. Dr. Bever has erroneously mentioned this as a complete translation of Duck's treatise. (Hist. of the Legal Polity of the Roman State, p. xi.)

[6] Burcardi Gotthelffii Struvii Historia Juris Romani, Justinianei, Græci, Germanici, Canonici, Feudalis, Criminalis, et Publici, ex genuinis monumentis illustrata. Jenæ, 1718, 4to.

of publications on the same subject, his Historia Juris may still be recommended as an useful book of reference. A more copious, and indeed a more able history of the law was written by his contemporary C. G. Hoffmann, a pro-fessor in the university of Frankfort on the Oder.[7] This work extends to two quarto volumes, which are however swelled by certain tracts of Hotman, Selden, Thomasius, and other writers. In the second volume, which is only to be viewed as supplementary to the first, he has collected and illustrated the fragments of the regal laws; of the Grecian laws, as elucidating the origin of those of the Romans; the fragments of the laws of the twelve Tables, and of the Edictum Perpetuum.

Brunquell's history of the Roman law was published in the year 1727.[8] The author was a professor in the university of Jena, and having been invited to the newly founded university of Göttingen, he died there in 1735, within three months after his arrival, and before he had completed the age of forty-two. He was conversant with elegant literature, and produced a very useful and read-

[7] Christ. Godofr. Hoffmanni Historia Juris Romano-Justinianei. Lipsiæ, 1718-26, 2 tom. 4to. The first volume was reprinted in 1734.—" Hoffmannus in Historia Juris, quæ duobus voluminibus in quarto 1734 Lipsiæ locupletissima prodiit, cæteris omnibus legum historicis palmam præripuit. Inter elementarios autem libellos Brunquelli Historia Juris Romani et Germanici eminet, quam in plerisque capitibus Heineccianæ multum præfero." (Hommelii Litteratura Juris, p. 53.)

[8] Jo. Salom. Brunquelli Historia Juris Romano-Germanici. Jenæ, 1727, 8vo. Amst. 1730, 8vo. Amst. 1738, 8vo. Amst. et Lugd. Bat. 1751, 8vo.—Haubold speaks of the author as "jurisconsultus omnino litteratissimus, e cujus Historia Juris Romano-Germanici multa minime vulgaria disci possunt." (Institutiones Juris Romani Litterariæ, p. 167. Lipsiæ, 1809, 8vo.) His other works are published under the title of " Opuscula ad Historiam et Jurisprudentiam spectantia. Collegit atque edidit D. Hen. Jo. Otto Kœnig." Halæ Magd. 1774, 8vo.

able book, which has not yet been entirely superseded. But he soon met with a formidable rival in Heineccius; whose "Historia Juris Civilis Romani ac Germanici," first printed in the year 1733, is to be classed among the best of his publications. It afterwards received considerable improvements from Ritter, whose annotations are learned and able.[9]   This work of Heineccius, together with most of those which have hitherto been enumerated, relates almost exclusively to the external history of the law ; but another publication of the same meritorious and indefatigable individual is justly regarded as a very important contribution to the internal history.   It was published in the year 1719, under the title of "Antiquitatum Romanarum, Jurisprudentiam illustrantium, Syntagma, secundum ordinem Institutionum Justiniani digestum;" and no fewer than nineteen editions have now appeared.   For the last, as well as the best edition, we are indebted to the learned and judicious Haubold,[1] whose loss will long be deplored by the lovers of ancient jurisprudence.

A copious and somewhat pompous history of the Roman jurisprudence was published during the middle of last century, by Antoine Terrasson, an advocate in the parliament of Paris, and afterwards professor of the canon law in that university.[2]   The work exhibits a suf-

[9] Jo. Gottl. Heineccii Historia Juris Civilis Romani ac Germanici. Halæ, 1733, 8vo. Lugd. Bat. 1740, 8vo. Cum observationibus Jo. Dan. Ritteri. Lugd. Bat. 1748, 8vo. Cum obs. Ritteri et Jo. Mart. Silberradii. Argentorati, 1751, 8vo. Cum obs. Ritteri et Silberradii. Argent. 1765, 8vo.

[1] Francofurti ad Mœnum, 1822, 8vo.

[2] Histoire de la Jurisprudence Romaine, contenant son origine et ses progrès, &c. Par Me. Anthoine Terrasson, Ecuyer, Avocat au Parlement. Paris, 1750, fol.

ficient parade of erudition, but is by no means remarkable for solid learning or accurate research. Even in that portion which specially relates to his native country, his information is less curious or interesting than might reasonably have been expected. A particular example will render this criticism more fair, and more intelligible. With no small parade, he produces an *arrêt* of the parliament, dated on the 2d of April 1576, and authorizing Cujacius to read lectures on the civil law in the university of Paris : this document, he assures his readers, had never before been communicated to the public ; and in the preface to his work he states in due form, " c'est encore à Monsieur Joly de Fleury père, Procureur Général, que j'ai obligation de la connoissance et de la communication de cet arrêt." But this very document, which is of some importance, had been inserted by Menage in his remarks on the life of Ayrault, seventy-five years before the appearance of Terrasson's history.[3]

A more masterly history of the Roman jurisprudence was published in 1754 by Jo. August Bach, an extraordinary professor of law in the university of Leipzig.[4] Four years afterwards, he died at the premature age of thirty-seven.[5] Being intimately acquainted with the

[3] Menagii Vitæ Petri Ærodii et Guillelmi Menagii, p. 164. Paris. 1675, 4to.

[4] Jo. Augusti Bachii Historia Jurisprudentiæ Romanæ. Lipsiæ, 1754, 8vo. Lips. 1765, 8vo. Lips. 1775, 8vo. Lips. 1782, 8vo. Cum observationibus Aug. Corn. Stockmann. Lips. 1796, 8vo. Cum iisdem. Lips. 1807, 8vo. There are other editions of a more recent date.

[5] According to the expression of Cramer, he was disputed to death by his colleague Sammet. " Er war ein gewaltiges *animal disputax*, hatte, wie er selbst erzählte, Bach zu Tode disputirt, und den Befehl bewirkt, dass bey seinem Erscheinen im Petrinum, die vier Decane sich einstellen müssten, um allenfalls Namens des Kurfürsten zu intercediren." (Haus-Chronik, S. 79. Hamburg, 1822, 8vo.)

classical languages and literature,[6] he possessed a manifest advantage over some of his predecessors. His history is written with learning, ability, and judgment; and in some respects it has not been surpassed by any that has yet appeared. It only embraces the external history, but in this department it has uncommon merit: the author traces the progress of public as well as private law; his information is carefully drawn from the original sources; and he exercises those critical talents which he had cultivated in the school of Ernesti, and which recommended him to the warm approbation of Wyttenbach.[7] The university of Leipzig has long been distinguished as a school of jurisprudence; and as it has long been one of the first classical seminaries in Europe, the study of the civil law is here supported by all the collateral aid that is to be derived from ancient literature. Ernesti, a philologer and theologian, who had no small influence in forming the recent character of this university, was suffi-

[6] One of his learned labours was an edition of some of the works of Xenophon. "Ξενοφῶντος τινά. Xenophontis Œconomicus, Apologia Socratis, Symposium, Hiero, Agesilaus, cum animadversionibus Jo. Augusti Bachii." Lipsiæ, 1749, 8vo. To this volume he has prefixed a critical epistle of his learned preceptor, "Jo. Augusti Ernesti Epistola ad Jo. Augustum Bachium de Xenophonteis Locis nonnullis," which concludes in the following manner: "Nihil jam amplius restat, quam ut tibi, doctissime Bachi, specimen hoc egregiæ eruditionis Græcæ gratuler, optemque ut et hujus et reliquæ tuæ elegantissimæ doctrinæ dignos et copiosos fructus capias, tuique ingenii, quod in te cognovi raræ felicitatis atque elegantiæ, lumen clarius indies eluceat. Ita vale, et amorem in me tuum mihi perpetuo conserva."

[7] Besides his history of the Roman jurisprudence, Bach had published "De Legibus Trajani Commentarius." Lipsiæ, 1747, 8vo. And after his death appeared a collection entitled "Jo. Augusti Bachii Opuscula ad Historiam et Jurisprudentiam spectantia. Collegit et præfatus est Christ. Adolphus Klotzius." Halæ, 1767, 8vo.

ciently aware of the importance of some knowledge of the
Roman jurisprudence to a classical scholar:[8] he recommended the study by his precepts, as well as by his example; and the importance of classical learning to the
civilian, was equally well understood by his contemporaries.　Bach was one of Ernesti's pupils; and, from that
period down to the present, the university of Leipzig has
in general been adequately supplied with able professors
and zealous students.

Pursuing the chronological order to which we have
hitherto adhered, we discover, after a considerable interval, " The History of the Legal Polity of the Roman
State," written by Dr. Bever, an advocate at Doctors
Commons.[9]　He was likewise a fellow of All Souls College at Oxford, and had read lectures on the civil law in
that university.　He has produced a copious, and we
fear a somewhat tedious work, which however is not
destitute of merit.　It was translated into the German
language by Völkel, who has corrected many of his
errors, for the author left many errors to correct.　Bever
writes like a scholar, and a man of ability; but he
laboured under the disadvantage of being in a great

[8] " Neque enim ignorabat, quam multa essent in libris Latinis, quæ
sine juris illius scientia satis intelligi et explicari non possent." (Ernesti
Narratio de J. M. Gesnero: Opuscula Oratoria, p. 327. Lugd. Bat. 1762,
8vo.)　In another of his works, Ernesti has formed a very high estimate
of the qualifications requisite in a lawyer, " si quis juris consulti perfecti
formam exprimere velit." (Opusculorum Oratoriorum novum volumen,
p. 74. Lipsiæ, 1791, 8vo.)　His merits in the department of jurisprudence have lately been commemorated in an " Oratio de Joh. Aug. Er-
nestii Meritis in Jurisprudentiam, auctore Emilio Ferdinando Vogel."
Lipsiæ, 1829, 8vo.

[9] The History of the Legal Polity of the Roman State, and of the Rise,
Progress, and Extent of the Roman Laws.　By Thomas Bever, LL. D.
Lond. 1781, 4to.

measure unacquainted with the best civilians of the continent, more especially those of a recent date: the only modern names which he mentions in his introduction are those of Bynkershoek, Vander Muelen, Hoppe, Gravina, Mascou, Heineccius, Ferriere, and his own countryman Dr. Duck. This is certainly a very scanty catalogue of " those writers who, having confined their researches to juridical subjects alone, come under the particular denomination of civilians." He appears at the same time to have been very indifferently acquainted with their personal history: Bynkershoek, who was president of the supreme court of Holland, he describes as a celebrated advocate; and Heineccius, whom every body knows to have been a German, he describes as " a Dutch writer of extensive learning and abilities." But instead of Dutch, his table of errata admonishes us to read Prussian. To some readers, such criticisms as these may appear minute, and even trifling; but we consider it of some consequence to warn the successors of Dr. Bever against this supine method of conducting their researches.

It was the plan of this writer to prosecute his learned enquiries to a much greater extent. " The volume," he remarks, " now respectfully submitted to perusal, (with which his inquiries might properly end), includes the whole history of the Roman laws, so long as they preserved their influence over this immense and variable empire. In the twelfth century, however, they revived in a new shape; not as an uniform body, to be received in any given country by the force of their original authority; but as a plentiful mine of miscellaneous and valuable materials, for the common use of all mankind. In this state, they became connected with the feudal and canon laws, which were generated from the barbarity and superstition of the intermediate ages; while the western world was held in a comfortless suspense between Paganism and Christianity. Every constitution of modern Europe being founded upon an union of these three celebrated systems, it will be a work of no less utility than entertainment, to follow them in their progress to these later times, and to point out their effects upon the government of those countries which have been pleased to adopt them. In the course of this pursuit, due attention will be paid to their various operations in the different parts of the British empire, especially in the maritime and ecclesiastical courts, wherein the civil and canon laws more immediately prevail, under the authority of the legislature. Should the present attempt, therefore, have the good fortune to merit a favourable reception from the public, the remainder will be made the subject of a second volume, as soon as ever the author's professional engagements will afford him leisure." But this plan was never carried into execution; and indeed such an undertaking was probably more laborious and difficult than the learned author might at first imagine.[1]

Dr. Bever's work was soon followed by an historical view of the Roman law, written by another member of the university of Oxford, Mr. Schomberg, a fellow of Magdalen College.[2] His mode of writing is much more

[1] A manuscript work of Dr. Bever, entitled "A short History of the Legal and Judicial Constitution of Great Britain," was lately sold at an auction in Edinburgh, for the sum of 6l. 10s. It is a quarto volume of 132 pages, written in a large and regular hand, and bearing the date of 1759.

[2] An Historical and Chronological View of the Roman Law, with notes and illustrations. By Alexander C. Schomberg, M.A. Fellow of Magdalen College, Oxford. Oxford, 1785, 8vo. It appeared in a French dress, under the title of "Précis Historique et Chronologique sur le Droit

concise, and he was more extensively acquainted with the works of the civilians; but his notices are generally too brief to satisfy the curious enquirer. Schomberg's book was translated into French, and, in that language, passed through more than one edition. But the English civilians have all been totally eclipsed by Mr. Gibbon, who in the forty-fourth chapter of his history has introduced a very able and a very striking sketch, partly historical, of the Roman jurisprudence. Of the necessity of acquainting himself with the Roman law, he seems to have been fully aware when he undertook to write the history of the Roman empire; and although his early studies had not received such a direction, he speedily discerned the spirit of the ancient and modern civilians, and he drew many valuable illustrations from their works. He even obtained, what he perhaps did not anticipate, a conspicuous place among the civilians of the age. Dr. Ferguson did not however profit by this example when he prepared his History of the Roman Republic: he has very rarely availed himself of the same copious source of information; and this cannot but be regarded as a manifest defect in a work which is not without an ample share of merit.[3] It must indeed be admitted that his volumes are deficient in general erudition, and that they display but a small portion of the eloquence which characterizes his earlier Essay on the History of Civil Society.

Romain, avec des notes et des éclaircissemens. Traduit de l'Anglais par M. H. Boulard." Paris, 1793, 12mo. Paris, 1808, 12mo. Mr. Schomberg, who died in the year 1792, is likewise the author of " A Treatise on the Maritime Laws of Rhodes." Oxford, 1786, 8vo.

[3] " In numero illorum prope infinito excellere videntur Britanni duo, Fergusonus et Gibbonus : quorum hic Cæsarum tempora, sive lapsum et interitum imperii Romani, ille liberæ reipublicæ historiam amplexus est." (Holtii Hist. Juris Romani, p. 6.)

A late writer, who was little disposed to doubt the in-
fallibility of his own judgment, has pronounced the following censure of Gibbon's chapter, and the subject to
which it relates. " The chapter," says Mr. Whitaker,
" is long and tiresome, from the ample nature of the
subject, and from the necessary dryness of the disquisition.   But nothing can subdue the native barrenness of
such a field as this." [4]   But the rector of Ruan-Lanyhorne
was no oracle of the civil law ; and here it only seems
necessary to make a very brief reply, in the words of
Menander :

$$\text{Οὐκ ἔστ' ἀνοίας οὐδὲν, ὡς ἐμοὶ δοκεῖ,}$$
$$\text{Τολμηρότερον.}^{5}$$

A different opinion was entertained by Hugo, who
translated this chapter into German, and illustrated it
with notes.[6]   A different opinion was likewise entertained by Warnkoenig, who published it in French, with
more copious illustrations.[7]

[4] Whitaker, Gibbon's History reviewed, p. 52.   Lond. 1791, 8vo.

[5] Menandri et Philemonis Reliquiæ, p. 251. edit. Meineke.

[6] Eduard Gibbon's historische Uebersicht des Römischen Rechts, aus
dem Englischen übersetzt, und mit Anmerkungen begleitet vom Professor Hugo in Göttingen.   Gött. 1789, 8vo.   These annotations have
lately been rendered more accessible to the English reader: " Survey of
the Roman Law, &c. with notes, by Professor Hugo of Göttingen, translated from the German by the Rev. W. Gardiner, LL.D."   Edinb. 1823,
12mo.

[7] Précis de l'Histoire du Droit Romain, par E. Gibbon; traduction
adoptée par M. Guizot. Revu, rectifié, et augmenté de notes, accompagné
d'une Introduction et d'un Tableau synoptique de l'Histoire du Droit
Romain, par L. A. Warnkoenig.   Liége, 1821, 8vo.—Professor Du Caurroy has expressed a more unfavourable opinion, and has pointed out
several inaccuracies in this part of Gibbon's work, with which however
he seems to be only acquainted in the French translation. (Thémis,
tom. ii. p. 485.)   It is, I think, sufficiently evident that the learned pro-

Hugo's translation of this celebrated chapter was published in 1789, and his history of the Roman law made its appearance in the course of the following year.[8] It is in many respects a work of great value, and contains a very able and masterly view of the internal as well as the external history.[9] The spirit of the laws, together with their successive changes and modifications, are generally traced in a striking, and very often in a satisfactory manner. It is the production of a writer possessing great natural perspicacity, improved by long and assiduous study. To many readers it is a subject of regret that this history is written in the German language, and that the author's style is not remarkably unentangled and perspicuous. The work has been translated into French, unfortunately not by a lawyer, but by a physician;[1] and the learned author is

fessor has not duly appreciated his rapid and masterly sketch, to which it would not perhaps be easy to find a parallel in the writings of the professed civilians.

[8] This work has now reached the eleventh edition: "Lehrbuch der Geschichte des Römischen Rechts bis auf Justinian." Berlin, 1832, 8vo. As a companion to it, we may here mention Hugo's "Lehrbuch der Geschichte des Römischen Rechts seit Justinian, oder der juristischen und meist civilistischen gelehrten Geschichte." Berlin, 1830, 8vo. This is the third edition. Nor must we overlook another curious and valuable work of the same author: "Beyträge zur civilistischen Bücherkenntniss der letzten vierzig Jahre, aus den Göttingischen gelehrten Anzeigen und den Vorreden, besonders zu den Theilen des civilistischen Cursus, zusammen abgedruckt und mit Zusätzen begleitet." Berlin, 1828-9 2 Bde. 8vo.

[9] Professor Schilling of Leipzig, another very able civilian, has published a volume, containing upwards of 400 pages, under the subsequent title: "Bemerkungen über Römische Rechtsgeschichte. Eine Kritik über Hugo's Lehrbuch der Geschichte des Römischen Rechts bis auf Justinian." Leipzig, 1829, 8vo.

[1] Histoire du Droit Romain, &c. Paris, 1822, 2 tom. 8vo.

far from being satisfied with this version, although it was revised by M. Poncelet, lecturer on the history of law in the university of Paris. Several years have elapsed since a Latin translation was commenced " a literarum et juris Romani cultore Batavo," that is, I believe, by Engelbronner, a doctor of Leyden; but the scheme appears to have been abandoned for want of sufficient encouragement. As Warnkoenig had undertaken to add a preface and notes, this publication had a fair claim to public favour, and, if brought to a conclusion, it would have proved more satisfactory to many English readers than either the German original or the French version.[2]

Gibbon has introduced a new method of arranging the principal eras in the history of the law. " The revolution," he remarks, " of almost one thousand years, from the twelve Tables to the reign of Justinian, may be divided into three periods almost equal in duration, and distinguished from each other by the mode of instruction and the character of the civilians." The first period extends from the age of the twelve Tables to the birth of Cicero; the second from the age of Cicero to that of Alexander Severus;[3] and the third from the age of Alexander to that of Justinian. This arrangement has been adopted by Hugo, who however has necessarily ascended to an earlier era.

[2] Historia Juris Romani usque ad Justinianum, auctore G. Hugo, &c. Præfatus est et notas literarias adjecit L. A. Warnkoenig, J. U. D. &c. Vol. primum. Amst. 1827, 8vo.

[3] The legislation of this emperor has been copiously illustrated in a work bearing the following inscription: " Aurelii Alexandri Severi, Imperatoris Romani, Axiomata Politica et Ethica. Ejusdem Rescripta universa, Alexandri Chassanæi commentariis illustrata. Ad Regem Christianissimum. Secunda editio." Paris. 1635, 4to.

The French revolution had at first a very unfavourable influence on the study of ancient literature and
ancient jurisprudence. Many of the principal actors in
its dreadful scenes were chiefly distinguished by vulgar
and unmitigated ferocity. The nation had too much
cause to complain of real grievances, and many essential
changes were expedient and even necessary; nor was it
altogether unnatural, in such a situation, for the minds
of men to be impelled with a blind and undiscriminating
zeal to alter whatever had been long established. The
study of the civil law languished in the native country of
Cujacius; nor did it begin to revive till after the restora-
tion of the ancient dynasty. While France was yet controlled by " the destiny of the emperor," M. Dupin,
an eminent advocate of Paris, attempted to publish a
very brief historical sketch of the Roman law; but as
some of his reflections on the past were supposed to admit of an inconvenient application to present times, his
harmless little work did not elude the vigilance of the
police. The first edition is said to have been suppressed in 1809,[4] and the second was not published till
after an interval of ten years.[5] A more copious work on
the same subject was soon afterwards produced by M.
Berriat St. Prix, a professor of law in the university of
Paris.[6] This history was not altogether unsuited to
the exigencies of the age and nation; but it has not re-

[4] See however what is stated in the " Revue de Législation et de Jurisprudence, publiée sous la direction de M. L. Wolowski," tom. iii. p. 67.

[5] Précis Historique du Droit Romain, depuis Romulus jusqu'à nos
jours. Par M. Dupin, Avocat à la Cour Royale de Paris. Paris, 1819,
12mo.

[6] Histoire du Droit Romain, suivie de l'Histoire de Cujas. Par M.
Berriat-Saint-Prix, Professeur de Procédure Civile, et de Droit Criminel,
à la Faculté de Droit de Paris. Paris, 1821, 8vo.

ceived unqualified praise from the civilians of other countries. It was reviewed in a somewhat sarcastic tone by Professor Rossi, who has evinced himself very capable of estimating the merits and defects of such a performance.[7] It solely relates to the external history; and we must admit that some portions of it are too superficial to be either interesting or useful. The author is unfortunately ignorant of the German language; and his acquaintance with the German civilians who have written in Latin, is very far from being extensive. The most valuable part of his volume is the appendix, which contains the most elaborate and satisfactory life of Cujacius that has hitherto appeared.[8]

They formerly ordered these things better in Poland, which is now subjected to the caprice of an insane and ferocious despot. Dr. Macieiowski, professor of the civil law in the university of Warsaw, published his historical work in 1820, and a second edition appeared in 1825.[9]

---

[7] Annales de Législation et de Jurisprudence, tom. ii. p. 383.

[8] Supplementary notices of Cujacius, communicated by Savigny and Berriat St. Prix, occur in the Thémis, ou Bibliothèque du Jurisconsulte, tom. iv. p. 193, 385.

[9] Historia Juris Romani. Scripsit Wenceslaus Alexander Macieiowski, J. U. D. Lycei et Universitatis Litterariæ Varsaviensis Professor, &c. Editio secunda. Varsaviæ, 1825, 8vo. After the German fashion, the work has two separate titles; the first of which is, " Principiorum Juris Romani tomus I. Historiam hujus ipsius Juris continens." Other two volumes are required to complete the author's plan; but this volume, embracing the external history of the law, may of itself be considered as forming an entire work. The prolegomena, extending to twenty-two pages, contain several interesting discussions, well calculated to give the reader a favourable impression of his acuteness and intelligence. In p. 11. he has inadvertently confounded Frontinus with Fronto: " Frontinus, cujus opera invenit nuper Angelus Majus." Frontinus has long been known as a writer on the stratagems of war: the

o

He has evinced an intimate acquaintance with the writings
of all the eminent civilians of Germany: he is fully
apprized of all the recent discoveries and speculations;
and possessing a sound and enlightened spirit of criticism,
he is always capable of applying his knowledge to a useful
purpose.   He is evidently a person of an acute intellect,
improved by systematic and persevering study, and is
little disposed to adopt without examination the statements or inferences of former writers.   Possessing such
qualifications as these, he has undertaken a task which is
by no means easy, but for which he is eminently prepared.
Of his Latinity we cannot indeed speak without some
small abatement of this general commendation: the
words which he employs are sometimes barbarous in
their origin or in their application; [1] and his combinations
of words are occasionally liable to objections equally
valid.   But if he does not rise to the elegance of Gravina,
neither does he descend to the barbarism of Thomasius:
he generally expresses himself, if not with idiomatic
purity, at least with vivacity; and, in one word, he uniformly writes like a man of talents.   In the general plan
of his work, he in a great measure adheres to the sub-
divisions of Gibbon and Hugo.   The history of each era
is distributed into three sections, which are again subdivided into different chapters.   The first section relates

fragments of Fronto were recently discovered by Angelo Mai, and after
having been published by him, were again edited by Niebuhr.

[1] Thus, for example, he always applies the word *periodus* in the un-
classical signification of a period of time.   The professor of Warsaw is
not however to be compared to a certain provost of Trinity College,
Dublin, who, at the examinations for fellowships, was accustomed to use
such phrases as "*quo* periodo."   See Dr. Duigenan's *Lachrymæ Academicæ*, or the present deplorable State of Trinity College, Dublin, p. 75.
Dublin, 1777, 8vo.

to the political condition of the people; the second to the sources of the law; and the third to the study of the law, including an enumeration of the most celebrated lawyers. His sketches of political history are generally very brief, and frequently very able. He is not a compiler from former compilers; he is not satisfied with borrowing the facts, and repeating the observations of his predecessors, but is always disposed to examine and judge for himself. In investigating the primitive history of Rome, he evinces his acuteness as well as his learning. This portion of history is involved in doubts and difficulties, which we can scarcely hope to see removed or overcome: here, as in many other cases, it is not so easy to build as to demolish. Of the historical labours of Niebuhr he expresses no unfavourable opinion, so far as relates to the ability of the author; but he is by no means prepared to acquiesce in all his conclusions.

Dr. Schweppe, who was successively a professor at Kiel and Göttingen, and afterwards a judge of the court of appeal at Lübeck, published a work which embraces the internal as well as the external history of the law.[2] Some errors, contained in the first edition, were corrected in the second, which made its appearance in 1828. The author died in the course of the following year. A history of the Roman law, upon a more ample scale, was about the same period undertaken by Dr. Zimmern, a professor in the university of Jena. The first volume was very favourably received; and, after an interval of three years, it was followed, not by the second, but by

[2] Römische Rechtsgeschichte und Rechtsalterthümer, mit erster vollständiger Rücksicht auf Gajus. Von Albrecht Schweppe, Dr. ehemaligem Professor zu Kiel und zu Göttingen, jetzigem Oberappellationsrathe zu Lübeck. Göttingen, 1822, 8vo.

the third volume.[3]   The learned author did not live to complete his plan; but it is expected that the intermediate portion of the work will be supplied by an individual competent to the task.

Something approaching to a history of the Roman law was published by Mr. Burke in the year 1827.[4]   The author, who at first concealed his name, was evidently a scholar and a man of talents; but he was not sufficiently acquainted with the writings of his predecessors, and therefore laboured under some obvious disadvantages. The only historians of the civil law whom I remember to have seen quoted in his book are Gravina, Heineccius,

---

[3] Geschichte des Römischen Privatrechts bis Justinian.   Von Dr. Sigmund Wilhelm Zimmern, ordentlichem Professor des Rechts in Jena. Erster Band.   Heidelberg, 1826.   Dritter Band.   Heidelberg, 1829, 8vo. The third volume is published separately, with the following title: " Der Römische Civilprozess in geschichtlicher Entwicklung bis auf Justinian."

[4] An Historical Essay on the Laws and the Government of Rome; designed as an Introduction to the Study of the Civil Law.   Cambridge, 1827, 8vo.   Camb. 1830, 8vo.   The first edition is anonymous; the second exhibits the name of the author, Edmund Plunkett Burke, Esq. of the Inner Temple, Barrister at Law.   My remarks, originally printed in 1829, are more particularly applicable to the first edition.   The author, who derived his lineage from Ireland, was born at Lisbon in the year 1802.   He received the rudiments of his education in England; and having afterwards spent three years in the Lyceum of Caen, in Normandy, he was entered of Caius College, Cambridge, where he took the degree of A. B.   He was a young man of no ordinary talents, but was depressed by res angusta domi, and became too desultory in his habits.   Unaided by other influence, the ability displayed in his Historical Essay, added to his proficiency in the French language, procured him in 1832 an appointment as one of the judges of St. Lucia, in the West Indies; and about a year after his arrival in that colony, the governor, General Farquhar, nominated him judge of the vice-admiralty court.   He died in 1835, in consequence of an injury which he had received at Dominica during a dreadful hurricane.   (Law Magazine, vol. xiii. p. 533.)

Hugo, and Berriat St. Prix. Hugo, of whose merits he seems to be fully aware, is only quoted in the French translation; and we may safely suppose the English author to be altogether unacquainted with the German language, which however is a very necessary acquisition for any person who now undertakes to write the history of the Roman jurisprudence. This ingenious writer concludes his work with the following paragraph: " The tide of desolation which inundated the whole of Europe during the early part of the middle ages, and swept away every vestige of civilization, carried with it the venerable fabric of the Roman jurisprudence. Those mutilated remains of it which had been inserted in the code of Alaric were all that were preserved; and it was not till the beginning of the twelfth century that the productions of Justinian's reign were rescued from oblivion. The eagerness with which they were then sought after, and the ardour with which they were studied throughout Europe, are well known to all who are conversant with the literary history of those times. And let it be remarked that the influence which the Roman law rapidly acquired was due to its intrinsic merits alone. Those who have pretended, on the authority of a few detached sentences, that the whole system was calculated to further the interests of despotism, have only shewn their entire ignorance of it. The zeal with which the study of it was cultivated, could have no such motive. The adoption of the many rules of legal wisdom, with which, by the confession of its most determined opponents, it abounds, did not necessarily entail a submission to two or three constitutional doctrines, which stand isolated as it were from the body of the law. By far the greater part of its regulations were quite as well fitted to a free as to

a despotical constitution: many of them, indeed, had
been actually framed at a time when Rome was a republic,
and the change of dynasty had altered nothing of their
spirit.   It was [as] a 'collection of written reason,' the
most flattering appellation a body of law can receive, that
the civil law of Rome forced its way into the favour of
the very small portion of the community, which, at the
time of its discovery, was competent to understand the
language in which it was written, or to appreciate its
merits.   The regulations that had maintained the order
and harmony of society in Rome, were found to be
equally capable of producing the same effects in France,
in Germany, or in modern Italy; and their intrinsic value
was enhanced by their practical utility.   It is not true,
therefore, that motives of personal interest, or of party
spirit, led to their adoption among the different nations
of Europe.   The nation among whom they had originated
was no more: neither the majesty of her name, nor the
terror of her arms, could longer inspire veneration, or
enforce submission; yet her laws were respected and
obeyed.   Even now, ages after the downfall of the Roman
empire, they still remain in force, and are unquestionably
the chief surviving record of its former greatness."   This
passage I quote with the double view of evincing that he
is no despicable writer, and that his information is nevertheless too limited for an historian of the civil law.
Here we have the antiquated tale of the temporary extinction of all knowledge of the Roman jurisprudence,
together with an obvious allusion to the sudden resuscitation after the notable siege of Amalfi.   For this student
of Cambridge, Savigny has in vain written his history of
the Roman law during the middle ages.

These are among the more conspicuous writers who

have undertaken to unfold the history of the Roman law; but to this list many other names might be added, provided we were to include all the authors who have presented, in whatever form, their contributions to this department of historical jurisprudence. Selchow, Martini,[5] Günther, Dabelow, and many others, have published more brief sketches. In the form of an outline for the use of his students, an able and judicious little work was prepared by Holtius, while a professor in the university of Louvain.[6] Since that period, he has returned to Holland, and he now occupies a chair at Utrecht. Of a similar denomination, the most recent work that has fallen under my inspection is that of Dr. Burchardi, a professor in the university of Kiel.[7]

The Roman jurisprudence, which has exercised an indirect influence in every civilized country of Europe, has immediately given rise to two systems of law, which long continued to regulate the civil and ecclesiastical affairs of modern nations. The first of these is the feudal, which is so intimately connected with the civil law, that the one is not unfrequently regarded as a component part of the other. The remaining system is denominated the canon law, well known to those who are familiarly acquainted with the history of the Romish

[5] Caroli Antonii de Martini, S. C. R. A. M. in Supremo Judiciorum Tribunali a Consiliis Aulicis, et P. P. O. Ordo Historiæ Juris Civilis, in usum Auditorii vulgatus. Editio tertia. Viennæ, 1770, 8vo.

[6] Historiæ Juris Romani Lineamenta. Quibus in academica institutione uteretur, adumbravit Adr. Cath. Holtius, Juris Professor in Academia Lovaniensi. Leodii, 1830, 8vo.

[7] Geschichte und Institutionen des Römischen Rechts. Ein Leitfaden für Vorlesungen von Dr. G. C. Burchardi, ordentlichem Professor des Rechts in Kiel, und Mitgliede mehrerer gelehrten Gesellschaften. Altona, 1834, 8vo.

church. A brief account of the general texture of both may perhaps be considered as no useless or superfluous supplement to the preceding observations.

The feudal law is that system of Gothic jurisprudence which reached its full maturity during the middle ages, and which long continued to regulate the tenure of real property in the principal countries of Europe. The relations of lord and vassal have undergone very essential changes, the knight no longer holds his estate on the condition of military service, and most of the feudal incidents have been gradually superseded as unsuitable to the spirit of modern times; but this law has left many deep traces behind it, and is so closely interwoven with our national institutions, that it could not without great difficulty be entirely disentangled. Where the substance has almost totally vanished, the form is in some instances not very advantageously retained.

Of the word feud many different etymologies have been proposed. According to Somner, who treads in the steps of Selden and Spelman, feud is a German compound, which consists of *feh, feo,* or *feoh,* signifying a salary, stipend, or wages, and of *hade, head,* or *hode,* signifying quality, kind, or nature; so that, in its primary acceptation, feudum, or land held in fee, was such as was held in *fee-hode,* by contraction *feud* or *feod;* that is, in a stipendiary way, with the acknowledgment of a superior, and a condition of returning some service for it, on the withdrawing of which, the land was revertible to the superior.[8] Sir Martin Wright has remarked that " this etymon not only suggests the most probable account of

---

[8] Somner's Treatise of Gavelkind, p. 106. Lond. 1660, 4to.

the word, but gives us the clearest description of the thing itself."[9]

The origin of the feudal system is a question which has been long and much agitated, and different authors have arrived at very different conclusions. "It has puzzled the learned," says Dr. Stuart, "to discover the nation of the barbarians which first gave a beginning to fiefs. No inquiry could be more frivolous. In all of them they must have appeared about the same period; and they prevailed in all of them in consequence of the similarity of their situation on their conquests, and in consequence of their being governed by the same customs. It is not therefore to the principle of imitation that their universality is to be ascribed."[1] But the most comprehensive and the most decided opinion is that of Mr. Pinkerton, who avers that "the feudal system, about which so much noise is made, is the natural fruit of conquest, and is as old in the world as conquest. A territory is acquired, and the state, or the general, bestows it on the leaders and soldiers, on condition of military service, and of tokens acknowledging gratitude to the donors. It was known in the Greek heroic ages. It was known to Lycurgus, for all the lands of Sparta were held on military tenure. It was known to Romulus, when he regulated Rome. It was known to Augustus, when he gave lands to his veterans, on condition that their sons should, at fifteen years of age, do military service. The reason it did not preponderate and corrupt in Greece and Rome was, that it was stifled by the necessary effects of cities, as above mentioned. In Persia, where there were no cities of any power or privilege, it preponderated

[9] Wright's Introduction to the Law of Tenures, p. 4.
[1] Stuart's View of Society in Europe, p. 218. Edinb. 1778, 4to.

and corrupted at an early period. The feudal system, whether in its original democracy, or corrupted into aristocracy, must limit the power of kings; for men who hold their possessions on military service, must of course have arms in their hands: and even in absolute governments the soldiers are free, witness the prætorian bands and armies of imperial Rome, and the Turkish janisaries. By the feudal system every man held arms and freedom in his hands.   Montesquieu has begun his account of the feudal system with that of the ancient Germans, given by Tacitus,[2] and prides himself in leaving off where others began. A writer more profound would leave off where Montesquieu begins."[3]   This last sentence may be considered as a modest attempt at impressing the reader with an opinion that Pinkerton is a writer more profound than Montesquieu; but, without acquiescing in all his notions, we may at least admit that of the feudal system many authors have taken a view much too narrow and limited.   The peculiar relation of lord and vassal, of territorial grants and the tenure of military service, is

[2] Montesquieu de l'Esprit des Lois, liv. xxx. chap. ii. seq.—Dr. Stuart commences his researches from the same point. " In the manners of the ancient Germans," he remarks, " I have found the source and spirit of the feudal law." See likewise the elaborate work of Meyer, Esprit, Origine et Progrès des Institutions Judiciaires des principaux Pays de l'Europe, tom. i. p. 4.   Haye, 1819-23, 6 tom. 8vo.

[3] Pinkerton's Dissertation on the Origin and Progress of the Scythians or Goths, p. 139. Lond. 1787, 8vo.—The same modest and candid writer has thus discussed the merits of a great historian: "Mr. Hume, who knew nothing about Goths, nor the Gothic constitution, who is so shallow, that, far from reaching the bottom, he has not reached the bottom of the surface, but merely skimmed its top, observes in his own Life, that it is ridiculous to look on the English constitution as a regular plan of liberty before the death of Charles I. A profound remark truly, and most sagacious !" (Dissertation, p. 142).

doubtless to be traced in very remote ages and countries. All the feudal incidents it may often be difficult to detect; but wherever we find portions of land granted to military vassals under the condition, express or implied, of following the standard of their lord, we there find the most essential characters of the feudal system. The order of chivalry may not be found completely engrafted: there may be no denomination equivalent to that of knight, and such incidents as those of relief, aids, and wardships, may be wanting; but instead of a faint analogy, there may still be a very close resemblance between one system and another.

" It has been very common," says Mr. Hallam, " to seek for the origin of feuds, or at least for analogies to them, in the history of various countries. But, though it is of great importance to trace the similarity of customs in different parts of the world, because it guides us to the discovery of general theorems as to human society, yet we should be on our guard against seeming analogies, which vanish away when they are closely observed. It is easy to find partial resemblances to the feudal system. The relation of patron and client in the Roman republic is not unlike that of lord and vassal, in respect of mutual fidelity; but it was not founded on the tenure of land nor military service. The veteran soldiers, and, in later times, some barbarian allies of the emperors, received lands upon condition of public defence; but they were bound not to an individual lord, but to the state. Such a resemblance to fiefs may be found in the zemindaries of Hindostan, and the timariots of Turkey. The clans of the Highlanders [1] and Irish followed their chieftain

---

[1] " They are at present," says Dr. Smollett, " as free and independent of their chiefs as the law can make them; but the original attachment

into the field; but their tie was that of imagined kindred and respect for birth, not the spontaneous compact of vassalage. Much less can we extend the name of feud, though it is sometimes strangely misapplied, to the polity of Poland and Russia.[5] All the Polish nobles were equal in rights, and independent of each other; all who were less than noble, were in servitude. No government can be more opposite to the long gradations and mutual duties of the feudal system."[6]

Macieiowski, a learned civilian of our own age, discovers manifest vestiges of the feudal system among the ancient inhabitants of Tuscany.[7] To the ancient relation of patron and client, the origin of feudal tenures was traced by Budæus, one of the first lawyers in modern times who applied a very ample store of classical erudition to the illustration of Roman jurisprudence.[8] The same opinion was adopted by Zasius, but it has deservedly been rejected by most of the subsequent commentators;

still remains, and is founded on something prior to the feudal system, about which the writers of this age have made such a pother, as if it was a new discovery, like the Copernican system. Every peculiarity of policy, custom, and even temperament, is affectedly traced to this origin, as if the feudal constitution had not been common to almost all the nations of Europe. For my part, I expect to see the use of trunk-hose and buttered ale ascribed to the influence of the feudal system." (Miscellaneous Works, vol. vi. p. 275.)

[5] With respect to the state of vassalage in those two countries, consult Mr. Coxe's Travels into Poland, Russia, Sweden, and Denmark, vol. i. p. 118. 137. vol. ii. p. 93. 110. Lond. 1784, 2 vols. 4to.

[6] Hallam's View of the State of Europe during the Middle Ages, vol. i. p. 200. sec. edit. Lond. 1819, 3 vols. 8vo.

[7] Macieiowski Historia Juris Romani, p. 36. " Antiquitus non videntur pertinuisse ad *populum* nisi patricii, moribus Etruscorum id ita serentibus; apud quos minime totus populus libertate gavisus est, sed jus, quod dicitur feudale, ibi valuit."

[8] Budæi Annotationes in Pandectas, p. 359. edit. Paris. 1535, fol.

nor is it easy to acquiesce in the speculation of Connanus, who deduces the principles of this law from the fraternities of Soldurii among the ancient Gauls.[9] The assignment of lands by the Roman emperors makes a nearer approach to the proper point. After Augustus had supplanted his rivals, he parcelled certain lands in Italy among his veteran soldiers;[1] and to the classical reader it is well known that, upon this occasion, Virgil was deprived of his little patrimony. The example was followed by other emperors. Alexander Severus allotted to officers and soldiers various lands which had been acquired on the frontiers, and which were to descend to their heirs on the condition of performing military service. This was a plan for securing a permanent guard in the outposts of the empire; and, as Taurellus and Gothofredus have remarked, it bears some resemblance to the feudal system;[2] but Hotman has very clearly pointed out the

[9] Connani Commentariorum Juris Civilis tom. i. f. 119. Paris. 1553, 2 tom. fol.—See Cæsar de Bello Gallico, lib. iii. cap. xxii. and Gebaveri Vestigia Juris Germanici antiquissima in C. Cornelii Taciti Germania obvia, p. 148. Gottingæ, 1766, 8vo.

[1] The example had however been set by Julius Cæsar; who to his veteran legions "assignavit et agros, sed non continuos, ne quis possessorum expelleretur." (Suetonii Julius Cæsar, § 38.)

[2] Taurelli de Militiis ex casu, ad Ant. Augustinum Epistola, p. 83. Gothofredus ad Cod. Theodos. lib. vii. tit. xv. p. 305. "Quæ pleraque ad feudorum naturam proxime accedunt," says this most able commentator. Haloander supposes feuds to be mentioned in the Novels under the name of *militiæ*. "Animus erat in finem adjicere Feudorum Consuetudines, quas veteres appellare solebant jura militiarum, et Imp. nominat στρατείας." See his dedication prefixed to Novellarum Constitutionum Dn. Justiniani Principis, quæ exstant, et ut exstant, Volumen. Norembergæ, 1531, fol. This opinion has however been refuted by different writers. "Militiæ enim," says Contius, "fuerunt officia certa ministris magistratuum assignata, quæ pecunia vendi poterant, et ideo in commercio erant, ut fuit officium apparitorum. Apparet ergo multum differre

distinction between these military retainers and the feudal vassals.[3]

Sir Thomas Craig has not overlooked the strong resemblance between the feudal tenures and the Turkish timars.[4] " The Spahyes," says Dr. Thomas Smith, " are another great support of the Turkish empire; soldiers who are obliged to serve on horseback by the tenure of the lands *(timars)* and estates they are possest of; these being not only the reward of their sweat and blood, but ties and obligations to further service in the field upon the first summons; each bringing so many horses with him according to the value of what he holds, which is the reason they do not receive an asper of pay out of the Grand Signior's exchequer, and are therefore known by the name of Timar-Spahyes, or *Feudatory*, to distinguish them from other Spahyes who live in the cities, and have not obtained a piece of land."[5] A more recent author represents this military establishment as still unchanged. " These," says Dr. Walsh, "are a kind of feudal cavalry, possessing hereditary lands, on the tenure of appearing in the field when called on. If they have no male children the lands devolve to the commander, who assigns them to others on the same terms, and so the corps is kept up. It consists of sixteen legions; who are perhaps the best mountain horsemen in the world."[6] Major Denham dis-

militiam a feudo. Nam militia est jus personæ; feudum in rebus immobilibus et quasi in possessione consistit." (Fornerii et Contii Tractatus de Feudis, p. 84. Leovardiæ, 1694, 8vo.)

[3] Hotomani Disputatio de Feudis, p. 10. Lugduni, 1573, fol.

[4] Cragii Jus Feudale, p. 27. edit. Baillie. Edinb. 1732, fol.

[5] Smith's Remarks upon the Manners, Religion, and Government of the Turks, p. 133. Lond. 1678, 8vo.

[6] Walsh's Narrative of a Journey from Constantinople to England, p. 186. Lond. 1828, 8vo.

covered traces of the same system at Bornou in the interior of Africa. " The feudal law," as he informs us, " exists here in full force ; and a man unwilling to serve, provides one or more substitutes, according to his means."[7] Here however we have but an inadequate representation of the feudal system. In the centre of India, this system is to be found in a more complicated and perfect form. Of its present character and condition in Rajast'han, some very curious and interesting details have been furnished by Colonel Tod, who supposes Asia to have been the cradle of feudalism. " The perfection of the system in England," he remarks, "is due to the Normans, who brought it from Scandinavia, whither it was probably conveyed by Odin and the Sacasenæ, or by anterior migrations, from Asia; which would coincide with Richardson's hypothesis, who contends that it was introduced from Tartary. Although speculative reasoning forms no part of my plan, yet when I observe analogy on the subject in the customs of the ancient German tribes, the Franks, or Gothic races, I shall venture to note them. Of one thing there is no doubt—knowledge must have accompanied the tide of migration from the east: and from higher Asia emerged the Asi, the Catti, and the Cimbric Lombard, who spread the system in Scandinavia, Friesland, and Italy."[8] Nor was this system confined to the continental part of Asia: Molina informs us that it prevailed to a great extent in the island

[7] Denham's Narrative of Travels and Discoveries in Northern and Central Africa, p. 150. Lond. 1826, 4to.

[8] Tod's Annals and Antiquities of Rajast'han, or the Central and Western Rajpoot States of India, vol. i. p. 132. Lond. 1829-32, 2 vols. 4to.

of Japan.[9]   That the germ of the feudal system first appeared in Asia, is at least highly probable.   Its earliest
traces have been discovered among the Gothic tribes of
Europe.   Successive swarms of Goths moved towards the
north-western parts of the old world; and when they had
subdued many different nations, it may be presumed that
they settled the conquered provinces according to some
general plan which they had learned in the east.   Of the
Asiatic tribes it is one great characteristic to adhere,
from one century to another, to the customs of their ancestors.   This remark is signally verified in the history
of the Chinese and Hindus; and it seems applicable to
all the other tribes of men who inhabit that quarter of
the globe.

Of the early progress of the feudal system, so able a
delineation has been given by Dr. Stuart, that I am here
tempted to introduce a long extract from his work.   Having quoted a passage from Tacitus,[1] he proceeds with
the subsequent commentary.   " This passage abounds in

---

[9] " Illud obiter dixerim," says Molina, " apud Japonenses nil videri
esse frequentius quam feuda. Cum enim bellis perpetuo in ea ingenti
insula principes inter se contendant, antiquo inter eos more, quæ unusquisque bello obtinet, continuo dividit inter suos duces, et alios quos
diligit, cum onere sibi serviendi in bello, et alia onera præstandi; mutatque
dominos de uno loco in alium, auferendo ab eis quæ possidebant, et alia
eis largiendo. Majores autem dinastæ sub supremo aliquo principe ita
constituti, divisa habent loca, quibus dominantur, in alios sibi inferiores,
cum eisdem oneribus sibi inserviendi in bello et præstandi alia realia onera,
et illi in alios, quousque devenitur ad infimos *tonos*, quos ipsi vocant, qui
similiter dominantur unusquisque in suo oppido, et simili fere lege, ut
vassalli ipsum comitentur in bellum, et servitia alia realia præstent.
Mores tamen et usus feudorum non iidem, sed diversi in aliquibus sunt
apud ipsos ab iis qui in Germania, Gallia, et Italia vigent." (De Justitia
et Jure, tom. ii. col. 1062. edit. Mogunt. 1659, 6 tom. fol.)

[1] Tacitus de Moribus Germanorum, cap. xxvi.

instruction the most important. It informs us that the German had no private property in land, and that it was his tribe which allowed him annually for his support a proportion of territory; that the property of the land was invested in the tribe, and that the lands dealt out to individuals returned to the public, after they had reaped the fruits of them; that, to be entitled to a partition of land from his nation, was the distinction of a citizen; and that, in consequence of this partition, he became bound to attend to its defence, and to its glory. With these ideas, and with this practice, the Germans made conquests. In conformity therefore with their antient manners, when a settlement was made in a province of the empire, the property of the land belonged to the victorious nation, and the brave laid claim to their possessions. A tract of ground was marked out for the sovereign; and, to the inferior orders of men, divisions corresponding to their importance were allotted. But while, in their original seats, such partitions were annual, it was expedient that they should now be invested in the possessor. A more enlarged idea of property had been gradually unfolding itself; and though it was convenient to, and suited the views of a narrow community, to take back its land, the measure was not practicable in an extensive society. Nations were no longer to shift their habitations. The boundaries of particular states were to be respected. The tribe ceasing to wander, the individual was also to be stationary. The lot or partition now received by him, was to continue in his possession, and to be an object of his industry. He was to take root, if I may speak so, in a particular spot. He was to bestow on it his affection; it was to feed and to enrich him with its produce. His family were to feel an interest in his

P

estate; his sons were to succeed him. Heirs were to fail in the blood of the proprietor. It affected him, that the crown or a stranger should possess the subject of his toils and attentions. The powers of sale and donation came to be understood. The right of holding a landed territory with no limitation, and of disposing of it at pleasure, was known and prevailed. . . . When we mount up to the origin of customs, we are to be struck with their simplicity. The lot or partition to the sovereign was to constitute his domains. It was to support his splendour, to defray the expences of government, and to maintain his household. The lot or partition to the individual was to give rise to allodiality. It was the land which was free, which was named *propriety*, in contradistinction to tenure; and, being still the mark of a citizen, it subjected him, as in Germany, to the general obligation of taking arms in defence of the community.[2] But the domains of the sovereign, and the lands of lot or partition to the people, could not exhaust all the territory of a conquest. They were principal and

---

[2] " The allodial lands," as Dr. Stuart remarks, " were enjoyed in full property, and are therefore opposed to feudal or beneficiary possessions, which were received with limitations, and under the burden of military service to the grantors." See Heraldi Quæstionum quotidianarum Tractatus, p. 109. Paris. 1650, fol. The word *al-od* is supposed to be equivalent to *all-hood*, and therefore to indicate completeness of possession. It is synonymous with *udal*, which is employed to denote the right of such lands in Orkney and Zetland; "whereby," as Lord Stair has stated, " without any infeftment, investiture, or other right or writ, they enjoy lands and hereditaments." (Institutions of the Law of Scotland, b. ii. tit. ii. § 11.) See likewise Lord Bankton's Institute of the Laws of Scotland, vol. i. p. 541. This word is evidently borrowed from the ancient Norwegian language. In the Islandic language, *ódal* signifies allodial property, but it also signifies *res derelicta*. (Haldorsonii Lexicon Islandicum, vol. ii. p. 121.) It is not therefore improbable that the term was originally applied to lands which, having been found deserted, were occupied without form or ceremony.

natural objects of attention; yet, after their appointment, there were much extensive property, and many fair possessions. The antient maxims of the people did not allow them to seize these by a precarious occupation. Men who had connected the property of land with the tribe, and not with the individual, could not conceive any title in consequence of which they might arrogate possessions to humour their fancy, or to flatter their pride. Their antient notions continued their operation: the community was concerned with what no man could claim. The lands accordingly which were assigned neither to the sovereign nor to the people, which formed not the domains of the former, nor the partitions of the latter, were the lands of the state or the fisc." [3]

Du Moulin has traced the origin of the feudal law to the Franks, by whom he supposes it to have been introduced into Gaul. [4] Grotius and other writers have, with greater probability, represented it as having been widely diffused at an early period. [5] Lombardy has frequently been regarded as the place of its origin, because to that country we are indebted for the ancient digest of this

[3] Stuart's View of Society in Europe, p. 24.—It is not the object of this sketch to attempt a developement of the feudal system, but merely a faint outline of the history of the feudal law. Besides the different works which I here have occasion to quote, particularly those of Stuart and Hallam, I may refer the English reader to Dr. Robertson's View of the Progress of Society in Europe, prefixed to his History of the Reign of Charles V.

[4] Molinæi Commentarii in Parisienses Consuetudines, p. 10. edit. Genev. 1613, fol.—The same opinion is adopted by many other writers, and, among the rest, by Hervé in his Théorie des Matieres Féodales et Censuelles, tom. i. p. 2.

[5] Grotius de Jure Belli ac Pacis, lib. ii. cap. vii. § 21. See the same illustrious writer's Historia Gotthorum, Vandalorum, et Langobardorun. prol. p. 64. Amst. 1655, 8vo.

consuetudinary law.[6]   The *Feudorum Consuetudines* are
said to have been compiled by Gerardus Niger, who is
likewise called Capagistus, and by Obertus de Orto or
Horto, who were both lawyers and consuls of Milan.[7]
They lived in the reign of Frederick the First, surnamed
Barbarossa, which commenced in 1152, and terminated
in 1190.   Whatever share they might have in preparing
the materials, it may perhaps be suspected that they did
not digest the work in its present form.   Their opinions
are on some occasions placed in opposition to each other,
and are quoted as if from distinct works.   Thus in lib. ii.
tit. li. § 3.   " Similiter si quis investitus fuerit de feudo,
ita ut ad fœminas transiret, et duas filias tantum relique-
rit, quarum una filium habeat, et altera filiam; utrum
post mortem illarum masculus tantum feudum habere debeat?   Secundum Gerardum, masculus tantum : Obertus contra."   And in § 6 of the same title : " Similiter
feudum lege commissoria datum non valet, id est, si ad
certum tempus pecunia non solvatur creditori, ut habeat
in feudum.   Gerardus.   Et secundum Obertum, valet."
On other occasions, both names are subjoined : " Gerardus et Obertus."   It might indeed be conjectured that
the work was arranged by their joint labour; and that

----

[6] Panciroli Thesaurus variarum Lectionum utriusque Juris, p. 130.
Venetiis, 1611, fol.   Giphanii Antinomiæ Juris Feudalis, p. 29.   Francofurti, 1606, 4to.   "Manet igitur verum," says Giphanius, "feuda,
quoad originem, ad clientelas Romanorum, vel ad homines Romanorum
referre posse.   Deinde, feuda sunt ex jure Longobardorum, non si specte-
mus originem, sed si respiciamus ad rerum distinctiones, ordinationes,
constitutiones, statuta, quæ ex moribus et quotidiana observatione Longobardorum fluxerunt."

[7] Dieck's Literärgeschichte des Longobardischen Lehenrechts.   Halle,
1828, 8vo.   Laspeyres über die Entstehung und älteste Bearbeitung der
Libri Feudorum.   Berlin, 1830, 8vo.

when any difference of opinion occurred, they took care
to state it in this formal manner. Du Moulin supposes
Obertus to have been the sole compiler. We are assured
by Odofredus, a commentator on the Code, who lived
about the year 1250, that Hugolinus, otherwise called
Hugo a Porta Ravennate, who died in the year 1168,
added the feudal law to the ninth collation of the Novels,
and that it was received as a tenth collation.[8] Some
writers consider the statement as a mere device, intended
to enhance the authority of this branch of jurisprudence.
The feudal law is commonly subjoined to the *Corpus Juris Civilis,* of which many of the older civilians regarded
it as a component part. " The last tome of the civile
law," says Sir Thomas Ridley, "is the Feudes, that is,
the books of customes and services that the subject or
vassall doth to his prince or lord, for such lands or fees
as he holdeth of him."[9] In the common editions, the
Feudorum Consuetudines are divided into two books; but
the edition of Cujacius, Coloniæ, 1588, 8vo, exhibits a
new arrangement, with a series of five books. The first
book he ascribes to Gerardus, the second and third to
Obertus; the fourth is taken from several ancient
authors, and the fifth consists of imperial constitutions
relative to matters of feudal cognizance. To the common editions in two books, are likewise appended constitutions of several emperors; and two of them, issued by
Henry the Seventh, are described by the term *Extravagantes;* a term which is also used in the canon law, to
denote documents which wander beyond the limits of a

[8] B. G. Struvii Historia Juris, p. 721. Jenæ, 1718, 4to.

[9] Ridley's View of the Civile and Ecclesiasticall Law, p. 68. sec. edit.
Oxford, 1634, 4to.

particular collection.[1]   The work itself is partly composed of such constitutions; and the entire collection closes with an instrument relative to the peace of Constance, *De Pace Constantiæ*, concluded, on the one part, between the emperor Frederick the First, his son Henry king of the Romans, and certain nobles of Germany, and, on the other, various cities of Lombardy, the march of Ancona, and Romagna.

These books of the feudal law are evidently written by individuals familiar with the doctrines and the phraseology of the civil law; and the new system of jurisprudence may be considered as a scion from the old.   The composition necessarily partakes of the general barbarism of the age to which it belongs, nor are the materials reduced to a systematic or lucid form.[2]   Some of the more classical civilians have therefore treated this law of Lombardy with the utmost contempt.[3]   As to the authority

[1] See F. A. Biener's Geschichte der Novellen Justinian's, S. 277. Berlin, 1824, 8vo.

[2] "Stilus forensis est, qualis jurisconsultorum ejus temporis esse potuit : scripti enim sunt seculo inerudito, neque fieri potuit quin aliquod ejus seculi vitium contraxerint.   Verba ipsa Latina, nisi si quæ sint fori propria.   Phrasis, sive, ut grammatici loquuntur, constructio Longobardica est, ut facile quivis sine interprete sensum percipere potest.   Tumultuarie sane sunt conscripti, ex adversariis sive schedis Gerardi et Oberti relictis, ab alio puto quam ipsis collectis.   Obertus enim et Gerardus, prout quæque facti species occurrerat, consulti quid de eo sentirent, scripto declararunt.   Hæc eorum adversaria, post eorum excessum, aliquis juris feudorum studiosus in libros redegit, sine delectu, sine methodo, quod non est negandum: ita tamen eorum responsa celebrata sunt, et in honore habita, ut pro jure certissimo a posteris adhuc sint usurpata." (Cragii Jus Feudale, p. 36.)

[3] "Feuda postremo," says Taurellus, "quæ non minus barbaro quam inepto, et sibi parum constanti, ac vix meo judicio legi digno volumine continentur." (De Militiis ex casu, ad Ant. Augustinum Epistola, p. 81.) See likewise Gravinæ Origines Juris Civilis, p. 103. edit. Mascovii.

which properly belongs to it, the feudalists have entered
into much discussion, and have maintained various opinions. Some of the early writers represent it as having
been sanctioned by different emperors, particularly by
the first three Fredericks, but others consider this sanction as more than doubtful. Craig is induced to suppose
that the feudal law must have derived its authority from
some imperial rescripts, although they have not descended to our time; for he cannot conceive that the emperors would otherwise have permitted it to be taught in
the schools, and observed in the judicatories. Du Moulin, on the other hand, considers the private part of the
compilation as unwritten law, " jus non scriptum," adopted at Milan, and the remainder, the constitutions inter-
spersed, as written law, "jus scriptum," retaining its
force within the limits of the empire.[4] This appears to
be a very sound opinion ; nor do I think it necessary to
mention the various suggestions and speculations of other
writers. In many different countries, this compilation
has been received and partly adopted as consuetudinary
law, and in all those countries has been modified by tacit
usage, or by express enactments, nor has it any other
authority except such as it has thus obtained. The
Lombardic body of law is described as " Feudorum Consuetudines," and " Jus Feudale commune ;" the first
title denoting that it is consuetudinary or unwritten law,
and the second that it has obtained more or less authority
wherever the feudal law has been adopted.

The substance of these books was digested into a new

[4] Molinæi Commentarii in Parisienses Consuetudines, p. 24.—See
likewise Duck de Usu et Authoritate Juris Civilis, f. 35. b. Bitschii Commentarius in Consuetudines Feudorum, p. 14. G. A. Struvii Syntagma
Juris Feudalis, p. 30.

form by Antonius Minuccius a Prato Veteri, a professor
in the university of Bologna, who was born about the
year 1380;[5] and his labours are said to have received the
sanction of the emperor Sigismund, as they certainly did
that of Frederick the Third.[6] Haloander had originally
intended to subjoin it to his edition of the Novels; but
it was not till after a long interval that the work was first
published by Schilter. Another digest of the same materials was afterwards undertaken by Bartholomæus Baraterius or de Barateriis, who was a native of Piacenza,
and was successively a professor at Pavia and Ferrara.
Having completed his work in 1442, he dedicated it to
the duke of Milan. It was first printed at Paris in the
year 1612.[7] Neither of these works seems to have obtained any permanent footing, even in the universities of
Italy. The books of the feudal law were exhibited in a
German dress by Dr. Lorenz Weidmann, who likewise

---

[5] Pancirolus de claris Legum Interpretibus, p. 198. Savigny's Geschichte des Römischen Rechts, Bd. vi. S. 255. Osservazioni e Disserta-
zioni varie sopra il Diritto Feudale, concernenti l'Istoria e le Opinioni di
Antonio da Pratovecchio, celebre Giureconsulto del Secolo xv. e Rifor-
matore dei Libri de' Feudi. Livorno, 1764, 4to. This elaborate volume,
which appeared without the name of the author, was written by Miglio-
rotto Maccioni, a professor in the university of Pisa.

[6] Laspeyres über die Entstehung und älteste Bearbeitung der Libri
Feudorum, S. 126. Berlin, 1830, 8vo. This is a work of much critical
research, and the author, who is now a professor in the university of
Halle, belongs to the school of Savigny. He has more recently published
a work under the following title: "Lex Salica. Ex variis quæ supersunt
recensionibus, una cum Lege Ripuariorum, synoptice edidit, glossas
veteres variasque lectiones adjecit Ernestus Adolphus Theodorus Laspeyres, J. U. D. et in Universitate Fridericiana Halensi cum Vitebergensi
consociata Professor Publicus Ordinarius." Halis Saxonum, 1833, 4to.

[7] The works of Minuccius and Baraterius are subjoined to Schilter's
Codex Juris Feudalis Alemannici. Argentorati, 1695, 4to.

introduced some changes of arrangement. His work, *Die Lehenrecht verdeutscht*, was printed by Schoiffer of Mainz in the year 1530.

The principles of the feudal law had soon begun to be taught in the universities. The text was illustrated by many glosses and commentaries; and many summaries and treatises have from time to time been added. The principal feudalists who preceded his own time, are thus enumerated by Dr. Duck: " Horum librorum authoritatem augent egregii illi jurisconsulti qui ad eos glossas, commentarios, et tractatus scripserint. Glossas in Feuda scripserunt Bulgarus, Pyleus, Ugolinus, Vicentius, Jac. Goffredus, aliique; sed Jac. Columbinus eorum ultimus omnes superavit, et post eum, ait Jason, nemo glossas in Feuda scribere tentavit.[8] Alii summas et tractatus de Feudis composuerunt, Odofredus, Jac. de Arena, Hostiensis, Jac. Ardizoni, Zasius, Rebuffus, Hannetonius, Henr. Rosenthall, aliique, qui omnem Feudorum scientiam amplissime tradiderunt. Commentarios in Feuda scripserunt Jac. de Belvisio, Andr. de Iserma, Baldus, Jac. Alvarottus, Math. de Afflictis, Fr. Curtius, Jac. Cujacius, aliique, in quibus eminet Cujacii elegantia et literarum splendor, authoritas et judicium Jac. de Belvisio et Baldi, quorum ille octies se legisse libros Feudorum Papiæ testatur, Baldus vero commentarios suos scripsit postquam jus civile per quadraginta septem annos professus insignem famam acquisiverat. Et inter hos omnes e glossographis Jacobo Columbino, e summistis Jacobo Ardizoni, e commentariis Jacobo de Belvisio primus locus ab omnibus conceditur."[9] To this enumera-

---

[8] See Savigny's Geschichte des Römischen Rechts im Mittelalter, Bd. v. S. 82. Heidelberg, 1815-31, 6 Bde. 8vo.

[9] Duck de Usu et Authoritate Juris Civilis, f. 38. edit. Lond. 1653, 8vo. A similar account is given by Pancirolus, Thesaurus variarum Lectionum

tion some names ought perhaps to have been added, particularly those of Hotman and Vulteius. Of the more recent commentaries on the text, the most copious is that of Caspar Bitsch, professor of law in the university of Strasburg.[1] Among the systematic treatises which have appeared since the publication of Duck's very useful work, it may be proper to mention the elder Struve's *Syntagma Juris Feudalis*, which contains much information in a form not very elegant or attractive.[2] Many elementary works, such as those of Schilter, Stryk, and G. L. Böhmer, and an immense number of detached dissertations, have from time to time been published in Germany, where every province of jurisprudence is most laboriously cultivated. Of separate tracts on the feudal law, an ample collection was published in Jenichen.[3] Various writers treat of this law as it has been adopted and modified in different countries. Thus the feudal law, as applied in Scotland, has been illustrated with much learning and ability by Sir Thomas Craig, one of the greatest lawyers whom his country has produced. One of the earliest books on the law of England is Thomas Littleton's treatise on tenures; and the feudal law of that country was afterwards discussed by Sir Henry Spelman, Sir Martin Wright, Sir Jeffrey Gilbert, and various other writers.

utriusque Juris, p. 131. Venetiis, 1611, fol. See likewise Rittershusii Partitiones Juris Feudalis, p. 15. edit. Argentorat. 1659, 8vo.

[1] Caspari Bitschii Commentarius in Consuetudines Feudorum. Argentorati, 1673, 4to.

[2] Geo. Ad. Struvii Syntagma Juris Feudalis. Francofurti ad Mœnum, 1703, 4to. This is the eighth edition.

[3] Thesaurus Juris Feudalis, continens optuma atque selectissima Opuscula, quibus Jus Feudale explicatur. Francof. ad Mœn. 1750-4, 3 tom. 4to.

In France the feudal law was embodied in the *loi cou-tumier* of different provinces; and many curious reliques of jurisprudence have thus been preserved. The most interesting of these are perhaps the *Coustumes de Beau-voisis*, digested by Philippes de Beaumanoir.[4] Montesquieu has described it as an admirable work,[5] and has quoted it upon many different occasions. " This treatise of Beaumanoir," says Mr. Barrington, " is so systematical and complete, and throws so much light upon our ancient common law, that it cannot be too much recommended to the perusal of the English antiquary, historian, or lawyer. He kept the courts of the Comte de Clermont, and gives an account of the customary laws of Beauvoisis (which is a district about forty miles to the northward of Paris) as they prevailed in the year 1283. He is consequently a more ancient writer than Littleton, and, to speak with all due reverence of this father of our law, perhaps a better writer. It need hardly be said

[4] Coustumes de Beauvoisis, par Messire Philippes de Beaumanoir, Bailly de Clermont en Beauvoisis, Assises et bons Usages du Royaume de Jerusalem, par Messire Jean d'Ibelin, Comte de Japhe et d'Ascalon, S. de Rames et de Baruth, et autres anciennes Coutumes; le tout tiré des manuscrits, avec des notes et observations, et un glossaire pour l'intelligence des termes de nos anciens autheurs, par Gaspard Thaumas de la Thaumassiere, Ecuyer, S. de Puy-ferrand, Bailly du Marquisat de Château-neuf-sur-Cher, Avocat en Parlement. Bourges, 1690, fol.—Of the *Assises de Jerusalem*, a new and complete edition, in three volumes quarto, was in 1830 announced by Cotta of Stuttgard. The editors are E. H. Kausler and J. C. Bluntschli, who promise a very careful revisal of the text, with copious and various illustrations; and, for the satisfaction of many readers, we may add that they write, not in German, but in Latin. Of the second part, the *Assise de la Court des Borgés*, the original has not yet been printed. Some extracts, relative to maritime law, may be found in Pardessus, *Collection de Lois Maritimes antérieures au XVIIIe Siècle*, tom. i. p. 275. Paris, 1828-34, 3 tom. 4to.

[5] Montesquieu de l'Esprit des Lois, liv. xxvi. chap. xv.

that the customs of the two countries were at this time
very similar, especially of the more northern parts of
France: if we wanted other proof, the commentators on
the oldest French law books cite Littleton as illustrating
their customs."[6] Of the customary laws of France the
other collections are very numerous.[7] Nor must we here
neglect to particularize a very curious relique of early
jurisprudence, the *Assises de Jerusalem*, which are decidedly of a French origin. After the conquest of the holy
city in the year 1099, the barons who led the crusade
elected Godefroy de Bouillon king of Jerusalem; and it
was one of the new sovereign's first cares to form a body
of laws for the government of his subjects. By the counsel of the patriarch, and of his princes and barons, "et
des plus sages homes qu'il pooit avoir," he appointed wise
men to make enquiry at persons from different countries
as to the particular usages of those countries. Having
received the desired information in writing, he again assembled his principal adherents; and having laid this
document before them, and caused it to be read, he
afterwards, with their counsel and concurrence, selected
what to him seemed good, " et en fit assises et usages
que l'on deust tenir et maintenir, et user au royaume de
Jerusalem, par lesquels il, ses gens, et son peuble, et
toutes autres manieres des gens alans, et venans, et de-
morans, fussent governés et menés à droit et à raison el
dit royaume." They were called *Assises* from the circumstance of their having thus been confirmed in an assembly
of the chief persons of the state. They were afterwards
modified and enlarged by this king and his successors;

[6] Barrington's Observations on the more ancient Statutes, p. 439.

[7] See Dupin's edition of Camus's Lettres sur la Profession d'Avocat,
tom. ii. p. 190.

and about the year 1250 were arranged by Jean d'Ibelin, Comte de Japhe et d'Ascalon, Seigneur de Rames et de Baruth. Having been adopted in the kingdom of Cyprus, they were revised in the year 1369 by sixteen individuals nominated in an assembly of the estates of that kingdom. They had been translated into Greek for the benefit of those subjects who did not understand the original language; and of this version some portions have been preserved in the Royal Library at Paris. After Cyprus had fallen under the dominion of the Venetians,[8] the book was translated into the Italian language.[9] It is generally admitted that the laws thus adopted in the kingdoms of Jerusalem and Cyprus, were in a great measure derived from the customs and usages of the kingdom of France.

The feudal system seems to have arrived at maturity during the reign and in the dominions of Charlemagne and his immediate successors. The reliques of their legislation are to be found in the *Capitularia Regum Francorum*. As the empire of Charlemagne not only included France and Germany, but likewise a great portion of Italy, and some portion of Spain, a certain uni-

---

[8] See Johann Paul Reinhards vollständige Geschichte des Königreichs Cypern. Erlangen und Leipzig, 1766-8, 2 Bde. 4to.

[9] Le Assise et bone Vsanze del Reame de Hyervsalem. Venetia, 1535, fol. The volume concludes with the following colophon: "A laude & honor del Omnipotente Iddio, finisce il presente libro, qual è de le Assise & bone Vsanze del Reame de Hierusalem, stampato in Venetia, regnante l'inclito Meser Andrea Gritti, Doxe di Venetia, nelli anni de la Natiuita del Signor nostro MDXXXV. del mese di Marzo, in la stamparia di Aurelio Pincio Venetiano." The name of the translator is Florio Bustron. This translation contains both the laws which relate to *L'alta Corte* and those which relate to *La Corte de li Borgesi*. Both parts may be found in the collection of Canciani, *Barbarorum Leges antiquæ*, vol. ii. p. 479. vol. v. p. 107.

formity of laws and usages was naturally promoted by this political union. "Feudal tenures," it is stated by Mr. Hallam, "were so general in the kingdom of Aragon, that I reckon it among the monarchies which were founded upon that basis. Charlemagne's empire, it must be remembered, extended as far as the Ebro. But in Castille and Portugal they were very rare, and certainly could produce no political effect. Benefices for life were sometimes granted in the kingdoms of Denmark[1] and Bohemia. Neither of these, however, nor Sweden,[2] nor Hungary, comes under the description of countries influenced by the feudal system. That system, however, after all these limitations, was so extensively diffused, that it might produce confusion, as well as prolixity, to pursue the collateral branches of its history in all the countries where it prevailed."[3] The prevalence of the feudal law in Lombardy has already been mentioned; and it sooner or later extended its influence to almost every corner of Italy, including the islands as well as the continental states.[4] In England and Scotland it struck a very deep and vigorous root. Its progress in the former country seems to be correctly stated by Blackstone. "This feudal polity," he remarks, "which was thus by degrees established over all the continent of Europe, seems not to have been received in this part of our

---

[1] See Dansk Lehns Ret af Peder Kofod Ancher. Kiöbenhavn, 1777, 8vo.

[2] Stiernhöök de Jure Sueonum et Gothorum vetusto, p. 276. Holmiæ, 1682, 4to.

[3] Hallam's View of the Middle Ages, vol. i. p. 201.

[4] The Sicilians, says Mr. Brydone, " still boast that they retain more of the feudal government than any nation in Europe. The shadow indeed remains, but the substance is gone long ago." (Tour through Sicily and Malta, vol. ii. p. 225. Lond. 1773, 2 vols. 8vo.)

island, at least not universally, and as a part of the national constitution, till the reign of William the Norman.
Not but that it is reasonable to believe, from abundant
traces in our history and laws, that even in the times of
the Saxons, who were a swarm from what Sir William
Temple calls the same northern hive, something similar
to this was in use; yet not so exclusively, nor attended
with all the rigour that was afterwards imported by the
Normans. For the Saxons were firmly settled in this
island, at least as early as the year 600; and it was not
till two centuries after, that feuds arrived to their full
vigour and maturity, even on the continent of Europe."[5]
Craig supposes the feudal law to have been established
in Scotland before it was established in England;[6] but

[5] Blackstone's Commentaries on the Laws of England, vol. ii. p. 48.
See likewise Dr. Sullivan's Historical Treatise on the Feudal Law, and
the Constitution and Laws of England, p. 18.   Lond. 1772, 4to.

[6] Cragii Jus Feudale, p. 47.   Brussii Principia Juris Feudalis, p. 5.
Edinb. 1713, 8vo.   See Dr. Stuart's Observations concerning the Public
Law and the Constitutional History of Scotland, p. 7.   Edinb. 1779, 8vo.
Lord Kames, whose speculations often rest upon a very insecure foundation, is pleased to express himself in the following terms: " I entertain
some doubts whether the feudal law was introduced into Scotland so early
as in the reign of Malcolm II.   What to me brought this thing first
under suspicion, is a fact that can be made extremely evident.   When
one dives into the antiquities of Scotland and England, it will appear that
we borrowed all our laws and customs from the English.   No sooner is a
statute enacted in England, but, upon the first opportunity, it is introduced into Scotland; so that our oldest statutes are mere copies of theirs.
Let the Magna Charta be put into the hands of any Scotsman, without
giving its history, and he will have no doubt that he is reading a collection
of Scots statutes or regulations.   Now it is a point settled among the best
English antiquaries, that the feudal law was introduced into England by
William the Conqueror.   I need not spend time upon this topick, after
what is said by the accurate Spelman, and by our countryman Craig.
Joining these two things together, a strong presumption arises, that the

this is an opinion which apparently must continue to rest
on conjecture, and not on historical evidence.

The capitularies, which have already been mentioned,
are certain laws enacted under the auspices of kings of
the Frankish race. They are called *capitularia*, by a word
of no classical authority, but derived from *capitulum*, the
diminutive of *caput;* and they are so described from the
circumstance of their being enacted or digested *capitula-
tim*, by heads or chapters.[7] The term is very frequently
used in a general sense, but in other instances capitularies are distinguished from laws.

The laws of the Franks were enacted " consensu populi, constitutione regis." Liberty was the chief inheritance of the ancient people of Germany, nor were they
governed by laws which they had no share in enacting.
It has been remarked by Dr. Stuart, that " the short,
but comprehensive and sentimental work of Tacitus, on
the manners of Germany, is the key to the institutions,
the capitularies, and the codes of the barbarians."[8] In
the opinion of the same able jurist, the foundation and
principles of the Anglo-Saxon constitution are to be
found in the institutions and manners of the ancient Germans; and he has accordingly endeavoured to trace the

---

feudal law made its progress from England to this country, as all the
English statutes, making improvements and alterations upon it, certainly
did. But this presumption receives additional force, when it is considered,
that if we had the feudal law before it came into England, it must have
been taken from some other people than the Normans, with whom we had
no commerce." (Essays upon several Subjects concerning British Antiquities, p. 4. Edinb. 1747, 8vo.) Of such random assertions as these,
it would be superfluous to attempt a formal refutation.

[7] Augustinus de Emendatione Gratiani, p. 327.

[8] Stuart's Historical Dissertation concerning the Antiquity of the English Constitution, p. 108. 2nd edit. Lond. 1771, 8vo.

most essential principles of that constitution to the forests of Germany. But the national assemblies of those who were capable and worthy of bearing arms, appear to have been gradually superseded by a select council, composed of the two orders of the clergy and nobility; and if the great body of the people attended their deliberations, it seems to have been more in the capacity of spectators, than of actual legislators. This was the form of the constitution in the time of Charlemagne, in whose name a great proportion of the capitularies were promulgated, though some of them belong to a more recent, and others to a more early period, the collection commencing with an enactment of king Childebert, dated in the year 554. The capitularies are written in the Latin language, and this task was doubtless performed by the ecclesias-tics. The Latin copies were deposited among the na-tional archives, but the laws were divulged to the people in their mother tongue.[9]

Savigny has supplied the following statement: " The imperial ordinances of the Franks, *capitularia,* which, after the extension of their empire, were distinguished from the national laws, *leges,* arose from the enlargement of the same principle. All royal enactments, particularly in later times, were called capitularia or capitula. The king had a double character; the one, as chief of each individual tribe, and the other, as head of the whole na-tion. Hence the capitularies are of two classes; those defining the laws of a particular race, e. g. " Capitula addita ad Legem Salicam," and those of general appli-cation over the whole Frank territory. In the kingdom

---

[9] Bieneri Commentarii de Origine et Progressu Legum Juriumque Germanicorum, part. i. p. 168.

Q

of the Franks, with which so many different nations were incorporated, the capitularies are so frequently general, under the Carlovingian dynasty, that when their character is not specially fixed, they may be understood as belonging to that class. In Lombardic Italy, on the contrary, where the Lombards and Romans were the only distinct people, most of the ordinances of Charles and his successors must be understood as constituting exclusively Lombardic law. For this reason, probably, they have been inserted in all the early collections of that law, and were consequently never obligatory on the Romans. It is, however, of great importance to determine accurately the limits of the general capitularies. The laws of the race of Charlemagne have been erroneously supposed to apply to all the subjects of their extensive empire. These princes reigned over three distinct kingdoms; the Frankish, Lombardic, and that which, under the name of Rome and the Exarchate, had recently constituted part of the Greek empire. No capitulary, however general, could overstep the boundaries of that state in which it had originated. The only exceptions to this rule were some clerical laws; and their universal validity arose from the unity of the church, and from the common old ecclesiastical authorities, on which they were founded. No example of a similarly general application is found in any of the temporal ordinances." [1]

[1] Savigny's Geschichte des Römischen Rechts im Mittelalter, Bd. i. S. 143. Cathcart's Translation, p. 155. See likewise Eichhorn's *Deutsche Staats-und Rechtsgeschichte*, Th. i. S. 346, and Conringius *De Origine Juris Germanici*, p. 88. edit. Helmestad. 1720, 4to.—The earliest editor of the Capitularies was Vitus Amerpachius, who published at Ingolstadt, in the year 1545, "Præcipuæ Constitutiones Caroli Magni de Rebus ecclesiasticis et civilibus." The history of the various editions we cannot here detail,

And now, as Sir Thomas Ridley speaks, "so much of the civile law, and the bookes thereunto pertaining. Now it followeth that I doe in like order speak of the canon law, which is more hardly thought upon among the people, for that the subject thereof, in many points, hath many grosse and superstitious matters used in the time of papistrie, as of the masse, and such other like trumperie; and yet there are in it, beside, many things of great wisdome."[2] Canon law is a term used to denote the ecclesiastical law sanctioned by the church of Rome, and possessing more or less direct influence in all countries which acknowledge the authority of the pope. The word κάνων signifies a rule, and this word was not at first considered as too feeble to express the claims of the

but must refer our more inquisitive readers to the copious and elaborate preface of Baluze, who has himself surpassed all preceding and all subsequent editors. His great collection appeared under the following title : " Capitularia Regum Francorum. Additæ sunt Marculfi monachi et aliorum Formulæ veteres, et notæ doctissimorum virorum. Stephanus Baluzius Tutelensis in unum collegit, ad vetustissimos codices manuscriptos emendavit, magnam partem nunc primum edidit, notis illustravit." Paris. 1677, 2 tom. fol. This valuable work was long afterwards reprinted in Italy, Venetiis, 1771. 2 tom. fol. Another edition, for which Baluze had himself made preparations, was published by Pierre de Chiniac: " Nova editio, auctior et emendatior ad fidem autographi Baluzii, qui de novo textum purgavit, notasque castigavit et adjecit. Accessere vita Baluzii, partim ab ipso scripta, catalogus operum hujus viri clarissimi," &c. Paris. 1780, 2 tom. fol. This edition is splendidly printed, but is somewhat disfigured by a French translation of the preface, exhibited column for column. The Capitularies may likewise be found in Georgisch's *Corpus Juris Germanici antiqui*, Halæ, 1738, 4to., and in Canciani's *Leges Barbarorum antiquæ*, Venetiis, 1781-92, 5 tom. fol. On the subject of the Formulæ, a recent work appeared with the subsequent title: " Commentatio de Marculfinis aliisque similibus Formulis, Liber singularis. Auctor Dr. J. A. L. Seidensticker." Jenæ, 1818, 4to.

[2] Ridley's View of the Civile and Ecclesiasticall Law, p. 73.

church to the obedience of her children; but, in the progress of priestly usurpation, the successor of St. Peter began to arrogate a more ample and definite jurisdiction, and to extend his regulations to many causes which are not strictly ecclesiastical. The stupendous fabric of papal dominion attained its full height in the eleventh century, under the auspices of Hildebrand, who was elected in the year 1073, and assumed the name of Gregory VII. It was one of his dictates that the church of Rome has never erred, and, according to the testimony of Scripture, never shall err;[3] and after this maxim was fully admitted, nothing remained to obstruct the progress of spiritual arrogance. What had formerly been described as a *rule*, was now dignified with the name of *law;* and from this period, a period of the deepest ignorance and superstition, the canon law obtained great influence in most countries of Europe. After the foundation of those seminaries of learning which we denominate universities, it acquired a distinguished place among the other faculties; and a knowledge of the canon law became a common road to the highest honours. It is a maxim of the commentators, that a Doctor of the Canon Law is to be preferred to a Doctor of Divinity in such dioceses as do not contain many heretics.[4]

The canon law is derived from many different sources. To the civil law its obligations are deep and extensive. The authority of the Scriptures cannot be entirely disregarded; but the writings of the fathers and doctors of the church, the decrees of councils, and the decretals of

---

[3] Mastricht Historia Juris Ecclesiastici et Pontificii, p. 297. Amst. 1686, 8vo.

[4] Lancelotti Institutiones Juris Canonici, tom. i. p. 232. edit. Doujat. Paris. 1685, 2 tom. 12mo.

popes, are much better adapted to the general views of the canonists.

The Greek church has bequeathed various reliques, which cannot be safely neglected by those who investigate the history of the canon law, as well as the general history of the church. Its *Codex Canonum*[s] is confirmed by the 131st Novel of Justinian, and is therefore considered as a portion of the civil law. From this collection the emperor borrowed those ecclesiastical constitutions which occur in the Code and Novels. We cannot however pursue this branch of enquiry, but shall merely direct the reader's attention to two very elaborate publications. The first of these is the " Bibliotheca Juris Canonici veteris : ex antiquis codicibus MSS. bibliothecæ Christophori Justelli, opera et studio Gulielmi Voelli et Henrici Justelli." Lutetiæ Paris. 1661, 2 tom. fol. For the other we are indebted to Dr. Beveridge, the very learned bishop of St. Asaph: " Συνοδικὸν, sive Pandectæ Canonum SS. Apostolorum, et Conciliorum ab Ecclesia Græca receptorum; nec non canonicarum SS. Patrum Epistolarum : una cum scholiis antiquorum singulis eorum annexis, et scriptis aliis huc spectantibus." Oxonii, 1672, 2 tom. fol. This publication was followed by his " Codex Canonum Ecclesiæ primitivæ vindicatus et illustratus." Lond. 1678, 4to. Nor must we here neglect to mention a very recent work by Professor Biener of Berlin: " De Collectionibus Canonum Ecclesiæ Græcæ Schediasma litterarium." Berolini, 1827, 8vo.

---

[s] Codex Canonum Ecclesiæ universæ, a Justiniano confirmatus. Christophorus Justellus, J. C. nunc primum restituit, ex Græcis codicibus editis et MSS. collegit et emendavit, Latinum fecit, et notis illustravit. Paris. 1610, 8vo.

Of the rules or laws received by the Latin church, there were many ancient collections. Dionysius Exiguus, an abbot who flourished about the beginning of the sixth century, formed two different compilations, one of the canons of the church, another of the decretals of the bishop of Rome; and this was the earliest collection of decretals. These were followed by the collections of Fulgentius Ferrandus, who flourished soon afterwards; of Isidorus Hispalensis, who was bishop of Seville from 595 to 636; of Cresconius, who flourished about the year 690; of Isidorus Mercator, otherwise called Pecca- tor, who wrote about the year 830, and is described as " impostor nequissimus;"[6] and of various other compilers, of whose labours we cannot at present enter into a full detail.[7] Burchardus, who was bishop of Worms from 996 to 1025, formed a compilation of the canon law, de- scribed as " Magnum Decretorum Volumen," and divided

[6] Archbishop Usher has described his practices in the following terms: " If this may be thought to prejudice the dignity of that church, which would be held to have sate as queene among the nations from the very beginning of Christianity, you shall have a crafty Merchant (Isidorus Mercator, I trow, they call him) that wil help the matter by counterfeit- ing Decretal Epistles in the name of the primitive bishops of Rome, and bringing in thirty of them in a row, as so many knights of the poste, to bear witnesse of that great authoritie which the church of Rome enioyed before the Nicene fathers were assembled." (An Answer to a Challenge made by a Iesvite in Ireland, p. 12. edit. Lond. 1631, 4to.)

[7] Besides the historians of the canon law, the reader may consult the following among other works: " Recherches sur plusieurs Collections inédites de Décrétales du Moyen Age, par Augustin Theiner, Docteur en Droit, etc." Paris, 1832, 8vo. The author, a very enthusiastic canonist, had previously published " Commentatio de Romanorum Pontificum Epistolarum Decretalium antiquis Collectionibus, et de Gregorii IX. P.M. Decretalium Codice." Lipsiæ, 1829, 4to. He has announced another work on a kindred subject: " Recherches Historiques et Critiques sur Ives de Chartres (mort en 1115), et son prétendu Ouvrage du Décret."

into twenty books. Ivo Carnotensis, bishop of Chartres from 1092 to 1115, is said to have been the author of a similar compilation, which bears the title of *Decretum;* and to him is ascribed another work on the canon law, sometimes called *Pannomia* and sometimes *Pannormia.* Both these works have been repeatedly printed.

Ivo was followed by Gratian, whose *Decretum* forms the first and most ample part of the *Corpus Juris Canonici.* He was a native of Clusium, or Chiusi, near Florence, and, according to a very improbable account, was the brother of Petrus Lombardus and Petrus Comestor. One of these three individuals was a native of Tuscany, another, as his name denotes, of Lombardy, and the third of France; but, in order to remove the difficulty which arises from this variety in the places of their nativity, some writers do their mother the honour of supposing that her three distinguished sons were the fruit of her unlawful intercourse with three different fathers, at different periods, and in different places. Gratian was a Benedictine monk of the monastery of S. Felice at Bologna. His work has long been commonly known by the title of *Decretum,* but is more correctly described as " Decretorum Collectanea;" and it is remarked by the very learned archbishop of Tarragona, that the old manuscripts scarcely ever bear the former title, but generally that of " Concordia discordantium Canonum."[s] According to the usual account, it was compiled in the year 1151 : this may indeed have been the period of its completion, but it evidently was not the labour of a single year. Cardinal Bellarmin has endeavoured to recon-

---

[s] Augustinus de Emendatione Gratiani, p. 3. edit. Baluzii. Paris. 1672, 8vo.

cile two conflicting authorities, by supposing that Gratian commenced his work in 1127, and completed it in 1151, thus allowing a period of twenty-four years for its composition.[9] The Decretum was presented to his holiness Eugenius III., who is said to have testified his approbation by conferring upon him the bishopric of Chiusi.[1] According to some writers, he was promoted to the rank of cardinal; but that he even became a bishop is not sufficiently proved, and it is certain that he never obtained a cardinal's hat.[2] His compilation never received the formal sanction of the pope; but although it is thus to be regarded as the work of a private individual, it speedily secured, and has ever since maintained, a degree of authority which makes a very near approach to that which belongs to written law.[3] The principal sources from which the Decretum is derived, are the sacred Scriptures, the spurious work described as the Apostolical Canons,[4] the decisions of ecumenical and local councils, the decretal epistles, partly genuine and partly spurious, of seventy-eight Roman pontiffs, the works of the Greek and Latin fathers and other ecclesiastical writers, the Theodosian Code and the *Corpus Juris Civilis*, the capitularies of kings of

[9] Bellarminus de Scriptoribus Ecclesiasticis, p. 187. edit. Colon. 1684, 4to.

[1] Pancirolus de claris Legum Interpretibus, p. 317. edit. Hoffmanni. Lipsiæ, 1721, 4to.

[2] Sarti de claris Archigymnasii Bononiensis Professoribus, part. i. p. 266. Tiraboschi, Storia della Letteratura Italiana, tom. iii. p. 453.

[3] Mastricht, p. 332. Doujat, Histoire du Droit Canonique, p. 92. Paris, 1677, 12mo. Doujat, Prænotionum Canonicarum libri quinque, p. 547. edit. Paris. 1687, 4to.

[4] See Joannis Dallæi de Pseudepigraphis Apostolicis, seu libris octo Constitutionum Apostolicarum apocryphis, libri iii. p. 412. Hardervici, 1653, 8vo.

France, and the rescripts of emperors. It is divided into three parts; of which the first and third are subdivided into distinctions, and the second into causes and questions.[5] Gratian, who wrote in an unenlightened age, is chargeable with many errors of ignorance or inadvertence, which the canonists have not scrupled to detect and expose. Augustinus has composed a series of dialogues *De Emendatione Gratiani*, in which the reader will find much learned and curious disquisition; and many other writers, editors as well as commentators, have endeavoured to rectify errors and supply defects. "To the compilations of Isidore and Gratian," says a catholic lawyer, "one of the greatest misfortunes of the church, the claim of the popes to temporal power by divine right, may in some measure be attributed. That a claim so unfounded and so impious, so detrimental to religion, and so hostile to the peace of the world, should have been made, is strange—stranger yet is the success it met with."[6]

The second collection which appears in the body of the canon law is entitled *Decretalium D. Gregorii Papæ IX. Compilatio.* It was formed under the direction and authority of this pontiff, who filled the chair of St. Peter from 1227 to 1241. He is himself commended for his skill in jurisprudence, and in the execution of this

---

[5] Of the usual method of quoting the Decretum and other portions of the canon law, the reader will find an account in Bishop Hallifax's *Analysis of the Civil Law*, p. 3. He likewise explains the method of quoting the books of the civil law. This latter subject is amply discussed by Thibaut, who refers to several other writers. (Civilistische Abhandlungen, S. 205. Heidelberg, 1814, 8vo.)

[6] Butler's Horæ Juridicæ subsecivæ, p. 170. 2d edit. Lond. 1807, 8vo.

plan he employed Raymundo de Peñafort, a learned Spaniard, who was afterwards enrolled in the catalogue of saints.[7] The work is divided into five books, and each book into various titles. These decretals are rescripts of the popes, in answer to prelates and other individuals by whom they have been consulted. They are sometimes called Decretalia, but commonly Decretales, the words Rescripta and Epistolæ being respectively understood. The work however is not strictly conformable to its title; for although the greater part of it is composed of decretals, the compiler has had recourse to various other authorities.

Gregory's decretals are followed by *Liber sextus Decretalium D. Bonifacii Papæ VIII.* which, notwithstanding the general title, is divided into five books. It was intended as supplementary to the other collection, and was compiled under the authority of Boniface, whose pontificate extended from 1294 to 1303. Besides the decretals of Boniface himself, and of preceding popes, ascending to Gregory IX., it includes decrees of the two general councils held at Lyon in 1245 and 1274.

The next work in the series bears the title of *Consti-*

---

[7] Antonii Bibliotheca Hispana vetus, tom. ii. p. 67. edit. Bayerii. The Spaniards have extolled him as a great saint, and we meet with divers relations of his life and miracles. One of these is entitled " Vita Sancti Raymundi de Peñaforti, Ordinis Predicatorum, per F. Petrum Marsilii, ejusdem Ordinis, olim conscripta." Barcinone, 1601, 8vo. This work, printed for the first time, is subjoined to Francisco Diago's " Historia del B. Cathalan Barcelones S. Raymundo de Peñafort, tercero Maestro General de la Orden de Predicadores." Barcelona, 1601, 8vo. Of the life and miracles of this saint there is another account, bearing the following title: " Relacion sumaria de la Vida, Milagros, y Actos de la Canonicacion de San Raymundo de Peñafort, de la Orden de Predicadores, escrita por Francisco Peña, Auditor de Rota." Cordova, *s. a.* 8vo. The work was originally composed in the Latin language.

tutiones Clementis Papæ V. in Concilio Vienensi editæ,
and is likewise divided into five books. Clement, whose
residence was at Avignon, presided in the council of
Vienne in the year 1312; and in addition to the constitutions there enacted, his collection comprehends some
other constitutions and decretals which he himself divulged before or after the holding of that council. After
his death, these *Clementinæ* were promulgated in the year
1317 by his successor John the Twenty-first, otherwise
called John the Twenty-second.

Of the same pope, who likewise resided at Avignon,
there is a collection of twenty constitutions, which bear
the name of *Extravagantes Joannis XXII.* They were
so called, because for some time they wandered beyond
the limits of the collection which contained the works
already enumerated as belonging to the body of the
canon law. The next work, which is entitled *Extravagantes Communes*, and is divided into five books, comprehends the constitutions of various popes, concluding
with Sixtus IV. whose pontificate extended from 1471 to
1484.

These are all the different compilations which constitute what is denominated the body of the canon law.[8] It
may be proper to add, that the best edition bears this
title: "Corpus Juris Canonici, Gregorii XIII. Pont.
Max. jussu editum: a Petro Pithœo et Francisco fratre,
Jurisconsultis, ad veteres codices manuscriptos restitutum,

---

[8] An ample collection, which may in some degree be considered as supplementary, was published by Augustinus. It was afterwards edited by
Charles Labbé in a splendid volume, bearing the following title: "Antiquæ Collectiones Decretalium, cum Antonii Augustini, Episcopi Ilerden-
sis, et Jac. Cujacii, Jc. celeberrimi, notis et emendationibus." Parisiis,
1609, fol.

et notis illustratum." Parisiis, 1687, 2 tom. fol. Of a more recent as well as more early date, there are many editions which we cannot here enumerate; and we shall only mention another, which was published by a protestant professor: " Corpus Juris Canonici. Justus Henningius Boehmer, J. C. recensuit, cum codicibus veteribus manuscriptis aliisque editionibus contulit, variantes lectiones adjecit, notis illustravit." Halæ Magdeburg. 1747, 2 tom. 4to.

The Institutions of Jo. Paulus Lancelottus, divided into four books, are inserted in different editions of the Corpus; and this circumstance has led some individuals, superficially acquainted with the subject, to suppose that they form an essential part of the authorized collection. They are however the production of a private lawyer, and having never received the sanction of the pope, they possess no authority beyond that which belongs to the character of the author as an able interpreter of the canon law. This work was undertaken with the approbation of Paul IV.: fifteen years elapsed before its completion; and Lancelottus having at length submitted it to the papal censors, and lingered two years in Rome, was compelled to abandon the hope of obtaining the sanction of his holiness Pius IV. The book was published in 1563, a few months before the dissolution of the council of Trent. The only favour which the author could obtain was that his Institutions might be added to the Corpus, but without any confirmation of their authority. They are sometimes inserted, and sometimes omitted; nor do they occur in that edition which we have already mentioned as the best. As they do not include the changes and modifications introduced by the council of Trent, they require the aid of a perpetual commentary.

The Institutions of Lancelottus are closely modelled upon those of Justinian. His subject does not easily admit of any high degree of classical purity, but the work is at least written with much neatness and perspicuity. The notes of Doujat form a very important addition: they evidently proceed from a man of ability and learning, and are generally composed in a style of pregnant brevity. The author whom he illustrates, named in Italian Giampaolo Lancellotti, was a professor of law in the university of Perugia, where he died at the age of eighty in the year 1591.[9]

The subsequent progress of the canon law, together with the more recent method of expounding it, must be learned from other writers. The most distinguished canonist of the last century was Dr. Van Espen, professor of the canon law in the university of Louvain, whose works extend to five volumes in folio.[1] His *Jus Ecclesiasticum universum* Mr. Butler has described as "a work which, for depth and extent of research, clearness of method, and perspicuity of style, equals any work of jurisprudence which has issued from the press; but which, in some places, where the author's dreary Jansenism prevails, must be read with disgust."[2] The life of the learned and conscientious author, it may be proper to state, has been elaborately written by Bellegarde."[3] There are other two recent works on the canon

[9] Tiraboschi, Storia della Letteratura Italiana, tom. vii. p. 786.

[1] The works of Van Espen may be found in the subsequent form. Scripta omnia. Lovanii, 1753, 4 tom. fol. Supplementum ad varias collectiones Operum Z. Bernardi Van Espen, J. U. D. Colon. Agrip. 1777, fol.

[2] Butler's Horæ Juridicæ subsecivæ, p. 184.

[3] Vie de M. Van Espen, Docteur ès Droits, et Professeur des Saints Canons dans l'Université de Louvain; où l'on trouve des éclaircissemens

law which I must recommend to the student's notice. " Caroli Sebastiani Berardi Commentaria in Jus Ecclesiasticum universum." Venetiis, 1789, 4 tom. 4to. "Joannis Devoti Institutionum Canonicarum libri IV." Florentiæ, 1816-7, 4 tom. 8vo. Neither of these is the earliest edition. Those who have any wish to ascertain how the canon law is taught by the catholics of Germany, may consult the following works. " Mauri de Schenkl Institutiones Juris Ecclesiastici communis. Editio emendata et valde adaucta a Josepho Scheill." Landishuti in Bavaria, 1830, 2 tom. 8vo. " Fundamenta Juris Ecclesiastici Catholicorum. In usus scholasticos conscripsit Jos. Anton. Sauter." Rotwilæ, 1825-6, 2 tom. 8vo. The canon law was ably illustrated by some of the German protestants, particularly by Ziegler, Thomasius, and Böhmer. Such was the reputation enjoyed by the last of these individuals, that difficult and intricate processes were frequently transmitted from Italy, to be decided by the law-faculty of the protestant university of Halle, during the period when Böhmer was dean.[4] Nor is this study neglected by either the papists or the protestants of the present day. Dr. Walter, professor of law in the university of Bonn, is the author of a work,

historiques sur tous les Ecrits ci-devant imprimés de ce Docteur, &c. par M. *** Licencié ès Droits. Louvain, 1767, 8vo. Pp. 871. According to a manuscript notice by *J. Le Plat, J. U. D.* contained in a copy in my possession, the book was written by M. Bellegarde. Le Plat was himself a professor in the university of Louvain, and is not altogether unknown in the annals of jurisprudence.

[4] " L'auteur a acquis une si grande réputation en Italie, qu'on envoyoit assez fréquemment des procès difficiles et compliqués à la décision de la faculté de droit à Halle, dont M. Boehmer étoit le doyen: j'en ai été témoin oculaire." (M. le Baron de Bielfeld, Progrès des Allemands dans les Sciences, les Belles-Lettres, et les Arts, p. 25. edit. Leyde, 1768, 8vo.)

published for the fourth time, under the title of " Lehrbuch des Kirchenrechts aller Christlichen Confessio-
nen." Bonn, 1829, 8vo. And a similar work has more
recently been published by Eichhorn of Göttingen, well
known for his history of the German law: " Grundsätze
des Kirchenrechts der Katholischen und der Evangelis-
chen Religionspartei in Deutschland." Göttingen,
1831-3, 2 Bde. 8vo.

While the papal power was yet in its meridian height,
this system of jurisprudence could only claim the proper
force of law within the papal dominions. It maintained
a very powerful and direct influence in every other country which acknowledged the bishop of Rome's supremacy;
but its dictates were controlled by the legislative authority, and modified by the practice of the courts, in each
of the countries where it found admission. Thus the
canon law of France differed in many respects from that
of Spain, and the canon law of England from that of
Austria. " All the strength," says Sir Matthew Hale,
" that either the papal or imperial laws have obtained in
this kingdom, is only because they have been received
and admitted either by the consent of parliament, and
so are part of the statute laws of the kingdom, or else
by immemorial usage and custom in some particular
cases and courts, and no otherwise, and therefore so far
as such laws are received and allowed here, so far they
obtain, and no further; and the authority and force
they have here is not founded on, or derived from themselves; for so they bind no more with us than our laws
bind in Rome or Italy." [5] These remarks, written in
protestant times, were equally applicable during the times
of popery.

[5] Hale's Hist. of the Common Law of England, p. 27.

The influence of the canon law in countries which have long abjured the authority of the pope, renders it even there a study of occasional importance to lawyers.[6] "So deep," says Lord Stair, "hath this canon law been rooted, that even where the pope's authority is rejected, yet consideration must be had to these laws, not only as those by which church benefices have been erected and ordered, but as likewise containing many equitable and profitable laws, which, because of their weighty matter, and their being once received, may more fitly be retained than rejected."[7] I cannot refrain from adding, that some knowledge of the canon law, at least of its history and external form, is of no small consequence to those who wish to understand the history and literature of the middle ages. This remark I shall endeavour to confirm by one or two examples.

Andrew Winton, the venerable prior of Lochleven, after having mentioned the irregular manner in which Walter Danielstoun took possession of the see of St. Andrews, subjoins this observation :

> Yeit be this electioune
> He dyd all ministratioune
> In jurisdictioune spirituale,
> And in all thingis temporale,
> All that quhile, rycht as he
> Had had lauchful autorite,
> Pretendand ay for his resown
> *Nichil de electione.*[8]

This passage, which to most readers must appear suf-

[6] Justi Henningii Boehmeri Jus Ecclesiasticum Protestantium, Usum modernum Juris Canonici juxta Seriem Decretalium ostendens. Halæ Magdeburgicæ, 1756-63, 5 tom. 4to. Of the first two volumes this is the fifth edition.

[7] Stair's Institutions of the Law of Scotland, b. i. tit. i. § 14.

[8] Winton's Cronykil of Scotland, vol. ii. p. 398.

ficiently obscure, the very accurate and intelligent editor, Macpherson, has left without explanation or conjecture. It bears an allusion to the Decretales Gregorii IX. lib. i. tit. vi. cap. xliv. § 2. *Nihil* is the first word of the chapter, and *de electione* denotes the subject of the title, or subdivision of the book. Danielstoun, whose election had not been confirmed by the pope, evidently relied on the authority of the subsequent passage: " Ita quod interim valde remoti, videlicet ultra Italiam constituti, si electi fuerint in concordia, dispensative propter necessitates ecclesiarum et utilitates, in spiritualibus et temporalibus administrent, sic tamen ut de rebus ecclesiasticis nihil penitus alienent."

Sir David Lindsay, another Scotish poet, makes the following allusion to the inordinate pretensions of the pope :

> His style at lenth gif thow wald knaw,
> Thow moste ga luke the cannon law:
> Baith in the Sext and Clementene
> His staitlie style thair may be sene. [9]

His editor, Mr. George Chalmers, who was guilty of a radical error when he supposed himself to be a man of learning, has subjoined this curious annotation: " The allusion is to the works of Pomponius Sextus, the great jurist of the third century." It is first to be remarked that Pomponius did not flourish in the third, but in the second century;[1] but if this "great jurist," of whom he speaks so familiarly, had actually written in the third century, how could he have illustrated the temporal power and splendour of the pope, before Christi-

---

[9] Lindsay's Works, vol. iii. p. 89.

[1] Guil. Grotii Vitæ Jurisconsultorum, p. 150. Bachii Hist. Jurisprudentiæ Romanæ, p. 477.

anity was established in the Roman empire? The *Sext*
to which Lindsay refers is manifestly the " Liber *sextus*
Decretalium ;" and the other authority which he appro-
priately quotes are the Clementinæ, or constitutions of
Clement V.

It is stated by Mr. Hallam, that " the stream of literature, that has so remarkably altered its channel within
the last century, has left no region more deserted than
those of the civil and canon law. Except among the
immediate disciples of the papal court, or perhaps in
Spain, no man, I suppose, throughout Europe will ever
again undertake the study of the one; and the new legal
systems, which the moral and political revolutions of
this age have produced, and are likely to diffuse, will
leave little influence or importance to the other." But
in all catholic countries, the canon law is a necessary
study; and even the protestants of Germany think it a
study which cannot be safely neglected. When to a
certain extent we recommend the study of the canon as
well as the civil law, we at the same time make a clear
distinction between the utility to be derived from the
one and from the other. A familiar acquaintance with
the civil law we are disposed to regard as the best foundation of all juridical science: the student, duly initiated
in classical learning, may thus acquire a concise and
elegant mode of reasoning on the multifarious topics of
jurisprudence; and he thus becomes familiar with those
maxims of law which have extended their influence to all
the civilized portions of Europe.[2] This species of know-

---

[2] The influence of the Roman law has even extended to the Ottoman
empire. " In the ordinary distribution of justice," says Dr. Shaw, " there
is in this, as in all other Turkish governments, an officer whom they call
the kaddy, who, for the most part, has been educated in the seminaries of
Stamboule or Grand Cairo, where the Roman Code and Pandects,

ledge is therefore highly valuable in itself, and it guides us to other knowledge, of more immediate application to the ordinary business of life. In several countries, the civil law continues to be studied with a degree of ardour which Mr. Hallam could not fail to consider as surprizing, and perhaps preposterous. But the canon law cannot claim the same pre-eminence, nor is it to be recommended to students on account of its intrinsic excellence : it is to be considered as the spurious offspring of the civil law, and as having gradually attained its full growth under the fostering care of priestly usurpation; what is most valuable, it has derived from the Roman jurisprudence, and its own peculiar maxims have all the same general tendency towards the power and aggrandizement of the church, that is, of churchmen.[3] Of the

translated into the Arabic language, are taught and explained as in the universities of Europe." (Travels, vol. i. p. 454. edit. Edinb. 1808, 2 vols. 8vo.) "Quin et Turcæ," says Matthias Stephani, "utuntur Codice Justinianeo, eoque utuntur in judiciis." (Commentarius in Novellas Constitutiones Justiniani Imperatoris, p. 36. Gryphiswaldi, 1630, 4to.) See likewise Leunclavii præf. in libros iii. Paratil. Duck de Usu et Authoritate Juris Civilis, f. 12. a. and Menagii Juris Civilis Amœnitates, cap. xxvi. An historical sketch edited by Crusius informs us, that not long after the taking of Constantinople, Maximus the patriarch, by command of the sultan, translated various books, and, among others, the royal or imperial codes; but whether by that expression we are to understand the Basilica or the laws of Justinian, may perhaps be considered as doubtful. Ὅστις καὶ ἀξιωθεὶς παρὰ τοῦ σουλτάνου, ὁρισμῷ τούτου μετεγλώττισε βιβλία πολλὰ ἐκ τῶν ἡμετέρων· καὶ πάντα τὰ γραμματεῖα, καὶ τοὺς κώδικας τοὺς βασιλικούς, καὶ ἄλλα χρειώδη. (Crusii Turcogræciæ libri octo, p. 27. Basil. 1584, fol.)

[3] "And indeed," says Sir Robert Wiseman, "setting aside some few special differences between the civil law and the canon as to some particulars, the canon law is nothing else but the civil law applied to the use of the church and church-matters. And such a conformity there is between them, that Rebuffus says, the canon law is but 'medulla legum et practica juris civilis;' the marrow and substance of the civil law, and the prac-

canon law, the study is therefore to be urged by other considerations than those of its real merits. Without some knowledge of this law, it is impossible to understand the history and the literature of the middle ages; and from the want of such knowledge of the most elementary kind, some of our writers, though by no means destitute of other learning, have been betrayed into the most palpable errors. A protestant divine, anxious to unveil the Man of Sin in his native deformity, ought to render himself familiar with the history and with the details of the canon law. Some of those who belonged to a very learned era, particularly Blondel and Daillé, were sufficiently aware of the value and importance of this branch of knowledge; and, in their controversies with the church of Rome, they were found to be very formidable antagonists.

Of the canon law there are many historical sketches; and more formal histories have been published by two able professors of law, the one a protestant, and the other

---

tical application of it to cases in fact arising. And Cujacius plainly averreth that the canon law ' fere omnia sumpsit ex jure civili, et omnino quicquid præclarum est in hoc jure, ex jure civili est; nec hujus interpres idoneus quisquam, nisi sit juris civilis peritissimus;' it is almost wholly taken out of the civil, but undoubtedly whatsoever is excellent in it, it has borrowed from the civil law ; neither can any one throughly understand the canon law, that is not first perfectly skill'd in the civil." (The Law of Laws, or the Excellency of the Civil Law above all other humane Laws whatsoever, shewing of how great Use and Necessity the Civil Law is to this Nation, p. 275. Lond. 1686, 8vo.) On the differences between the civil and the canon law, there are various works, but it may be sufficient to mention the following two: "Cunradi Rittershusii Differentiarum Juris Civilis et Canonici seu Pontificii libri septem." Argentorati, 1668, 4to. " Johannis Frederici Böckelmanni Tractatus postumus de Differentiis Juris Civilis, Canonici, et Hodierni." Traj. ad Rhen. 1697, 8vo. Neither of these is the original edition. Rittershusius was a professor in the university of Altdorf, Böckelmann in that of Leyden.

a papist. Mastricht's history displays good sense, as well as learning; and the author being a protestant, and writing in a protestant country, had, according to our estimate, a manifest advantage over Doujat. Both their works are of considerable value to the student of history, as well as of the canon law; but a very complete and satisfactory history of the canon law is still wanting. A Romanist, however liberal and enlightened, could not safely write with any degree of freedom; and we should therefore wish the task to be undertaken by some able and learned protestant, fully capable of detecting the Mystery of Iniquity, and not more zealous in exposing false than in defending true religion. All these qualifications could not perhaps be so easily found in the same individual; but for most, if not all, we must evidently look to the universities of Germany, where powerful talents are so frequently united with indefatigable industry. The light which Savigny's history of the Roman law has reflected on the institutions of the middle ages, might in some degree be paralleled by the history of the canon law, written with equal judgment, ability, and research. In one respect, it might be rendered more instructive, as it would trace the progress of some of the most gross impositions and most audacious exactions which the few have ever practised upon the many. The history of this law, during the period of its full vigour, involves the history of the Christian church in its lowest state of corruption; nor are human fraud and folly more glaringly displayed in any other record of the history of our species.

APPENDIX:

CONTAINING

CRITICAL NOTICES OF SOME WORKS

RECENTLY PUBLISHED IN GERMANY.

☞ OF the two articles contained in the following Appendix, the first was originally printed in Cochrane's Foreign Quarterly Review, and the second in the Foreign Quarterly Review, vol. xvii. published by Adolphus Richter & Co.

APPENDIX.

———————

No. I.

1. *Prodromus Corporis Juris Civilis a* Schradero, Clossio, Tafelio, Professoribus Tubingensibus, *edendi. Inest totius Operis Conspectus; Subsidiorum ad Institutionum criticam Recensionem et Interpretationem spectantium Enumeratio; Editionis ipsius Specimen.* Berolini, 1823, 8vo.
2. *Corpus Juris Civilis. Ad fidem Codicum manuscriptorum aliorumque subsidiorum criticorum recensuit, commentario perpetuo instruxit* Eduardus Schrader, Jctus. *In operis societatem accesserunt* Theoph. Lucas Frider. Tafel, Philologus, Gualth. Frider. Clossius, Jctus. *post hujus discessum* Christ. Joh. C. Maier, Jctus. *Tomus primus. Institutionum libri IV.* Berolini, 1832, 4to.

NEARLY thirty years have now elapsed since Professor Schrader formed the design of preparing an edition of the *Corpus Juris Civilis;*[1] and during this long interval he has devoted himself to the undertaking with a degree of ardour and perseverance of which it is not easy to convey an adequate idea. One of his learned coadjutors, Professor Tafel, is not a professional lawyer, but a philologer. Dr. Clossius, formerly a professor of law at Tübingen, was several years ago invited to the Russian university of Dorpat; and, after his departure, Professor Maier undertook to lend his friendly aid. These have been the regular labourers;

---

[1] Schrader's Abhandlungen aus dem Civil-Rechte, S. 193. Hannover, 1808, 8vo. He was then a professor of law and of philosophy in the university of Helmstädt. Of his preparatory labours we find further traces in his Civilistische Abhandlungen, S. 355. Weimar, 1816, 8vo.

but the lawyers of every country in Europe where the civil law is much studied and well understood, have felt a deep interest in the progress of the work, and have evinced a strong inclination to promote its success. Early and rare editions have been supplied from many different quarters; manuscripts have been examined and collated in many different countries; and the advice and suggestions of all the first civilians of the age have been freely communicated to Schrader, as to a person eminently qualified for the difficult task which he has undertaken.

The editions of the Corpus are very numerous; and as the book has continued to be in great request since the invention of printing, it is not to be imagined that a small number could supply the regular demand. The early editions are in many instances accompanied with the glosses of Accursius, and other civilians of the middle ages. Such an edition is described as the *Corpus glossatum*. The earliest editor, sufficiently provided with critical learning, was perhaps Gregorius Haloander, a young German, who was prematurely lost to the cause of literature and jurisprudence, a cause to which he had devoted himself with uncommon zeal and perseverance.[1] The Institutions and Pandects he published in 1529, the Code in 1530, and the Novels in 1531. Of the Greek text of the Novels this is the first edition, all the former editors having merely printed the old Latin version. Haloander rejected the old, and inserted a new translation of his own; but his edition of this and of the other books of the civil law is not illustrated with a commentary. It was the prevalent taste of the age to hazard very bold emendations, founded on mere conjectures, and to this taste he appears to have been sufficiently disposed to conform. At a subsequent period, various editions of the Corpus were illustrated by the notes of Contius, Russardus, and Charondas; but all the other editors were in a great measure eclipsed by Dionysius Gothofredus, who died in the year 1622. The editions which bear his name amount to a large number, and they are divided into two classes, those which contain and those which omit the

---

[1] See Conradi Parergorum libri quatuor, in quibus Antiquitates et Historia Juris Romani illustrantur. Helmstadii, 1740, 8vo.

glosses: these are the "editiones glossatæ," and "editiones non glossatæ."[3] An edition, containing the notes of Gotho-fredus, was printed at Amsterdam in 1663, under the superin-tendence of Simon van Leeuwen; and this has long retained its authority in the universities and the courts. The editor, who was an advocate at the Dutch bar, has added various readings, together with select notes of Augustinus, Govea, Cu-jacius, Contius, Grotius, Salmasius, and other learned civilians. He has likewise endeavoured to contribute his own share of an-notation; but this was a task for which he was indifferently qualified, either by his sagacity or erudition. The elegance of the typography recommends the book to many individuals who cannot form a very adequate judgment of its merits or defects.[4] The want of a more accurate and critical edition was sufficiently felt; but in a work of so formidable a character and extent, the deficiencies were more easily perceived than supplied. After a long interval this very heavy labour was undertaken by Gebauer, an eminent professor of law in the university of Göttingen ; and he was chiefly encouraged in his design by obtaining possession of the manuscript collections of Brenkman, who had devoted many years to the study of the Pandects, and had made great preparations for a new edition.[5] Gebauer was well known as the author of several learned works,[6] and of his intended edition high expectations were formed, but he did not live to bring it to a conclusion. The first volume, containing the Institutions and Pandects, was published in Göttingen in 1776 ; and many

---

[3] G. A. Struve wrote a large volume bearing the subsequent title:—
"Gothofredi *Immo*, hoc est, Conciliatio Legum in speciem pugnantium, quas in Notis ad Pandectas Juris Civilis, Dionysius Gothofredus, JCtus, verbum *Immo* usurpando, indicare atque arguere, omissa plerumque solu-tione, assueverat." Francofurti ad Mœnum, 1695, 4to.

[4] "Charta quidem bona est, sed editio non satis bona." (Reinoldi Opuscula Juridica, p. 716. Lugd. Bat. 1755, 8vo.)

[5] Gebaveri Narratio de Henrico Brenkmanno, de Manuscriptis Brenk-mannianis, de suis in Corpore Juris Civilis Conatibus et Laboribus. Gottingæ, 1764, 4to.

[6] A collection of Gebauer's smaller works appeared under the title of *Exercitationes Academicæ.* Erfordiæ, 1776-7, 2 tom. 4to.

years after his death, namely in 1797, the second volume was added by Spangenberg, a professor in the same university. This edition, though probably containing a more unadulterated text than any of those which preceded it, did not fully satisfy all the favourable anticipations which it had raised.

Besides the collective editions of the different works which constitute this body of law, there have been various editions of those works in a separate form. Few books have been more frequently printed than the Institutions of Justinian. Of the separate editions of the Pandects, there is one which claims particular attention, namely that of Taurellius, published at Florence in the year 1553, and representing the text of the famous Florentine manuscript. In this labour he was more or less engaged during the space of ten years; and in the Greek department he received the able assistance of Victorius. The book, which besides its intrinsic value has the recommendation of splendid typography, was at once regarded as a most important acquisition, and it still continues to be held in great estimation. The real editor was Lælius Taurellus, although he was willing to transfer the credit to his son Franciscus.[7] Of the Novels a separate edition was published by Henry Scrimger, the first professor of the civil law in the academy of Geneva, and a man of whom Scotland has some reason to be proud. He laboured much in Greek literature; but although he had prepared editions of several ancient authors, his labours were almost entirely lost to the public. His edition of the Novels, printed by H. Stephanus in the year 1558, contains the text materially improved upon that of Haloander. It is introduced by twelve pages of preliminary matter, but he has given no translation or notes. The volume however contains "Henrici Stephani Castigationes in Leonis Imperatoris Constitutiones." Scrimger mentions his design of publishing his annotations at a subsequent period, but this design he never carried into execution. A separate edition of the Novels, with a new version, was long afterwards published by J. F. Hombergk zu Wach, professor of law in the university of Marburg.

---

[7] Brenkmanni Historia Pandectarum, p. 350. Traj. ad Rhen. 1722, 4to.

The detached editions of the Institutions amount to a prodigious number. Many of an early date include the glosses of Accursius, which have long been considered as more curious than useful. The text of Haloander was admitted into many of those which succeeded. Soon after the commencement of the sixteenth century, various annotators applied their learning to the illustration of the Institutions. To adopt the slang of the present day, some of them were no doubt *talented* individuals; but they laboured under many disadvantages, which the lapse of a few years imperceptibly removed. One of those editors, who for some time enjoyed an ample share of reputation, was Sylvester Aldobrandinus, a native of Florence, and the father of Pope Clement VIII.[8] His dedication is dated at Ferrara, on the 1st of October 1538, and the edition was very frequently reprinted. Of one edition bearing his name, Lugduni, 1553, 8vo, a copy is now before us. It is elegantly printed, with a tasteful mixture of black and red ink; and the text and notes are distributed in different columns. The printing is however superior to the Latinity. Notes and commentaries on the Institutions now began to be produced in sufficient abundance. Ferrettus published an edition with notes in 1543; Baron, an edition with a commentary in 1545; Balduinus, an edition with a commentary in 1546; and Hotman, an edition with a commentary in 1560. These editors were all French professors of the civil law, and were men of high reputation. The commentary of Balduinus, like most of his other writings, is learned, copious, and excursive; nor was Hotman less profoundly skilled in ancient erudition. Another ample commentary, written by Schneidewin, was printed in 1571. At the head of those who illustrated the Institutions with shorter annotations, we cannot fail to place Cujacius, the prince of modern civilians. In another work, he has spoken in disparaging terms of those who had spent much superfluous labour in illustrating a book which is so clear as to require no illustration.[9] What might

[8] Pancirolus de claris Legum Interpretibus, p. 307.
[9] " Ex libris juris civilis, quibus solis nos uti Justinianus voluit in respondendo, litigando, judicando, libello Institutionum neque comptior

be clear to a person of his great sagacity and consummate learning, is not however equally clear to every ordinary student;
and he at length condescended to furnish notes, both critical
and explanatory. They are generally very brief, and are written
in his usual manner, which approaches to the oracular. His first
edition appeared in 1556, and it was followed by various others.
His notes are described and known as *notæ priores*, and *notæ
posteriores*. Both classes of them are inserted in the edition
of Fabrot, Parisiis, 1645, 12mo; but the one class is there
distinguished from the other. We ought not perhaps to pass
unnoticed the commentaries of Giphanius and Rittershusius,
two civilians who were deeply imbued with ancient literature.
Of Harpprecht's immense commentary on the Institutions, the
first volume was published at Tübingen in the year 1609.
Schrader has inadvertently assigned the date of 1709. The
work was reprinted in quarto; and another edition, probably the
last, was published by Vicat at Lausanne, in the year 1748, in
four volumes folio. The commentary of Bachov was first printed
in 1628, and he is still considered as one of the most able and
accurate expounders of the Institutions. That of Vinnius, which
followed in 1642, has obtained a much higher reputation, but,
in the opinion of Schrader, is inferior in intrinsic value; and
he is indeed disposed to think that for this reputation the author
is in no small degree indebted to the clearness and fluency of
his style. An edition of his commentary was published by
Heineccius in 1726, and it contains some valuable additions,
which were printed in a separate form in 1732. Vinnius, whom
we still regard as an able commentator, likewise published a
small edition of the Institutions, accompanied with brief notes,
which have long been found extremely useful. The commentary of Janus a Costa, or Jean de la Coste, who was succes-

neque facilior ullus est, quive interpretem desideret minus, ut plane
illorum videatur esse otium ignobile qui eum libellum longissimis onerant
commentariis, quod positum est in una cognitione in infinita dispartientes,
quo scilicet plura scire videantur, ut illis quidem videtur, nostro judicio,
ostentatione vana quo ceteris nihil scire videantur." (Cujacii Observationes, lib. xi. cap. xxxviii. p. 531. edit. Colon. Agrip. 1598, 8vo.)

APPENDIX. 255

sively a professor of law in the universities of Toulouse and
Cahors, is also entitled to particular attention on account of the
learning and subtilty which it displays. It was first printed at
Paris in 1659, after the death of the author, and was republished at Utrecht in 1714, under the superintendence of J. vande Water, who has subjoined the notes of Marcilius and Muretus, together with some other appendages. Copies of the same
edition bear the imprint of Leyden, with the date of 1719.
Another large commentary, written by Hoppe, was published in
1693, and has passed through various editions, one of which
was elaborately prepared by C. F. Walch, and printed in 1772.
The book must therefore have attained to no inconsiderable
reputation; and Dr. Taylor describes the author as " a most
admirable and useful writer."[1] Very different however is
the opinion of Dr. Schrader, who dismisses him with this brief
character, " Centies dicta ne bona quidem methodo repetiit."
Ludewig has with justice remarked, that Hoppe was deficient
in the knowledge of philology and legal antiquities.[2] A more
learned annotator was J. H. Böhmer, chancellor of the university of Halle, who published two different editions of the
Institutions in 1719 and 1728. They were both printed at
Halle in quarto. He has bestowed some labour in amending
the text, but his notes are neither very copious nor very elaborate. The commentary and critical notes of Everard Otto,
which were published in 1729, and were more than once reprinted, are deservedly commended by Schrader for the valuable and interesting mixture of philological and juridical information which they contain. Otto, a native of Germany, was
then professor of law at Utrecht, and was afterwards syndic

[1] Taylor's Elements of the Civil Law, p. ix. " The turn and manner of
his comments is such, that I think they might very successfully serve for
an introduction to the more diffusive and comprehensive work of Vinnius,
where we commonly set out. Above all, the *lemmata*, or axioms, which
he is constantly gathering up, in the course of his notes, are the happiest,
the clearest, and the most faithful compendium of law that I ever met
with; and, with the help of a small comment, would make a valuable
system by themselves." See Schrader's Prodromus, p. 264.

[2] J. P. de Ludewig Vita Justiniani, p. 59. Halæ Salicæ, 1731, 4to.

of Bremen. He was the author or editor of many other works, which are well known wherever the civil law is much studied. One of the latest critical editions of the Institutions in a separate form is that of Professor Biener of Berlin, published in the year 1812. He has carefully revised the text, and, besides availing himself of the labours of former editors, has noted the collation of eight different manuscripts.

It is not to be supposed that this is a complete enumeration, even of the more elaborate editions and commentaries. Of the merits and defects of previous editors and commentators, Schrader seems in general to have formed a very correct and impartial judgment : nor have his enquiries respecting manuscripts been less indefatigable. One hundred and sixty-three manuscript copies of the Institutions are enumerated and described in his Prodromus ; and of these his edition exhibits collations of no small proportion. His assiduity and perseverance in procuring such collations, is well known to his friends at home and to his correspondents abroad. The libraries of many different countries were eagerly ransacked. Sanguine hopes were entertained that in those of England and Spain, which had seldom been explored by skilful eyes, many precious treasures might be discovered ; and it was imagined that some works of the ancient civilians, hitherto considered as irretrievably lost, might be found amid the dust of the Spanish libraries. It was chiefly from an impression of this kind that Dr. Hänel was induced to devote so much time and labour to his researches in that country. [3] These high expectations were not indeed

---

[3] Catalogi Librorum Manuscriptorum, qui in Bibliothecis Galliæ, Helvetiæ, Belgii, Britanniæ M. Hispaniæ, Lusitaniæ asservantur, nunc primum editi a D. Gustavo Haenel. Lipsiæ, 1830. 4to.—In a passage, which is well worth quoting, the author gives a most lamentable account of the state of literary research in Spain, and makes some remarks on the character and prospects of that unfortunate and distracted nation, which are as apposite at the present moment as at the time they were written. " Non sine quodam animi dolore commemorare possum, bibliothecas ab Hispanis ipsis ita nunc negligi, ut, cum iter per Hispaniam facerem, solus semper fere in bibliothecis essem. Per integros dies, quos in bibliothecis Hispalensibus et Toletanis consumsi, præter me unum nemo venit qui librum inspicere vellet. Quid vero nostrates dicent audientes, nonnullas

realized; but he found many manuscripts of juridical works already known, and communicated much information to Schrader. The examination of the English libraries was undertaken by several young civilians; and one of those who entered upon the task with most zeal and ardour, was the late Dr. Jourdan, whose name we cannot mention without feelings of deep regret. He studied in the university of Paris, where he took the degree of doctor of laws; and having been called to the bar, he was less distinguished as a mere practitioner than as an able civilian. By his talents and zeal he had no small influence in reviving, among his countrymen, a study which had fallen into unmerited neglect. He became one of the editors of the " Thémis, ou Bibliothèque du Jurisconsulte," to which he contributed many ingenious articles; and he maintained a correspondence with all the most eminent civilians of the age, particularly those of Germany and the Netherlands. He was a candidate for a professorship of the civil law at Paris; and although it may very safely be affirmed that his qualifications were greatly superior to those of any individual brought into competition, they were disregarded by incompetent and partial judges. He was a man of an ardent temperament, very decided in the expression of his opinions; and as he entertained an undisguised contempt for the disciples of the old school of Heineccius, he exposed himself to no small share of personal animosity. He afterwards directed his views towards a chair in the university of Louvain, where his friends Warnkoenig and Holtius then taught with high reputation; but during one of his visits to Britain, he was seized with a fever,

literarum in Hispania universitates, e. g. Granatensem, bibliotheca publica carere ? Utinam ii, quibus in Hispania rei publicæ cura tradita est, intelligerent, civitatum fundamentum, quo firmius nullum poterit inveniri, in animis civium, literis ad omnem humanitatem recte institutorum, positum esse. Omnes, qui Hispanos accuratius cognoverunt, vota faciunt, ut populus, qui mentis animique dotibus excellit, atque ingenium acerrimum cum singulari quodam pertinacia miro modo ita conjungit, ut medius quasi positus inter frigidissimarum atque calidissimarum plagarum populos utrorumque virtutibus præditus sit, e vinculis, quæ monachi et vecordes quidam viri, sed summo loco constituti, ei imposuerunt, tandem aliquando liberetur."

S

which his debilitated frame could not resist, and he died at Deal on the 27th of August, 1826.[1]

In the Prodromus, Schrader has given a very particular account of his plan, and of the various *subsidia* for the completion of his edition. This volume, itself a work of no inconsiderable labour, is well deserving of a place in the library of a civilian. The plan which he originally proposed is in some degree modified; and as one entire portion of the edition is brought to a conclusion, the public is now enabled to estimate the value of his services, and those of his learned associates. According to the best opinion which we are capable of forming, this is the most valuable edition of the Institutions that has hitherto made its appearance; and if the other portions of the *Corpus Juris Civilis* were published with equal diligence and ability, the names of those fellow-labourers would deserve to be mentioned with signal honour in the annals of jurisprudence. The rules of sound and sagacious criticism are most carefully applied to the adjustment of the text. The notes which relate to the various readings are, by an arrangement very proper and convenient, separated from the commentary. This commentary, concise rather than diffuse, is very able and elaborate, and contains a suitable mixture of jurisprudence and philology. Illustrations are drawn from a great variety of ancient writers, Greek as well as Latin; and here the classical erudition of Professor Tafel must have been very beneficially employed. The recent discovery of the Institutions of Caius has given this edition a signal advantage over almost all those by which it has been preceded; and many other advantages it derives from the combined talents and learning of the editors.

It is earnestly to be wished that they may be enabled to bring their great undertaking to a conclusion; but, at all events,

---

[1] In the *Zeitschrift für geschichtliche Rechtswissenschaft*, Bd. vii. S. 43-89, Warnkoenig has given an interesting sketch of his life and character, under the title of " Der Rechtsgelehrte Dr. Jourdan in Paris und sein Verhältniss zur Reform der Rechtswissenschaft in Frankreich." A notice of him by A. Taillandier, advocate, occurs in the *Revue Encyclopédique*, tom. xxxii. p. 259. See likewise Lerminier's *Introduction générale à l'Histoire du Droit*, p. xviii. Paris, 1829, 8vo.

what they have already published is complete in itself, and there is a separate title for their edition of the Institutions. Of all the reliques of ancient jurisprudence, the Institutions of Justinian have been the most widely circulated. Of the immense variety of separate editions we have already had occasion to speak; and the translations into different languages amount to a very formidable number. Here we are induced to mention an early Spanish version, which we believe to be of great rarity, and unknown to most of the writers on the literary history of the law: " Las Institvciones Imperiales (ô Principios del Derecho Ciuil) dirigidas al Principe Don Philippe nuestro señor. Traduzidas por Bernardino Daza, Legista, natural de Valladolid. Con licencia y priuilegios. En Tolosa, por Guion Bodauila, Impressor y Iurado de la Vniversidad, 1551." 8vo. As a further proof of the singular popularity of the Institutions, it may be stated that several poetical versions have been executed in different ages. At a very early period, a French poet was induced to undertake

> Pour Institutes roumancer.

The name of this versifier is unknown, and the only copy of his translation which we have seen is without a date; but it must apparently have been printed several years before the close of the fifteenth century. It is a folio volume, printed with Gothic letters, having illuminated capitals, and bearing this inscription: " C est le liure des institutions des drois appelle Institute, translate de latim en francois, & corrige en deligence ꝑ plusieurs docteurs et souuerains legistes." The translator first introduces a metrical prologue of his own, and afterwards proceeds to the *prœmium* of Justinian, which he commences thus:

> La maieste de lempereur,
> Qui du mõde est gõuerneur,
> Doit estre darmes hõnoree,
> Et de loys garnie et armee;
> Si que en temps de paix et de guerre
> Soit bien gouuernee la terre,
> Et que par lempereur de rõme,
> Qui de lempire tient la sõme,

Soient trestous ses enemis
Par force darmes desoubz mis;
Si que plus fort de luy ne truisse,
Et par les loys refrener puisse,
Et ramener a esgaulte
Des mauluais la desloyaulte;
Qui les bons du tout excillassent,
Se la iustice ne doubtassent;
Et ainsi seroit lempereur
En deux manieres vainqueur,
Par armes prince glorieux,
Par loys sage religieux.

One of the Latin paraphrases was published under the following title: "Elementa Ivris Civilis, sev Institvtiones Imperiales in carmē cōtractæ, autore L. Honorato Dracone Iurisconsul. Eiusdem de Iurisprudentiæ Studio et Iustitiæ Laudibus Sylua. In gratiā studiosorū additi sunt Caij Iurisconsulti Institut. libri duo. Coloniæ, apud hæredes Arnoldi Birckmanni, 1556." 8vo. Another appeared after a long interval: "Institvtionvm, sev Elementorum Divi Justiniani, Sacratissimi Principis, libri qvatvor, a Joanne Baptista Pisacane, V. I. Doctore, ac Regio Auditore Castri Novi Neap. in carmina redacti. Neapoli, typis Iosephi Roselli, M.DC.LXXXXIV. Superiorvm Permissv." Fol. "Dr. Parr thinks this the scarcest book in his library. He saw it about forty years ago in White's catalogue, and eagerly secured it. He never saw it in any other catalogue; he never found a scholar who knew its existence; he has in vain inquired for it in the university libraries, and the libraries of collectors. The learned Mr. Hamley of New College, Lady Oxford, and, at her request, Mr. Windham, the English minister at Florence, and the Russian minister, who was a collector, could not find it in Milan, Florence, Venice, and other parts of Italy. Mr. Blunt, the ingenious son of a Birmingham surgeon, was for several years busy in inquiring at the libraries and booksellers' shops in Paris, but could not hear of it. At length Mr. Hobbs Scott, in 1819, rummaging some old neglected books in the back room of a bookseller at Rome, met with it. The bookseller knew not its value. Mr. Scott paid a few shillings, and brought the book to Hatton. Dr. Parr then gave his other copy, as a rarity, to adorn the library of his honoured friend Mr. Coke, of Holkham."[5] Of this rare book he might however have found another copy in the Advocates Library at Edinburgh. The paraphrase of Pisacane is more amplified than that of Draco, and his versification is more easy and elegant. The former commences the *proœmium* with the following lines:

> Ut studiis Augusta fieri est ornanda Gradivi [6]
> Majestas, sic est placitis armanda Themistos
> Æque, ut prudenter tempus moderetur utrunque
> Et belli et pacis; ne tantum terror et horror
> Hostibus immineat, ne tantum clara triumphis
> Gloria contingat vincenti, quin et iniquos
> Legitimæ mulctent methodi, atque calumnia cesset.
> Quorum utranque viam vigilantia nostra peregit
> Sedula, supremi nutu præsente Tonantis.
> Nam quantum bello sudarimus, Africa testis
> Et non parva orbis pars nostro Marte recepta,
> Hostilesque procul pulsi domitique furores,
> Cæsaque barbaries trux: porro legibus orbis
> Omnis jam regitur, quas aut invenimus ipsi
> Autores, aut ex veterum collegimus amplis
> Innumerisque voluminibus.

Pisacane has thus versified the same passage:

> Qui regit imperio populos, orbemque gubernat,
> Legibus armandus justis, decorandus et armis,
> Tempus ut utrumque et belli pacisque regatur,
> Victor et existat princeps Romanus in hostes
> Bella gerens, fraudes hominum depellat iniquas
> Tramite legitimo, fiat sanctissimus æqui
> Cultor, et hostili victor de gente triumphet.
> Quorum utramque viam, cœlesti numine ducti,
> Nos satis insomnes mira perfecimus arte.
> Barbaricæ gentes, fuerant quæ nostra redactæ
> Sub juga, sudoris noscunt quem fudimus imbrem;
> Africa, et innumeri populi, quos vicimus, urbi
> Addidimusque iterum nostræ post tempora longa,
> Numinis auxilio, referunt quæ gessimus armis.
> Utitur et nostris generatim legibus orbis,

---

[5] Bibliotheca Parriana, p. 489.   Lond. 1827, 8vo.

[6] This verse is very deficient in sense as well as metre. For *fieri*, we must evidently read *feri*.

Ordine dispositis, lectisque ex jure vetusto.
Et cum confusas leges digessimus ante,
Ad veterum prudentum immensa volumina, et omnis
Antiqui juris curam protendimus, undas
Æquoreas veluti emensi mediumque profundum,
Divina insperatum opus hoc implevimus aura.

In the subsequent verses, this poetical civilian has paraphrased a portion of the title *De Nuptiis*.

Non celebrare licet nobis connubia cuncta;
Nam thalamos natura vetat conjungere natas
Cum patribus; vetitum inter avum neptemque, nepotem
Atque aviam socii consortia jungere lecti.
Lineola in recta cuncti hoc servare minores,
Ipsi ut si coeant, sit uterque nefarius æque
Incestus nubens : adeo hoc verum esse putatur,
Ut quamcunque pater natam sibi liber adoptet,
Hanc sibi non possit vinclo sociare jugali.
Illius ergo nequis lecti sacra jura subire,
Quam tibi vel neptem vel fecit adoptio natam,
Jure potestatis fuerit licet illa soluta.
Inter personas transverso ex ordine junctas
Est quædam similis, non observatio tanta;
Namque soror fraterque jugalia vincula lecti
Nectere non possunt, vel eadem matre creati
Ac patre, utrovis fuerint vel stipite nati.
Sed si germanam tibi fecit adoptio, donec
Ipsa manet stabilis, constans, eademque, jugales
Inter te atque illam nequeunt consistere tædæ.
Cum vero solvetur adoptio, ducere nulla
Hanc tibi jura vetant : sin patris nulla potestas
Te premit, haud vetitum socialia nectere vincla.

No. II.

1. *Lex Romana Burgundionum. Ex Jure Romano et Germanico illustravit* August. Frideric. Barkow, J. U. Doctor, et in Universitate Literaria Gryphiswaldensi Antecessor. *Gryphiswaldiæ*, 1826, 8vo.

2. *Corpus Legum, sive Brachylogus Juris Civilis. Ad fidem quattuor codicum scriptorum et principum editionum emendavit, commentarios criticos, locorum similium annotationem, notitiam litterariam, indicesque adjecit, ineditam incerti scriptoris Epitomen Juris Civilis, medio duodecimo sæculo factam, ex codice Tubingensi edidit* Eduardus Böcking, Juris utriusque Doctor, et in Universitate Frider. Guil. Rhenana E. O. Professor Publicus. *Berolini*, 1829, 8vo.

3. *Lex Dei, sive Mosaicarum et Romanarum Legum Collatio. E codicibus manuscriptis Vindobonensi et Vercellensi, nuper repertis, auctam atque emendatam edidit, notis indicibusque illustravit* Fridericus Blume Hamburgensis, in Academia Georgia Augusta Antecessor, Magn. Brit. Hannoveræque Regi ab Aulæ Cons. *Bonnæ*, 1833, 8vo.

4. *Dissensiones Dominorum, sive Controversiæ veterum Juris Romani Interpretum qui Glossatores vocantur. Edidit et adnotationibus illustravit* Gustavus Haenel Lipsiensis. *Insunt anonymi vetus Collectio, Rogerii Dissensiones Dominorum, codicis Chisiani Collectio, Hugolini Diversitates sive Dissensiones Dominorum super toto Corpore Juris Civilis; quibus adcedunt Excerpta e Rogerii Summa Codicis, Hugolini Distinctionibus et Quæstionum Collectionibus. Omnia præter Rogerii Dissensiones nunc primum e codicibus edita, et indicibus rerum, glossatorum, legum, glossarum instructa. Lipsiæ*, 1834, 8vo.

Of the ardour and enthusiasm with which the study of the civil law is now prosecuted in Germany, these four publications afford a signal proof. In what other country would the same books find such able editors, or indeed any editors whatsoever; and in what other country would they have found publishers? Here we are not presented with the precious reliques of the classical civilians, of such writers as Caius, Ulpian, and Paulus, but with those of nameless writers of the lower and middle ages. Every scattered remnant of ancient jurisprudence, however mutilated or disfigured, attracts the eager attention of the learned jurists, with whom that country so conspicuously abounds: they possess sufficient industry, as well as sufficient skill, to separate the gold from the dross; and from the most unpromising materials, from what to less practised eyes might appear a heap of rubbish, they sometimes extricate fragments of no inconsiderable value. It is besides to be noted, that men of erudition have their own peculiar recreations, in which the uninitiated cannot participate, and of which they cannot form an adequate conception; nor is it very hard to conceive, that Haubold or Hänel may have been as much entertained with the *Dissensiones Dominorum*, as any slender damsel with the most bepuffed of all the novels that have issued from a certain metropolitan shop. We must certainly admit, that the entertainment is neither identical nor similar; but different palates are gratified by dishes of the most dissimilar flavour.

The book here described as *Lex Romana Burgundionum*, was originally printed under the perplexing and inappropriate title of " Papiani liber Responsorum," and under that title it has generally been quoted and recognized. In the year 1566, it was first published by Cujacius, who subjoined it to his edition of the Theodosian Code. The name of Papianus was utterly unknown in the annals of jurisprudence; nor does the book contain the opinions of a lawyer on particular cases, but a formal treatise on various titles of the law. It seems indeed to be ascertained beyond all doubt, that the name of the author, as well as the title of the book, is only to be traced to an error of the copyist, and inadvertency of the editor. Of the Breviarium of Anianus, all the complete manuscripts conclude with a minute fragment of an illustrious civilian, " Papiniani lib. I. Responsorum;" but in this as well as in other passages where the name occurs, it is uniformly written *Papianus*, instead of *Pa-*

pinianus.[7] As the error is thus repeated in different places, it may have originated from the use of a contraction in writing the name. Cujacius is supposed to have printed from a manuscript, in which the fragment now mentioned was immediately succeeded by the *Lex Romana,* and to have mistaken the rubric of this fragment for that of the succeeding treatise. In the Vatican Library there is a manuscript which exhibits the very same contents and arrangement. In a subsequent edition, printed at Paris in 1586, he varied the title of the book, describing it as " Burgundionis J. C. qui Papiani Responsorum titulum præfert, liber." This description refers us to the true origin of the book, which appears very clearly to have been compiled for the use of the Roman subjects belonging to the ancient kingdom of Burgundy.

In the preamble to the *Lex Burgundionum,* we meet with the following passage : " Inter Romanos vero interdicto simili conditione venalitatis crimine, sicut a parentibus nostris statutum est, Romanis legibus præcipimus judicari : qui formam et expositionem legum conscriptam, qualiter judicent, se noverint accepturos, ut per ignorantiam se nullus excuset."[8] This passage was written in the second year of the reign of Gundebald, that is, in the year 517. His barbarian subjects were to be governed by one code of laws, and his Roman subjects by another. When the first code was completed, the second was promised : the Roman subjects, indulged with the privilege of being governed by their national laws, were to be furnished with such a form and exposition as should regulate the judicial proceedings in which they were solely concerned. Lindenbrog perceived that the work ascribed to Papianus was precisely such a compendium as might be supposed to suit this purpose ; and Cujacius had evidently arrived at the same conclusion, when he described it as the work of a Burgundian lawyer. Gothofredus and other writers remarked that the order of arrangement was almost the very same in both works ; and

[7] Conradi Parerga, p. 101. Savigny, Bd. ii. S. 24.

[8] Lindenbrogii Codex Legum Antiquarum, p. 267. edit. Francof. 1613, fol.

as this order is not such as obviously presents itself, we naturally
infer that, so far as relates to the distribution of the titles, the
one book served as a model for the other. A strong presumption likewise arises from the barbarian regulations which this
civilian borrows from the laws of the Burgundians. The second title, *De Homicidiis*, concludes with the subsequent passage : " Et quia de pretiis occisorum nihil evidenter lex Romana
constituit, dominus noster statuit observandum, ut, si ingenuus
ab ingenuo fuerit interemptus, et homicida ad ecclesiam con-
fugerit, ipse qui homicidium admisit, cum medietate bonorum
suorum occisi heredibus serviturus addicatur, reliqua medietas
facultatis ejus heredibus relinquatur. Si vero servus cujus-
cunque occisus fuerit ab ingenuo, et ipse homicida ad ecclesiam
convolaverit, secundum servi qualitatem infra scripta domino
ejus pretia cogatur exsolvere, hoc est, pro actore c. sol., pro
ministeriali lx., pro aratore, aut porcario, aut virvicario, aut
aliis servis xxx., pro aurifice electo c., pro fabro ferrario l.,
pro carpentario xl. inferantur. Hoc ex præcepto domini
regis convenit observari." The Roman law had not, like the
barbarian codes of the middle ages, regulated the price of
blood ; but the Roman subjects of this barbarian king were not
to be left without a table of fees. The prices for the homicide
of different classes of persons generally correspond with the
regulations established by the code of the Burgundians.

This anonymous writer appears to have drawn his materials
from the Institutions of Caius, the Sententiæ Receptæ of Paulus,
the Gregorian, Hermogenian, and Theodosian Codes, and from
the novels of several emperors. What he has derived from
these different sources, is distinguished with great care and accuracy by the learned editor. The work, as now published,
consists of forty-seven titles, which are generally very short
and simple; nor is it to be supposed that all the leading objects
of legal cognizance can be comprized within such narrow limits.
As little is it to be expected, that this civilian of Burgundy,
writing during the sixth century, and at a distance from Constantinople and Berytus, can always be found a safe guide in
questions of pure Roman law. The incidental value of his
work has however been recognized by the most competent

judges, and among the rest by Savigny, who remarks that it contains many passages of ancient jurisprudence, of which no other traces are now to be discovered.[9] The author had access to many pure sources, which have long been closed by the mouldering ruins of time. But he did not possess sufficient skill to preserve unsullied the valuable fragments which he incorporated in his motley fabric; and to render it available for the illustration of ancient jurisprudence, required no inconsiderable effort of learning, ingenuity, and industry. Such was the principal part of the task undertaken by Dr. Barkow; and this task he appears to have executed in a manner highly creditable to his professional character. The work, as appended to several early editions of the Theodosian Code, is without any commentary or notes. Schulting inserted Papianus in his collection, entitled "Jurisprudentia vetus Ante-Justinianea," which was first printed at Leyden in the year 1717, and he added some annotations, which are not very elaborate. He was a man of great erudition, and of eminent knowledge of the civil law, but it was not consistent with his general plan to bestow much time and space upon this particular tract. After the lapse of half a century, the task of illustration was more ambitiously attempted than successfully performed by Amaduzzi. The text was next printed in the "Jus Civile Antejustinianeum," which appeared at Berlin in the year 1815. This collection was published by an association of civilians; and the care of the *Lex Romana* devolved upon F. A. Biener, who has more recently distinguished himself by different works. He has subjoined various readings, but no commentary. Hitherto the book had never been published in a separate form; and this edition of Barkow is therefore recommended by many different circumstances. The volume commences with a preface, which extends to sixty-six pages, and embraces all the preliminary information that any reader could be supposed to require or wish. A very elaborate commentary is placed under the text; after which follow the various readings, consisting of thirty-seven pages.

[9] Savigny's Geschichte des Römischen Rechts im Mittelalter, Bd. ii. S. 32.

The work entitled *Lex Dei* is apparently a production of nearly the same age.[1] The author is supposed by Gothofredus to have been contemporary with Cassiodorus, who flourished about the middle of the sixth century. A- conformity has been traced between the sentiments as well as the style of the two writers; and Blume has remarked that *quia*, instead of *quod*, and *incipit* governing an accusative, seem to indicate that the anonymous author could scarcely have written before the year 500. When his work was first discovered in the sixteenth century, Du Tillet, Charondas, Cujacius, and others, ascribed it to a certain Lucinius Rufinus; but upon what authority, or according to what conjecture, it appears extremely difficult to ascertain. They evidently could not confound him with an eminent lawyer of the same name, who was contemporary with Julius Paulus, and therefore belonged to a much earlier age. Zimmern, a recent and distinguished historian of the Roman law, is inclined to believe that he may have been a Jew; but we perceive no adequate reason for departing from the current opinion, which represents him as a Christian. Freherus and Otto suppose him to have been a monk: Blume replies that, before the age of St. Benedict, there were very few monks in the western parts of Europe, and still fewer who could have cultivated the study of letters. Cassiodorus, whom we have mentioned as the supposed contemporary of the anonymous writer, was himself the founder of a monastery in a remote part of Calabria, and in this retreat he closed a long life, which had been much devoted to profane as well as sacred literature. It is at least highly probable, that the writer in question was an

---

[1] Various writers of a more recent age have instituted a formal comparison between the Jewish and Roman laws. One of these is William Wellwood, professor of law in the university of St. Andrews, who published a work bearing the subsequent title: "Juris Divini Judæorum ac Juris Civilis Romanorum Parallela; sive utriusque e suis undequaque sedibus ad verbum transcripti ocularis Collatio: authore Gulielmo Velvod." Lugd. Bat. 1594, 4to. This work is followed by an appendix, with a regular title-page containing the same date: "Ad expediendos Processus in Judiciis Ecclesiasticis, Appendix Parallelorum Juris divini humanique."

ecclesiastic of some denomination. The knowledge which he displays of the sacred writings, renders this an obvious conjecture. From his mode of addressing the lawyers, " scitote jurisconsulti," it has been inferred that he was not himself of their numbers, for this is not like a man addressing a body to which he himself belonged. Blume, by some inadvertence, has stated that such an argument was first employed by Finestres, in the prolegomena to his edition of Schulting's " Jurisprudentia Ante-Justinianea." Ceruariæ, 1744, 12mo. In two different works, Gothofredus had anticipated this argument by an entire century.[2]

The chief value of such a work as this obviously lies in its preserving scattered fragments, which might otherwise have been lost. The author had access to many treatises which have utterly perished, or of which we only possess the mutilated remains; and as he collected his materials with a considerable degree of industry, his labours have found due acceptance with the most learned of the modern civilians. Nor are they without some degree of interest to theologians.[3] The editor is inclined to believe that the passages of the Old Testament he must either have quoted by memory, or rendered from some Greek version. " Quamobrem mea quidem sententia eo potissimum inclinat, collectorem ea loca quæ adfert, vel memoria minus exacte tenuisse, vel ex Græca quadam interpretatione ipsum vertisse." Venema, a learned divine, was of opinion that he must either have employed a version of his own, or quoted from some version now unknown. The supposition of his relying to any extent upon his memory in digesting so long a series of quotations, seems to fall considerably short of probability.

This relique of ancient jurisprudence has already appeared in about twenty different editions, of which the earliest was published by Pierre Pithou in the year 1573. Another was published by H. Stephanus, in a small volume, entitled " Juris

[2] Gothofredi Manuale Juris, p. 63. Prolegomena Codicis Theodosiani, cap. iii.

[3] See Bishop Münter's Fragmenta Versionis antiquæ Latinæ Antehieronymianæ, in the *Miscellanea Hafniensia*, tom. ii. p. 89.

Civilis Fontes et Rivi," which made its appearance in 1580. The tract was inserted in the collections of Van Leeuwen and Schulting. In the Berlin collection of 1815, it was printed under the superintendence of Biener. Notwithstanding the labours of so many precursors, Dr. Blume has found ample room for the exercise of his learning and industry. He has produced an elaborate and critical edition, which will be found of no inconsiderable value to those who prosecute similar studies with suitable ardour, with such ardour as is now displayed in the universities of Germany. His prolegomena, consisting of forty-four pages, exhibit a copious account of the book, of the manuscript copies which have hitherto been traced, and of the various editions and commentaries. One manuscript he himself discovered in the library of the chapter of Vercelli. His more brief notes, relating to the adjustment of the text, and containing references to the original sources from which it is derived, are placed at the bottom of each page; and, under the title of *Excursus Critici*, he has subjoined some more extended annotations, which however are neither numerous nor diffuse. Several useful indices, prepared with due care and accuracy, close this curious volume.

The *Corpus Legum* evidently belongs to a more recent age. Senckenberg supposes it to have been written soon after the reign of Justinian, and he concludes that it must have been written by a native of Italy or Africa; but the arguments with which he supports these opinions are so extremely slender, that he appears to have made very few converts. A very different theory was proposed by Saxius, who conjectured that the real author of the work was no other than Apel, by whom he erroneously supposed it to have been originally published. Joannes Apellus, or Johann Apel, was born at Nürnberg in 1486, and died there in 1536. After completing his law studies, he became a canon of Würzburg, and councillor to the bishop; but having been compelled to leave the diocese in consequence of marrying a nun, he was in 1524 appointed professor of law in the university of Wittemberg, and for this office he was partly indebted to the friendship of Luther. In 1530 he became chancellor to the duke of Prussia; and it was during his residence at Königsberg that he found a manuscript of the work now under consideration. The manuscript he has described in his "Isagoge per dialogum in IIII. lib. Institutionum." This work was subjoined to an edition of the ancient treatise, printed at Louvain in the year 1551; and from his mention of such a manuscript being discovered on the remote shores of the Baltic, as well as from the similarity of his own method of expounding the law, Saxius, who imagined that this was the first edition, and that it was published by Apel himself, was led to suspect that he was the author of the work which he pretended to have rescued from oblivion. This opinion was adopted by Püttmann, Stockmann, and Hummel, but was sufficiently refuted by Cramer and Weis, and more recently by Savigny. Apel was never a professor at Louvain, and this edition appeared fifteen years after his death. The first edition of the Brachylogus was published in 1549, and several manuscripts of a much earlier date are still preserved. The fourth book, p. 131, contains a passage which furnishes us with some materials for chronology: "Quod autem clericus adversus laicum testis esse non possit, vel contra, in capitulari legis Longobardicæ cautum est; in legibus autem Romanis non memini me invenisse; immo contrarium in multis locis constitutum esse cognovi." Here the author refers to a capitulary of Louis the Pious, who began his reign in the year 814. Senckenberg, finding this note of time irreconcileable with his theory, rejects the passage as an interpolation; but as it contains nothing to excite suspicion, and occurs in all the known manuscripts and editions, we find it impossible to approve of his trenchant mode of obviating a critical difficulty. From the passage lately quoted, Savigny infers that the book was written in Lombardy. He is disposed to refer its composition to the commencement of the twelfth century, and he even hazards a conjecture that it may have been the production of Irnerius.

None of the manuscripts, except that of Vienna, has any title prefixed, and the title which it exhibits is altogether inappropriate: "Summa Novellarum Constitutionum Justiniani imp." The first two editions bear the inscription of "Corpus Legum;" and the third, published by Pesnot in 1553, is entitled "Bra-

chylogos totius Juris Civilis, sive Corpus Legum." Both titles
have since been used in their turn. The plan of the work is
nearly the same as that of the Institutions of Justinian, which
the anonymous writer has partly abridged, and has partly derived
his materials from other sources, the Pandects, the Code, and
the Novels. In his quotations from the latter collection, he
seems uniformly to have employed the epitome of Julianus,
whom he has frequently copied word for word. Savigny is of
opinion that he has made no use of the Breviarium of Anianus,
but, with respect to this point, Böcking arrives at a different
conclusion. As to the value of the work, they are sufficiently
agreed. This value, it may easily be conceived, does not consist in any originality of discussion on the principles of the
Roman law; but, in an historical point of view, the Brachylogus
is of no small importance. It apparently belongs to the era
immediately preceding that of the *glossatores ;* and, as Savigny
remarks, it serves to evince that some individuals then possessed
a knowledge of the law by no means despicable.[4]

Dr. Böcking has enumerated twenty-two previous editions of
the work. The first of these is appended to an edition of the
Institutions, printed at Lyon in the year 1549, " apud Senne-
tonios Fratres." Several of the early editors have added notes.
The edition of Reusner, Francofurti, 1585, 8vo., appeared " cum
paratitlis ejusdem, ac notis perpetuis, quæ commentarii vice
esse possunt." A more pompous edition was at length published by Senckenberg, a professor of law in the university of
Giessen. Francofurti et Lipsiæ, 1743, 4to. In a long preface, which he is pleased to call *præfamen,* and which is written
in a peculiar style of Latinity, the merits of his author are very
highly estimated; and he there expresses his determination to
adopt the Brachylogus as a text-book for his academical pre-
lections. The choice cannot be considered as very judicious,
nor is it to be supposed that his example found many imitators.
Böcking has reprinted the prefaces of former editors, has subjoined an account of the different manuscripts and editions, and

---

[4] Savigny's Geschichte des Römischen Rechts im Mittelalter, Bd. ii.
S. 255.

has discussed the age of the writer, as well as the merits of his work, and the sources of his knowledge. The preliminary matter occupies one hundred and twenty-eight pages, and contains very ample information. He has subjoined critical annotations, and, apart from these, perpetual references to the ancient texts; nor has he excluded the glosses and notes of the manuscripts and former editions. He seems to be completely qualified for the task which he has undertaken, and the book is now exhibited in a very satisfactory state. The Epitome inserted at the end of the volume had been previously noticed by Savigny and Schrader.

We now descend to the age of the *glossatores*, or those writers who used their best endeavours to elucidate the civil law soon after that study began to be prosecuted with renewed vigour. They laboured under many disadvantages, incident to a period of intellectual darkness. In the knowledge of philology and history, so requisite for understanding the scope and spirit of ancient jurisprudence, they were unavoidably deficient, and were therefore chargeable with mistakes and misconceptions into which no modern tyro could easily fall. But these peculiar faults must be imputed to the barbarous age in which they lived; their merits as acute and indefatigable expounders of the law were entirely their own. Some of the more recent and more elegant civilians, particularly Alciatus, Duarenus, Hotman, Govea, and Muretus, have treated them with undeserved contempt; but many others, and among these Cujacius, Gravina,[5] and Bynkershoek, have amply commended the sagacity and perseverance with which Accursius and the rest of that family have investigated the most intricate questions of law. Their merits were highly extolled by Wieling, in his "Oratio pro Glossatoribus";[6] and Hänel has discussed their character with ability and discrimination.[7] Brunquell published a learned

---

[5] Gravinæ Origines Juris Civilis, p. 113.

[6] Wieling Lectionum Juris Civilis libri duo, p. 291. edit. Traj. ad Rhen. 1740, 8vo.

[7] " Quod vero glossatorum scripta edo," says Hänel, " neminem fore arbitror, qui in malam partem interpretetur. Etsi enim sunt, qui illos renascentis juris Romani auctores contemnant, eosque meras ineptias protulisse audacter adfirment, tamen isti glossatorum scripta non modo non

T

prolusion on their sects and controversies,[a] which necessarily find a place in the general histories of the civil law; and, at a very recent period, the character and the works of the *glossatores* have been rendered more conspicuously known by the profound and masterly researches of Savigny.[b]

The first and oldest tract which occurs in Dr. Hänel's collection, he conjectures to have been written in Italy about the middle of the twelfth century. The author, whose name has not been discovered, begins by stating that there are said to be four lilies of the laws, yielding good and various odours: "Quoniam quatuor esse legum dicuntur lilia, varios bonosque odores referentia." These fragrant lilies are Martinus, Bulgarus, Hugo a Porta Ravennate, and Jacobus Hugolinus, who were all professors of the civil law in the university of Bologna, and whose differences of opinion in expounding particular doc-

legisse, verum ne inspexisse quidem videntur, quum si unius Azonis Summam et præcipue Lecturam Codicis leviter tantum gustassent, æquius fortasse judicium fecissent. Debemus enim in illis non solum acumen ingenii, verum etiam animi constantiam admirari, qui omnibus fere subsidiis, quibus nostra ætate instructi sumus, destituti ex ingentis molis voluminibus, sæpissime corrupte scriptis, disjecta doctrinæ membra conquirebant atque ordinabant, et quæ inter se pugnare viderentur, tam perite conciliabant, ut etiamnunc in jure controverso multas eorum opiniones, quamquam auctorum nomen reticentes, teneamus et in foro sequi non dedignemur. Omnino illi juris libros, quos possidebant, tam diligenter tractabant, ut eos memoria tenerent, tam docte et jucunde interpretabantur, ut incredibilis nobilissimorum ex omnibus Europæ partibus juvenum multitudo ad illorum scholas concurreret, quibus rebus tantam erant auctoritatem consequuti, ut de gravissimis causis, qui summam rerum illo tempore tenebant, ad eos referrent. Itaque glossatores semper colui, quum nitor et summa in excolendis operibus manus magis videri debeat temporibus quam ipsis defuisse, ut veteris quæ dicitur scholæ picturas magni habeo, etsi nunc eadem res adcuratius ad artis regulas pingi potest. Adjuvat præterea glossatorum lectio historiæ studium. Multæ enim opiniones multæque controversiæ etiamnunc agitatæ jam in glossatorum scriptis leguntur."

[a] Brunquelli Opuscula ad Historiam et Jurisprudentiam spectantia, p. 305. Halæ Magd. 1774, 8vo.

[b] Savigny's Geschichte des Römischen Rechts im Mittelalter. Heidelberg, 1815-31, 6 Bde. 8vo.

trines he undertakes to specify. But his attention is chiefly directed to the opinions of Martinus and Bulgarus.

The second tract, that of Rogerius Beneventanus " De Dissensionibus Dominorum," was first printed in the year 1537. An edition of it was published by Haubold,[1] to whose learned labours the students of ancient jurisprudence are so much indebted. Wenck, another very able professor in the same university who has illustrated the history of the *glossatores*, is inclined to believe that the author wrote between 1127 and 1158; but Hänel fixes upon a period somewhat more recent, and places the composition of the work between 1150 and 1162. Of the materials supplied by his anonymous predecessor, Rogerius seems very freely to have availed himself.

Another work of a nameless author, described by a good alliteration as " Codicis Chisiani Collectio," follows in the order of arrangement. Hänel supposes it to have been written about the close of the twelfth century. The author mentions the names of many recent writers on the civil law, all of whom, so far as can be ascertained, were natives of Italy, and it is highly probable that he likewise belonged to that country. From the two previous collections he has transcribed entire paragraphs.

The " Dissensiones Dominorum" of Hugolinus form a work of much greater extent than the other three combined. It comprehends no fewer than 470 paragraphs. Savigny and Hänel are both of opinion that the author must have written about the beginning of the thirteenth century. He has to a great extent incorporated the collections of his three predecessors, and has made many additions of his own. He mentions most of the writers whose names occur in the third collection, together with several others, and among these Azo, Odericus, and Vacarius; of whom the latter is best known to our countrymen, as having been the first professor of the civil law in England. His history was however involved in much obscurity till the appearance of Wenck's very elaborate and accurate work.

---

[1] Rogerii Beneventani de Dissensionibus Dominorum, sive de Controversiis veterum Juris Romani Interpretum, qui Glossatores vocantur, Opusculum. Emendatius edidit D. Christianus Gottlieb Haubold, &c. Lipsiæ, 1821, 8vo.

All these reliques of jurisprudence are published with the most scrupulous care and diligence ; nor can it escape the observation of any one who inspects the volume, that the editor must have bestowed upon it no small portion of time and labour. He commences with a preface of sixty pages, and has illustrated his different authors with a double series of annotations, the one containing references to a variety of writers who have discussed the same subjects, and the other relating to the readings and emendation of the text. His references to manuscript authorities, and to other obscure sources of information, are very numerous. His style of annotation is concise, and he compresses much erudition within a narrow compass. Four different indices, very laboriously compiled, complete a volume of nearly eight hundred pages.

Dr. Hänel is a professor of law in the university of Leipzig, and is a worthy successor of Haubold and Wenck. To his ardour in exploring the libraries of various countries, France, Switzerland, the Netherlands, Britain, Spain, and Portugal, we have elsewhere had occasion to allude. To this learned peregrination he devoted several years of his life, as well as a considerable share of his private fortune; and returning to his native country with a very ample stock of materials, he speedily began to communicate to the public some portions of his literary wealth. The earliest of his works was his catalogue of manuscripts: the *Dissensiones Dominorum* followed after an interval of four years; his edition of the Gregorian and Hermogenian Codes after an interval of another year; and he now meditates an edition of the Theodosian Code; a task for which he is eminently qualified, not only by his learning and acuteness, but likewise by the previous course of his researches.

INDEX.

Dabelow, 162. 199.
Daillé, 244.
Dalrymple v. Dalrymple, 120.
Damman, Hadrian, 133.
Daza, Bernardino, 259.
Debtors, their treatment, 21.
Decretals of Boniface VIII. 234.
Decretals of Gregory IX. 233.
Decretum of Gratian, 231.
Demente, 145.
Desuetude of laws, 123.
Devoti, 238.
Dickens, Dr. 111, n.
Dieck, 212, n.
Digest, or Pandects. V. Justinian.
Dionysius Exiguus, 230.
Dionysius of Halicarnassus, 14.
Dirksen, 4, n. 12, n. 23, n. 90.
Dissensiones Dominorum, 274.
Doctors Commons, 113.
Donellus, 132. 135. 150.
Dorotheus, 54. 58.
Doujat, 177. 232, n. 237. 245.
Draco, L. Honoratus, 260.
Drummond, Alexander, 134, n.
Duck, Dr. Arthur, 175.
Dunbar, Dr. James, 19.
Dupin, 192.
Dupont, Everard, 147.

Eck, Cornelius van, 141.
Edinburgh, university of, 133.
Eichhorn, 226, n. 239.
Elvers, 28, n.
England, law of, 95. 107. Study of the civil law there, 84.
Ernesti, 184.
Espen, Z. Bernard van, 142. 237.
Evelyn v. Evelyn, 99.
Extravagantes, 213.
Extravagantes Communes, 235.
Extravagantes of John XXII., 235.

Fabroni, 80, n.
Fabrot, 66. 254.
Ferguson, Dr. Adam, 188.
Ferrettus, 253.
Ferriere, 180.
Feudal law, 199.
Fischer v. the Earl of Seafield, 167, n.
Fleta, 93.
Forsterus, Valentinus, 174.
France, study of the civil law there, 132. Its loi coutumier, 219.
Franeker, university of, 136.
Fulbeck, William, 97, n.
Fulgentius Ferrandus, 230.
Funccius, 9, n.

Gaius. V. Caius.
Gebauer, 140. 158. 205, n. 251.
Geldart, Dr. 113.
Gentili, Alberico, 97, n. 151.
Gentili, Scipione, 150. 152.
Georgisch, 227, n.
Gerardus Niger, 212.
Germany, study of the civil law there, 2. 149. 165. 263.
Ghent, university of, 142.
Gibbon, 12. 45. 189. 191.
Gilbert, Sir Jeffrey, 218.
Giphanius, 150. 254.
Glanville, Ranulph, 92.
Glossatores, 7, n. 273.
Gobidas, 68.
Göschen, 26.
Gothofredus, Dionysius, 65. 76. 150. 250.
Gothofredus, Jacobus, 23. 40. 174.
Gouvea, or Goveanus, 169. 251.
Grandi, Guido, 81.
Gratama, Serpius, 20.
Gratian, 231.
Gravina, 23. 178.
Greece, Roman embassy to, 12.

THE END.

LONDON:
W. M'DOWALL, PRINTER, PEMBERTON ROW,
GOUGH SQUARE.